Song of the Self

The Keys to Love:

*Song of the Self Tarot Deck Explained
with Activations for Self-Growth*

David Robbins

Library of Congress Cataloging-in-Publication Data

Robbins, David.

Song of the Self: The Keys to Love, Song of the Self Tarot Deck Explained with Activations for Self-Growth

ISBN: **979-8-218-20109-8** (paperback)

ISBN: **979-8-218-20110-4** (eBook)

1. OCC024000 **BODY, MIND & SPIRIT** / Divination / Tarot 2. SEL021000 **SELF-HELP** / Motivational & Inspirational 3. OCC019000 **BODY, MIND & SPIRIT** / Inspiration & Personal Growth

Cover Art by David Robbins

Empowered Whole Being Press

www.EmpoweredWholeBeingPress.com

Dedication

I dedicate this book to my late partner, Michael Santa Cruz.

His love provided a life for me to remain employed and continue to write many works designed to help humanity heal.

Thank you, Michael, for sharing your life with me. Your love filled a yearning in my heart only you could fill. We shall meet again.

Symbol of The Self

The Four Archetypes of the Self
united with the Infinite Flow of Compassion

*The Song of the Self is our Ego's journey through Shadow, Soul, and
Spirit; the Four Archetypes of the Self.*

Table of Contents

Introduction

Having explored many areas of spirituality and self-growth, I believe we are divine beings having a human experience. The universal wisdom I have absorbed has culminated into the Song of the Self Tarot, expressing our collective path for Self-Becoming.

Song of the Self Tarot is the mythic journey of Prince **Ego** uniting with Sister **Shadow**, Sister **Soul,** and Brother **Spirit**. The twenty-two cards of the Major Arcana are the Keys to Love he travels through to complete the process. The ego's journey of Self Becoming is mainly about healing the Shadow; expressing the Beauty, Passion, and the Wisdom of the Soul; and accessing and expanding our divine qualities, such as compassion and forgiveness.

Each tarot card has a story, and a song illustrating the archetype. The images are explained spiritually and psychologically, referencing myth, literature, and film.

The *In a Reading* section for each card, describes their meanings and questions to ask to help the querent relate to the archetype for deeper understanding. The reader is provided with Activations for Soul Growth, Creativity and Dreamwork, along with Affirmations, References and Recommended Reading to assist your journey of the Self. Also included are personal examples of how I relate to them.

The Ten Universal Symbols of Manifestation are a condensed version of the minor arcana: showing the evolution of a thought for Self-Becoming to its realization. This process is applied creatively and can be used in working with dreams for your life and understanding the divine guidance we receive while sleeping.

Please Note: Although the Song of Self Tarot deck illustrations in this book are presented in grayscale, in the eBook and on the website they are in color. SongoftheSelfTarot.com

Using the Deck

I recommend the three-card spread for past, present, and future to get a wider perspective of your trajectory in the moment. Begin by focusing on how the center card of the present relates to where you're at now. Notice thoughts, feelings and images coming up for you. Is your intuition providing guidance? How do your impressions relate to the card? Do the cards validate where you're at, where you've been and where you're going? Are you getting confirmation for moving forward with an area of personal growth, a project, job, career, or relationship?

The Reader may use the cards as they are inspired to. Another option is to choose one card to reflect upon.

Invitation to the Song of the Self

Please join me in the Song of the Self we are all meant to sing in our own unique way. You may think of each card or archetype as a verse in your song of self-realization. Give yourself the gift of healing. Take what resonates and let what doesn't go. Please reach out to your local mental health providers if you need further assistance. You're welcome to laugh and cry at the drama and comedy and tragedy of life. May you be inspired to deeper healing and to shine your light more brightly. May you celebrate who you really are in your own unique Song of the Self. Thank you so much for beginning or continuing on your journey. Transforming ourselves, we have the power to collectively transform the world. With an open mind and heart, the impossible is made possible.

Song of the Self Tarot

Part I

Mystic Mirrors of Self Transformation

Hall of Mirrors

In a magical kingdom, Brother Spirit ushers Prince Ego into the great hall of the castle where the mystical mirrors hang on the wall.

Introduction to the Journey of the Tarot

The images the prince observes are the major arcana of the Song of the Self Tarot I designed. The journey through the archetypes helps us remember who we really are. We are meant to access all parts of our consciousness to experience wholeness. With Free Will, the Fool begins the journey of the soul:

Song of the Fool

The prince stares at the image of a white-winged angelic being in the red garb of a jester. Fearlessly poised at the edge of a cliff, The Fool prepares to dive into the earth below. Behind the figure is the sun bursting through the clouds from the heavenly darkness.

Brother Spirit informs, "this depiction of the Four Archetypes of the Self, represents your consciousness before incarnation: the dog, by the fool, represents the animalistic ego, the red court jester garments indicate the shadow or the dark forces of the self; the angel wings represent the spirit, and the sun depicts the soul. Prince Ego, become one with the figure of the Fool, to understand where we come from and where we go."

The prince uses his mind to inhabit the character in the picture; "I sense all the parts of me are merged together. It's difficult to differentiate between them."

"The Fool is the undifferentiated state of being, desiring to know itself," Brother Spirit informs. "Incarnating on the earth, consciousness develops as the ego, learning to understand the material world. Shadow, Soul and Spirit will be pushed back into the recesses of the mind."

"I hear a heavenly choir," the prince says.

"Sing the Song of the Fool," Brother Spirit advises. Prince Ego, sings:

> *To unite ego with spirit, shadow, and soul,*
> *I must differentiate before I can be whole.*
> *Earth is like a prison to become awake,*
> *the keys are within for the jail break.*
> *The winding process is depicted in the tarot,*
> *the road taken is not straight and narrow.*
> *Spiraling in, spiraling out,*
> *to become a spiritual spout.*
> *It's a path difficult and sometimes painful,*
> *to be who we are is our path most gainful.*
> *When I made my descent into matter,*
> *I acted the Fool, like the Mad Hatter.*
> *From Oneness in the cosmic soup,*
> *I incarnated in the earthly loop.*
> *The foolish ego takes a great leap,*
> *landing on the great earth heap.*
> *The fool's dip into the oceanic pool,*
> *begins the lessons of Earth school.*
> *The ego split from God the father,*
> *becomes the bereft prima matter.*
> *Floating like jetsam in the unconscious sea,*
> *the fool gathers the pieces with curiosity.*
> *Shadow, Soul, and Spirit become unspun,*
> *so, the Four Archetypes can reunite as one.*

The prince expresses his desire to be part of world, "It's so beautiful, and mesmerizing, I feel drawn to experience this reality." He jumps off the cliff and dives into the consciousness of physical manifestation.

Brother Spirit explains, "the materialistic earth and the oceanic spirit, depicted as a fish, represents the duality of incarnation.

Song of the Self Tarot: The Fool O

This tarot card of a strange creature perched on a cliff, the sun breaking through the clouds and the earth below, symbolizes the undifferentiated human consciousness. The Four Archetypes of the Self are present but not incorporated at this stage. The winged white figure of the Fool indicates Spirit; the red jester hat, collar, and shoes, signify the Fool's desire to be flesh and blood ego on the material plane.

The dog, representative of our animalistic mind-body, seems to push the Fool off the cliff; expresses the ego's free will to choose incarnation.

The earth below, depicted as the oceanic fish within the green earth circle is symbolic of the spirit within the body.

Gnosis: To Know Self

The Fool desires gnosis, to know himself as a divine being in human form. Gnosticism is a mythic story describing the development of our consciousness. Briefly, the spiritual source or Divine Father envisions itself in human form. He births from himself the Divine Mother. She uses her power of desire to give form to the image of human consciousness. This merging of divine masculine imagination and the Divine Feminine power of desire, results in the Divine Child, symbolic of Human Consciousness.

Sophia, the Divine Feminine, emulated Divine Masculine by birthing on her own, the Demiurge. The Demi-urge, jealous of the higher creation of the Divine Child created the world to entrap the souls. In this simulated world, the divine child forgets his spiritual origin and is made subservient to the ruling powers of the matrix.

As the Fool, we know the world is a simulation, but we willingly enter it to begin the journey of gnosis, to know thyself. Adam and Eve, eating the apple from the Tree of Knowledge represents the ego desiring self-knowledge. The Fool in heaven incarnating to earth, is symbolic of Adam and Eve leaving the Garden of Eden to enter the harsh earthly world of survival and toil. We, like Adam and Eve, the biblical personification of the Fool, realize the earth is really a school challenging us to know who we really are.

As the Fool, we come to earth to release the spirit within us to be aware of the matrix of control and enslavement and transcend our beingness into a higher consciousness. It is what is meant to be in the world but not of it. The Gnostic Myth, the Hymn of the Pearl, expresses our mission on earth; to retrieve the pearl of feminine wisdom, a symbol for the soul.

The film, the matrix is an excellent overview of Gnosticism. It shows the character Neo taking a red pill to become aware of what is really happening. Neo sees artificial intelligence controlling and feeding off humanity. The agents of the demi-urge try to destroy Neo to prevent him from freeing humanity from their ignorance.

In the movie Avatar, the characters enter a body with their consciousness to inhabit a foreign world; is a very clear depiction of gaining knowledge of a fantastic world and the opportunity for gnosis of one's own divinity.

Rider Waite Tarot: The Fool 0

The prince of the Song of the Self is analogous to the princely figure of the Rider Waite character, The Fool 0, about to happily walk off a cliff.

In his right hand the Fool holds a stick on his shoulder, appears to pass through the crown of his head into the rays of the shining sun; indicates he's directly connected to the divine light. The red feather emerging from his head represents his desire to be an incarnation of flesh and blood. The white rose he holds in his left hand depicting his state of purity and innocence is symbolic of his divine feminine nature.

His right hand also forms a line with his leg to a white dog urging him to take the leap of faith into incarnation; or is he warning the Fool of the danger he's about to step into? The dog represents The Fool's animal instincts of the ego mind-body.

Interestingly, the two lines stemming from the Fool's right hand form a 90-degree angle, depicts the spiritual and material opposing forces. Simultaneously, the dog directly under the sun, indicates the conjunction of the spiritual and material consciousness. Therefore, the ego is divinely inspired to leap into incarnation.

The staff of the Fool is associated with kundalini energy flowing along the spine. The sack at the end of the bindle, represents the Fool carrying his potential to manifest his divinity on earth.

On the Fool's clothing, the asterisks within circles, represent the potential of the divine star to shine in the form of human consciousness. The eleven circle symbols coincide with the ten plus 1 sephiroth of the Kabballah Tree of Life. These spheres are symbolic of the different aspects of human consciousness and development.

The snow-capped mountain in the background may depict the mountainous spirit, the source of creation.

The Fool in a Reading:

The Fool in a reading means, having faith to leap into a divinely inspired enterprise. Using our free will, we have the opportunity to begin new adventures in our lives as well as our interior world. We have the potential to manifest who we really are.

Questions to Ask in a Reading:

Are you thinking of starting a new adventure, job, relationship, creative project? Is there any thought, emotion or understanding trying to burst through your consciousness?

Activating the Fool

Personal Growth: Curiosity

We develop the curiosity to search within to begin the journey of the ego to heal the Shadow, reclaim the Soul and Spirit. When we start to think about who we really are, we activate the archetype of the Fool. We can begin a meditation practice to form a connection with the divine.

Creativity: Mandalas of the Mind

Using the curiosity of the Fool, we can explore our consciousness; by allowing symbols to emerge from the mind and putting them down in a circle, we create a landscape of the psyche at that moment in time, known as a mandala.

Dreamwork: Allowing

In terms of dreamwork, we can allow our dreams to enter conscious awareness. We can become curious what the symbols and events mean.

Experiencing the Fool

I experienced the curiosity of the Fool as a child reading about astrology and reincarnation. Expressing myself creatively as an artist, I enter the world of imagination. Considered a foolish enterprise by society, I pursued a career in the arts by going to art school. I studied Graphic Design to in the hopes I could make my creativity marketable.

Affirmations

I leap into being an individualized expression of the divine.

Summary of the Fool

The Fool represents our undifferentiated consciousness as a jumble of Ego, Shadow, Soul, and Spirit.

References

The Secret Book of John: The Gnostic Gospels—Annotated & Explained Hardcover – Feb. 1 2005 by Stevan Davies (Translator)

The Secret Book of John -- gnosticismexplained.org

Gnostic Scriptures and Fragments: The Hymn of the Pearl - The Acts of Thomas -- gnosis.org

The Matrix: Film

Avatar: Film

0. The Fool, by Anne-Marie Wegh -- anne-marie.eu

The Four Archetypes of the Self:

Magical Ego I, Shadow II, Soul III
and Spirit IV

In this section I explore the Four Archetypes of the Self, cosmically as the creation of consciousness and psychologically as the ego's journey uniting with the archetypes.

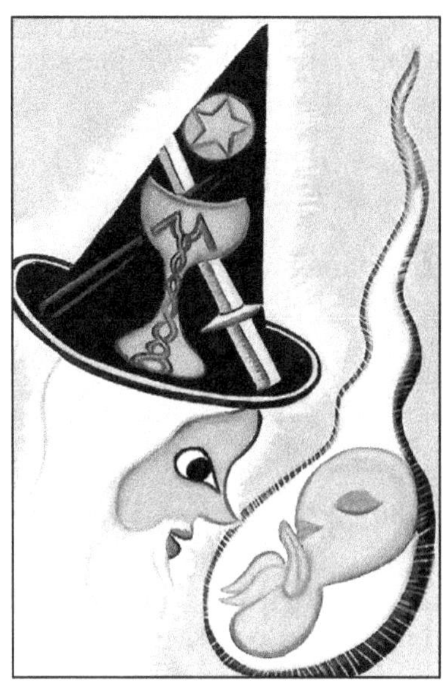

Song of the Magical Ego

The prince merges with the figure of the magician, looking at a fetus in a sperm-shaped container. Decorating his conical hat are a pentacle in a coin, a sword, a wand, and a gold cup, symbolizing the four functions.

The prince sings, the Song of the Magical Ego:

My conscious mind is essential,
the magical ego is my potential.
Thinking, feeling, intuition and the senses five,
are the four functions, helping me to thrive.
With awareness I can be whole,
raising my spirit is my goal.
For divine consciousness to be of the earth,
the magical ego is the gateway of birth.
Consciousness splits into day and night,
Ego ushers the dark into the light.
To become a divine enlightened force,
Ego is guided to unite with the source.

The Four Functions

The prince explains, "I feel like we are each a seed of universal consciousness containing all we need to find our way back to God.

"The Four Functions are the tools of the Magician for uniting the Four Archetypes of the Self," Brother Spirit informs.

The prince takes from his hat the golden coin with the five-pointed star; "This coin represents the five senses of sight, hearing, touch, smell, and taste.

The prince grasps the magic wand, "the wand represents the power of intuition."

The prince grabs the sword from his hat and brandishes it about. "The sword is the power of the intellect. It represents the function of thought. I can speak my truth and I can cut away the lies and deceptions. I can gain clarity using the power of my mind."

The prince returns the sword and picks up the golden goblet. "The golden cup represents the ability to express emotions. The Snakes of Transformation on the goblet indicate, through our emotions is how we heal our consciousness.

"The letter M indicates the four functions as well as the branches of the Four Archetypes of the Self: the first vertical line is the developing ego, the diagonal line downward is the ego entering the shadow; the diagonal line going up is the soul, and the last vertical line is bringing down spirit to earth," Brother Spirit explains.

The prince continues, "We are magical beings, but we forget the magic is inside of us. Our mission is to remember the magic and use it to make us healthy and then help others heal and be whole.

Song of the Self Tarot: The Magical Ego I

The Magical Ego is our personal consciousness used to perceive and interact with the world. The ego or personality of the Self has the potential to bring into awareness the other three archetypes: Shadow, Soul, and Spirit, comprising the fourfold nature of the psyche.

The yellow background behind the Magician and the fetus, illustrates the Divine Father in its state of Oneness. Meaning, his pure unconditional love glows in its unmanifested state. Through imagination, the Divine Masculine begins the creation of human consciousness.

The Divine Father, depicted as Merlin the Magician, envisions the consciousness of humanity, represented as the fetus. The spermatic shaped container around the unborn child represents the Divine Mother gives form to consciousness. In essence, the source of who we are imagines the Magical Ego and how it will be manifested.

The Magician's nose piercing through the receptacle of creation, mindfully places the template of four functions: thinking, feeling, intuition and the five senses within the ego. The fetus is symbolic of the potential of humanity to develop the intellect, pursue passion, receive divine guidance. In the simulated world, it can perceive and experience with sight, hearing, taste, smell, and touch.

The caduceus design on the cup, featuring the Snakes of Transformation are associated with serpentine kundalini energy, traveling the human spine to enlighten consciousness. Interestingly, the entwined snakes cross seven times, refers to the seven chakras. Above the snakes, sits the letter M, indicating the Four Archetypes of the Self implied in the four lines creating the letter. It signifies the ego with the Snakes of Transformation has the power to unite the separated entities of the psyche. The letter M also refers to Mercury or Hermes, the messenger of the gods associated with healing and Hermeticism, a philosophy for enlightenment.

Perception: Ego Tool of Awareness

Our egos are the archetype of the personality with the magical ability of perception. Comprised of the four functions, we have a great power to perceive within our consciousness and the world around us.

Rider Waite Tarot: Magician I

Song of the Self Tarot, the Magical Ego I, compares with the Rider Waite Tarot: The Magician I. A man dressed in a white tunic and red robe holds up a white wand in one hand and points down at the ground with the other. The symbols of the four suits of the minor arcana are displayed on a table. The foreground is filled with red roses and white lilies.

Above the Magician's head floats the infinity sign, analogous to the Infinite Flow of Compassion, signifies his divinity. The wand in his right hand forms a diagonal with his left down-pointing finger, indicates the spirit descending into the material dimension.

The concept of the spiritual and material is also represented in the white and red alchemical stages. White is the purity of spirit and red is the desire for consciousness to manifest in the physical body. The magician uses his free will, (magic) to incarnate his divine consciousness into human form.

The four objects on the table; sword, wand, cup, and pentacle are the four functions of ego consciousness. The red table appearing to be an extension of the red robe indicates these functions are manifested in the material dimension.

The yellow background of this card presents the oneness of divine solar consciousness. The Magician in front of it, in his dual-colored clothing, represents the duality of the spiritual and the material aspects of consciousness. In other words, divine human consciousness is birthed from the oneness and simultaneously imagines the ego mind as a vessel for spirituality. The tools on the table are created for the ego to navigate the material world.

The belt the Magician wears is a snake eating its own tail, known as the ouroboros, symbolizes sexual intercourse. In extension, it represents the union of opposites such as male and female, spiritual and material.

The Magical Ego in a Reading:

When the Magical Ego turns up in a reading it may indicate a vision from the divine you have had or will soon have. You may have constant thoughts for manifesting your dream. The querent may feel inspired by a vision or divine guidance.

Question to Ask in a Reading:

Have you been thinking about starting something new? Have you had a vivid dream recently? What is it trying to communicate to you? What are your thoughts, feelings, intuitions regarding the idea taking form? How can you make the vision into a reality?

Activating the Magical Ego

We experience the magical ego using our free will to begin the process of manifestation. Recall a time when you used your free will to manifest your desire. For example, you decided you wanted to purchase an item of clothing or buy groceries and went out and got it right away. In many ways we have the power of instant gratifications, deriving a great sense of power, gratifying our materialistic desires. Through the media we are manipulated to use our purchasing power to serve the controllers of society to make them more powerful and wealthy. Instead, we can use our powers to access the divine within to topple the system that enslaves us.

Personal Growth: Envisioning

Imagine yourself as the magician, envision who you really want to be in the world. Hold up your wand to the heavens above, bring down your divine powers to manifest your dream. Say the magic words, "I am Love," or "I am a divine expression of love." Feel this power resonating within you.

Allow a space in your heart to open to fill it with love. Let your divine self guide you to your purpose and how to fulfill it.

Creativity: Imagination

Allow your imagination to reveal the creation desiring to be expressed through you.

Dreamwork: Remembering

The Magical Ego in remembering a dream, begins the process of understanding the divine guidance you're receiving.

Experiencing the Magical Ego

The magic I most wanted to wield was finding my purpose in life. This topic, discussed in another book, began as a desire to use my creativity to survive childhood; blossomed into using creativity as a healing modality to be an art therapist. That dream did not manifest into a career, but it laid the groundwork for using creativity to be of service to humanity as a writer of metaphysical books, screenplays, and the designer of the tarot deck.

The manifestation for casting this spell has been a lifelong process, indicating our magical egos are always at work if we just tune into our divinely ordered higher fate. I can't say for sure, but I believe the ego mostly remains in a materialistic matrix until it desires to know its divinity. In choosing to be aligned with the divine, we begin to activate our highest fate. Which in essence is the purpose of this book.

Ego Activation: Developing Self Esteem

Much of what our egos perceive is a reality we are manipulated to accept. It is part of a dark agenda to keep us separated from our powers from soul and spirit.

Developing self-esteem, we will not be at the mercy of the authoritarians who say or behave as if they know better. We can use the power of discernment to question the truth; are the authoritarians reporting fake science to make us believe, and behave as they dictate?

We can access the power of our intuition to determine truth from lies. We may have no way of proving anything, but we can determine what truly resonates with us.

Before blindly following the propaganda of the media, we can investigate other sources of information to get a balanced view of what is happening. In my thinking, censored information is more likely the truth; otherwise, they wouldn't censor it. There are many doctors who state there is no covid or it was downgraded. They attest to what we are told is a vaccine, is really a harmful gene therapy.

Affirmations

I am love.
I am a divine expression of love.
With free will I manifest my highest destiny.
I have the power and tools to manifest my divine reality.
I use my intuition to determine the truth.
I free myself of the external despotic mind-control.

Summary of the Magical Ego I

The Magical Ego is the archetype of the personality with the ability of perception. Comprised of the four functions, we have a great power to perceive within our consciousness and the world around us.

Cosmically, the Magician is the Divine Masculine Father of Creation. He creates the Divine Feminine Mother as a container for his vision of the Magical Ego.

Psychologically, the Magical Ego is our consciousness with the mission of accessing soul and spirit. With his tools to navigate the simulated world, he begins the process of individuation.

References

The Magician, by Anne-Marie Wegh -- anne-marie.eu

Ouroboros, By Prof. Geller -- mythology.net

Ouroboros Meaning: Snake Eating Itself, The Infinity Symbol Tattoo

Meaning -- symbolsandmeanings.net

Ouroboros, by Catherine Beyer -- learnreligions.com

Hermes Trismegistus -- brittanica.com

Hermes Trismegistus & the Consciousness Revolution of the Renaissance, by Gary Lachman -- newdawnmagazine

Hermes Trismegistus-- unimedliving.com

Shadow II

Song of Shadow

The prince and Brother Spirit enter a tribal dance around a campfire. They sing with the ancient clan, the Song of Shadow:

Mountain majesty, Mother Earth,
mind-body consciousness we birth.
Impregnated by Spirit divine,
when her water breaks, we cross the line
from an astral being into a body of matter,
learning the truth for illusions to shatter.
Coiled within are the Snakes of Transformation,
they activate healing for Self-reformation.
Taming the inflated ego from running wild,
begins the birthing of the Divine Child.
Repression erupts in the fire of hate,
releasing pain, ends our tortured state.
Emotional expression undoes the self-hating hex,
reclaim sexuality to be High Priestess of Sex.
We share Beauty, Passion and Wisdom, our goddess gift,
then we detach from goddess to make the god shift.

Mother Earth

"The archetype of the Shadow is depicted as Mother Earth; representing the physical body for your consciousness to reside," explains Brother Spirit.

"But there really is no physical reality?" asks the prince.

"The material world is a simulation, like a computer-generated world," Brother Spirit confirms.

"But it seems so real," the prince remarks.

Brother Spirit explains, "You can think of life, like reading a book. You're not in the story, you're imagining it through the words."

"It exists only in my imagination," the prince clarifies.

Brother Spirit continues, "The life we choose to live is like a computer program we have accepted as reality in order to learn who we really are. We have options to choose from."

"What do you mean?" the prince asks.

"Mostly, the computer-generated reality is fixed into place, and we have to go by the rules of the programming; but we do have free will to decide how we experience the events of our lives. With our minds, we can understand the world around us and process the feelings within our psyche. If there is a buildup of emotions, we can express our feelings with words and movement. We can choose how we relate to others and which behaviors; thoughts and beliefs will help us progress into higher states of consciousness."

"I feel like I have some feelings I need to release," the prince states.

"By connecting with your feelings, you can feel them and let them go at any time."

The prince merges his consciousness with the Earth Mother. "I feel a lot of anger brewing under me."

"Allow it to come to the surface," Brother Spirit advises.

"It's the anger at authoritarian figures at school for having to comply with their requirements to pass their classes. I am paying these people to help me be a great art therapist and not to be a great writer of papers. I want to feel confident in my ability to help people, I don't feel like they're supporting me."

Brother Spirit explains, "Being a healer is really about accessing your compassion. This you already do. Your teachers are jealous of your power of compassion and unconsciously try to make the training more difficult. They think they are preparing you for the real world. You have had enough experience in the world to know how unaccommodating people are. You're learning in the healing profession, it's no different."

"That makes me angry," the prince states loudly. A tiny puff of smoke exits the hole of the volcano. What really makes me angry was when one of my teachers gave me an incomplete. She thought she was being generous not actually failing me." The lava starts to flow from the volcano. "She put me in charge of her groups when she was on vacation, indicates I was doing my internship adequately. I facilitated a breakthrough with a patient that was really amazing experience and yet she judged me.

Brother Spirit offers, "It gives you the opportunity to disallow the judgment of others to determine your self worth."

The prince continues, "It's very upsetting when the people you expect to be supportive and encouraging do the opposite. I just want to explode." The lava erupts and flows down the sides of the volcano.

Brother spirit inspires, "Keep allowing all your feelings to flow. Their behavior is not a reflection of who you are; they project their own deficiencies on to you. Have compassion and forgiveness for them to complete this process of healing yourself."

"I release all my anger; I return to my inner peace." The divine child within the mountain takes form within the mountain. "I feel inspired to forgive those that have hurt me and made my life unnecessarily difficult." Water flows from the cave opening at ground level.

"Look, the river of soul runs from within you," Brother Spirit remarks joyfully.

"It feels so good to allow myself to heal my anger and pain in this way."

"By healing yourself, you have the ability to help others heal," Brother Spirit clarifies.

"So, the ordeal gave me the opportunity to see the truth, release my feelings and access my divine qualities," the prince happily summarizes.

Song of the Self Tarot: Shadow II

A female figure resembling an exploding volcano, symbolizes the divine Earth Mother. The flow of lava forming her head of divine intelligence, depicts her desire to birth divine human consciousness.

Impregnated by the Divine Masculine, depicted as the Magician holding the sperm with fetus, the Divine Feminine gives form to the creator's vision with the power of her desire.

The process of creation is really the source of imagination, splitting off a part of itself and then unites with that part to realize the vision. Put another way, the singularity splits into duality and their union of divine feminine and divine masculine is the divine child or divine human consciousness.

The two giant palm trees, the pregnant Earth Goddess sits between symbolize the birth portal of duality. Meaning, the ego experiences itself as both material and divine.

The Divine Mother's water breaking, represent the flowing waters of the soul. The face emerging from her abdomen is the divine child, about to be born into the duality of matter and spirit. We can perceive the Shadow as the container of Soul and Spirit as well as the threshold into the material plane. Life on earth requires us to first develop our ego to navigate the material domain; in so doing, for most of us, our soul and spirit have recessed into our consciousness. The Shadow as the repository of the subconscious, holds our divine archetypes until we desire to heal ourselves and make our soul and spirit conscious. The Snakes of Transformation undulating up the palm trees are symbolic of the kundalini energy helping us heal and activate our power centers to eventually manifest our divinity on the earth plane.

The 12 lines of lava may indicate the genetic strands of DNA. The crescent moon and owl represent the Divine Feminine Wisdom.

Rider Waite Tarot: High Priestess II

In the Rider Waite tarot deck, the High Priestess, analogous to the Shadow II of Song of the Self tarot; sits between two pillars, one black, one white, symbolizes the duality of consciousness.

The High Priestess is the personification of the Divine Feminine is indicated by her crown of a full moon within two crescent moons and the crescent at her feet. Her blue gown draping down her is symbolic of the water of soul. The depiction of the moons and the tide behind her represent the influence the divine feminine has on our emotions.

The Divine Feminine uses her power of desire to bring forth the magician's vision for divine human consciousness. The Kabbalistic Tree of Life behind her with pomegranates is the template of humanity. The pomegranate symbolizes the sephira, the spheres of power, we can activate to be divine on earth. The High Priestess within us, holds the spiritual seeds of our divine qualities to bring them into consciousness. She can also be considered the kundalini energy awakening our seeds of divinity to reach fruition.

Crossing the threshold of the High Priestess, we enter the world of duality. The High Priestess bridges the split between inner and outer consciousness through expression, depicted as her flowing garment appearing as the waters of soul.

Her foot on the crescent moon, demonstrates she is in control of her feelings. The cross over her chest symbolizes, her heartfelt intention to unite heaven and earth; spirit and matter; light and dark; ego and shadow.

Shadow II in a Reading:

The Shadow in a reading expresses our desire to give birth to our divine self. She may be guiding us to meditate to stimulate our energy to activate our power centers.

Her appearance in a reading may indicate our desire to give birth to something in our lives; it can be a child, a relationship, a new career, job or creative idea.

Pulling the High Priestess or Shadow card in a reading may indicate an emotion festering below the surface. It can be seething anger, repressed pain, volcanic vengeance, or rapid lava flow of resentment. Psychologically, we are allowing our negative feelings to explode into a volcanic meltdown, indicating there is emotional work to be done for our consciousness to flow in peace.

The toxic feeling states are very much attached to the ego, having nothing to do with the eternal part of who we are, the soul. By shifting the focus to our eternal consciousness of soul, we allow the release of the destructive flow of negativity coursing through our ego mind and body.

Questions to Ask in a Reading:

What is your desire; personally, spiritually, and creatively? What feeling(s) are you trying to ignore or push away? Are your negative thoughts and feelings hurting yourself and others? Are you over-reacting with rage, can you let it go? How can I release the feelings engulfing my every thought and action? Have you had an emotional meltdown recently? Are you feeling depressed, can you express the emotions you're repressing?

Activating the Shadow

Soul Growth: Accessing Desire

Imagine yourself as the Divine Earth Mother desiring to give birth to your divine self. Become the embodiment of this desire, let it flow through your heart and mind.

Personal Growth: Releasing Toxic Feelings

Our Shadow may hold repressed feelings causing us to employ defense mechanisms. We may try to detach from uncomfortable feelings by projecting them on others. Or, we may over-react in a violent display of emotions. Instead, we can become aware of the emotions driving our destructive thoughts and actions and let them go. To help create a distance from reactivity, take a few deep breaths. Creating this healing space, gives you the opportunity to express your feelings in a healthy way.

Releasing painful feelings, from minor resentments to homicidal revenge, we expel the toxic emotions trapping us in victim mode. Rather than be dragged down into the whirlpool of emotions, we rechannel our flow of feelings like a river emptying out into the ocean. It means we drain ourselves from drowning in sorrow to return our consciousness to a peaceful state.

In summary: In the unconscious Shadow, our feelings cause great harm to self and others; bringing the emotions into consciousness, the darkness is enlightened; Shadow becomes Soul.

Personal Growth: Authenticity

The Shadow can be experienced by imagining a large python wrapped around yourself. Visualize yourself as the High Priestess, being squeezed by the enormous snake. The python's grip intensifies to cause us so much pain, we cry out for mercy and finally admit, we are being inauthentic.

My inner python caused me migraines until I accepted being gay. How are you behaving inauthentically? Are you seeking approval from your parents instead of pursuing your dreams? Are you being promiscuous to get others to like you or manipulate them? Once you express your truth to yourself the stranglehold of the python ceases. Allow the python to shrink to the size of a pet snake wrapped around your arms. Use the power of your python to guide you to living your most authentic life.

Creativity: Expressing Your Passion

Like the Earth Goddess bursting with lava, what is your burning passion? How can you pursue it. What's stopping you? Perhaps you're mentally and emotionally blocked; unlike a volcano, allow your repressed feelings to be **healthfully** expressed. Journaling and art provide a safe place to release your feelings.

You may discover your passion by remembering your childhood and the activities you enjoyed. Can they be adapted and incorporated into your life now?

Dreamwork: Emotional Healing

In dream work it's important to get the overall feeling of the dream, the feelings experienced throughout the dream, and how we felt after the dream. The dream feelings are more than likely, the emotions we need to express. Allow the dream feelings to stimulate emotional healing.

Working With My Shadow

The desire to be of service to humanity was strongly activated in me to be an art therapist. This career path did not work out as planned; instead, it was a steppingstone to being a writer.

After completing my thesis about mandalas, I continued to create the magic circles to explore metaphysical concepts which I analyzed and put into an unpublished book, The Art of Self Becoming. With continued study, my ideas culminated in the Four Archetypes of the Self. I analyzed myth, fairytales, literature, and movies to depict this fourfold journey in several unpublished works. Delving into understanding the archetypes, many areas of spirituality, self-help, and psychology, resulted in creating the Song of the Self Tarot deck.

I explored my Shadow through analyzing the contents of my dreams. Writing them down and interpreting them also became an unpublished work.

The log I kept for my internships, I typed up and added additional commentary to help others in similar situations went unpublished as well.

My rhyming poems expressing my feelings and insights, became an unpublished book titled, Testimony of the Self. As I'm doing with this current book, I hope to rework my earlier pieces for publication.

Affirmations

I am a powerful Divine Feminine human being.

My emotions are powerful tools for creation.

I desire to live my highest purpose.

I release and let go of all that is not who I really am.

I release negative thoughts and beliefs to be my authentic Self.

I am peace. I am love. I am healed.

Quotes

"Authenticity is the daily practice of letting go of who we think we're supposed to be and embracing who we are."
- Brene Brown.

"The greatest act of courage is to be and to own all of who you are — without apology, without excuses, without masks to cover the truth of who you are."
- Debbie Ford.

"We need to find the courage to say no to the things and people that are not serving us if we want to rediscover ourselves and live our lives with authenticity."
- Barbara De Angelis.

"The strongest force in the universe is a human being living consistently with his identity."
- Tony Robbins.

"Authenticity is about being true to who you are, even when everyone around you wants you to be someone else."
- Michael Jordan.

"The privilege of a lifetime is to become who you truly are."
- C.G. Jung.

Summary of the Shadow II

The singularity separates into the duality of Divine Father and Divine Mother. Through the magic of her desire, she becomes the womb of creation. Meaning, the vision of source has a space to manifest the form of consciousness.

Psychologically, the Shadow holds repressed emotions, the Waters of Soul, and the Divine Child (Spirit) desiring to be birthed into consciousness. Looking within the Shadow, the Ego begins the healing process, soul reclamation and spiritual resurrection.

References

The High Priestess, by Anne-Marie Wegh –– anne-marie.eu

Soul III

Song of Soul

I assume the form of a nude Isis riding on my golden barge. Framed by a bright yellow sun, I'm seated on a throne as I hold a golden ankh in my hands. I pass by beautiful giant sized lotus blossoms as I travel to reconnect with my divine child. I sing the Song of Soul:

The trickle turns into waters of Soul,
the ego as goddess is not yet whole.
As Isis, I take my place on the barge,
as the goddess soul, I'm now in charge.
The rising sun shines as my personal power place,
my crown, throne and ankh, my imperial grace.
Beauty, Passion, and Wisdom, I'm blossoming forth,
guide the soul to the spirit on the Nile flowing north.
On the waters of soul, I ride,
desiring to be spirit's bride.
I'll resurrect the spirit, I have the key,
stranded on his island, I'll set him free.
With mystical insights from the eye-land of Horus,
I'll go to the mountain to hear Buddha's chorus.

Reenacting the Myth of Isis and Osiris

"I'm feeling confident in who I am," the prince as Isis, communicates to Brother Spirit.

"You have become Beauty, Passion and Wisdom personified," confirms Brother Spirit.

"Your evil brother Set, prevented you from resurrecting your spirit. He has chopped up your husband Osiris into fourteen pieces and scattered them along the Nile."

"Please Brother Spirit help me find them," Isis asks.

Brother Spirit taking on the image of the Egyptian God, Thoth, holding a staff; stands next to Isis on the barge nods his ibis head, I will help you find and gather the pieces of the unmanifested Self.

The Goddess Nephthys, besides Isis says, "I will help you, my sister.

"Thank you, Thoth, illustrious god of the moon, magic, wisdom, and writing. Thank you, Nephthys, shadow sister.

"Resurrecting the spirit is the greatest undertaking you will ever do in your life," Nephthys informs Isis.

"We were about to unite and then Set did this terrible thing," Isis cries.

"The dark forces are very powerful, they are jealous of humanity's capacity to be divine," Thoth explains.

"If love is the greatest force, how can he continue to stand in my way? Isis asks.

"Our journey on earth has taught us to access love and allow it to grow, so you can be more powerful than the dark," Nephthys explains.

"Becoming who you really are is a process," confirms Thoth. "Remember how it all started?" he asks.

"Yes, Set made a special coffin for Osiris. He tricked Osiris to lay down in it. Then seventy-two of his demons nailed him inside it and then threw the coffin into the Nile. "

"Shutting Osiris in the coffin is really the psyche being trapped in illusion of the material world," Thoth clarifies.

Isis continues her tale, "Then I heard about the coffin growing in the roots of a tamarisk tree and then it was placed in a palace as a pillar. I found the pillar and took the coffin with me but did not know how to perform the magic to resurrect Osiris. Before I could get your help, Set found the body and dismembered him and scattered fourteen pieces all over Egypt."

"With magic you can become a falcon to locate all the pieces of Osiris," Thoth advises.

Nephthys and Thoth assist Isis with a spell,

> *Grounded on earth is like being blind,*
> *with higher perspective you will find,*
> *the pieces of your groom,*
> *be a falcon, rise and zoom.*

Isis becomes a falcon and retrieves the parts of her husband. Isis informs Nephthys and Thoth:

> *I found all his parts except for one,*
> *it no longer exists under the sun.*
> *His phallus was eaten by a fish in the Nile,*
> *resurrecting Osiris may take a while.*
> *For the resurrection to unfold,*
> *we'll create a phallus made of gold.*
> *For Osiris to unite with the soul,*
> *we wrap the pieces into a whole.*
> *Our union produces the divine child,*
> *brings to consciousness the spirit exiled.*

Isis performs sex magic with the resurrected Osiris. She is impregnated with Horus, who will battle Set and win.

Song of the Self Tarot: Soul III

On a barge, the goddess Isis sits naked on her throne, she holds the ankh like a bridal bouquet and wears a crown of a moon and horns. The sun encircling the goddess fills the barge. The ship connects with the isle of Horus, where the Divine Child holds a sistrum, a musical instrument in one hand and a Snake of Transformation in the other.

The Goddess Isis is symbolic of the feminine soul existing in each individual. In the center of the sun, she sits on a throne, signifying the seat of the soul. The sun is symbolic of the solar chakra, the personal place of power located in the abdomen.

The horns holding the pearl of wisdom of her crown, signifies the embodiment of the soul in the animalistic, material world of the ego-mind body. The pearl can also be seen as the moon, a symbol of the Divine Mother. As the sun centered Isis, the Archetype of Soul, she illuminates the Moon, her Shadow sister; expressing the process of the unconscious made conscious.

The ankh she holds, symbolizing the union of heaven and earth, or the soul centered ego uniting with spirit. The ankh appears as a bridal bouquet, indicates the soul is prepared to wed her Divine Masculine counterpart. The ankh viewed as a key to love is our desire to know our divinity. Our soul centered ego has the power to open the door to divine consciousness.

Crowned with the Pearl of Feminine Wisdom, she glides upon the waters of emotion; signifies she has mastered her feelings and channels her desire for spiritual evolution. Her barge connecting with the Island of Spirit, depicts her readiness to make the transition from goddess to god.

The Divine Child, Horus, offering Isis the singular snake, depicts the transformative energy needed for the ego-soul to achieve spiritual enlightenment. The four palm trees on the islet, represent the four archetypes united. The tree trunk can be seen as the ego, and the leaves are the shadow, soul and spirit made conscious. The rainbow crossing through the trees and above the divine child is another reference of this union. The rainbow is a symbol of uniting the seven chakras, symbolic of enlightenment.

The musical instrument, with its four strings is yet another depiction of uniting the Four Archetypes of the Self. The instrument is the divine child's gift to the soul, symbolizing her future alignment with the heavenly music of divine oneness.

Solar Barge

The barge can be a symbol of traversing the psyche. We can return to our own isle/eye of Horus, to seek the guidance we need. We can use our third eye as a portal to heal our past lives, as well as be connected to the future in order to manifest it in the present. Accepting the idea all time is one, this is possible; although ego experiences time linearly, our shadow, soul and spirit have access to a higher perspective.

My painting, depicting Isis on a barge with the sun, can be compared with the Ancient Egyptian God Ra's solar barque, a ship carrying the sun across the sky. The solar deity in many ancient cultures is really the story of the journey of the sun throughout the year. The shortest day of the year is considered the death of the sun and three days later it is resurrected. December 25th associated with the winter solstice and the birthday of Jesus was also the date of birth for several ancient deities. The name change for the solar god is often due to the new ruling family or dominating culture, much like how Romans latinized the names of the Greek Gods.

The resurrection of Osiris or the sun god represents our divine self, becoming conscious. The rainbow over the solar deity of Horus indicates divine manifestation. In William Henry's book, The Secret of Sion, he analyzes many images of Jesus and compares them with the rainbow bodies portrayed in Thangka paintings.

Lotus of Religions

The large lotus in the lower right corner depicts a five-pointed star denoting Christianity, and the six-pointed star of Judaism represent conventional religion. The cross with the Infinity sign denoting the Symbol of the Self, presents another option, the religion of the Self. Religion, etymologically, is to bind; refers to the individual uniting with the divine. In Song of the Self, the separated archetypes of the psyche are meant to be bound in unity by the ego.

The depiction of the fish beneath each religious symbol, represents the spirituality underpinning most religions. The fish symbol, often linked with Jesus; is understood as Christ Consciousness. Christ Consciousness, associated with Buddha consciousness, represents the individual's divinity. The fish in several Song of the Self tarot cards represents the divine rising into consciousness for the ultimate goal of spiritual enlightenment.

Analysis of the Myth of Isis & Osiris

The story of Osiris and Isis can be viewed as the creation of consciousness. Nailing Osiris in the coffin, symbolizes consciousness housed in the body. This "hermetic seal" referring to the Greek God, Hermes is associated with the Egyptian God Thoth. The principles of Hermes Trismegistus explain the nature of reality. The coffin symbolic of the alchemical vessel becomes a psychological process of self-transformation.

Set in orchestrating Osiris' confinement is comparable to the demiurge of Gnosticism creating an earthly domain for the souls. Both of them, jealous of their divine human counterparts trapped the consciousness of souls into a simulated reality. So, the Gnostic myth of creation appears to be a retelling of the Egyptian myth of Osiris and Isis.

"The All is Mind; the Universe is Mental." — The Kybalion

The sarcophagus becoming part of the tree roots can be viewed as the seed of divine human consciousness taking root in the material world. The sarcophagus resurrected as the pillar in the palace, represents the divine consciousness of the newborn prince.

Isis becoming a nurse to the prince and then interrupted in magically giving the child immortality; indicates the life span of the ego in the simulated world was made finite.

Isis rescues the body of Osiris and seeks help from the lunar deities; Thoth, Nephthys and her son Anubis, the jackal headed god to resurrect Osiris long enough to impregnate her. Set prevents this from happening by cutting up the body into 14 pieces and scattering them throughout Egypt. Isis becomes a bird and locates all the pieces except the phallus of which was eaten by a fish.

Isis and her helpers used a piece of wood to serve as a penis. The phallus can be symbolic of a staff for kundalini to flow up on; can be compared with the spine for our own kundalini to move along. Osiris' seemingly dead body is really our dormant spirit waiting for our ego-soul to resurrect it into consciousness.

Isis and her helpers using magic for resurrection is really the power of desire, necessary in creation. Personally, we use the magic of meditation for the process of manifesting our divinity into consciousness.

Osiris impregnating Isis is the inception of the spiritualized ego. The birth of Horus, the divine child, represents the birth of divine human consciousness. The myth of Isis and Osiris is a template of the creation of divine human consciousness as well as a path for us to birth our own divine child.

Interestingly, the thirteen found pieces may refer to Death XIII tarot card. By adding the missing piece, we get fourteen, associated with the Song of the Self Tarot XIV, Infinite Flow of Compassion. This dynamic between Set and Osiris demonstrates, death and resurrection are required in the process of creation and Self transformation.

In the ancient Sumerian tablets, we learn the genetic experimentation on humans resulted in turning off ten strands of human DNA, leaving only two. We have been misled to believe the deactivated genetic material is junk DNA. Can we assume the pieces of Osiris made whole, represent our DNA strands being activated? Perhaps the scattered pieces of Osiris refer to the power centers in the chakra system or the sephiroth of the Kabbalistic Tree of Life. Can the pieces placed along or in the Nile River refer to kundalini energy, flowing like water up the spine activating the power centers?

Isis giving birth to Horus is the creation of divine human consciousness as the Magical Ego. He is depicted as a human being with the head of a falcon, symbolizing the human mind-body united with divine spirit.

When Horus matures, he battles Set for his father's throne to the underworld and succeeds. Set, a powerful being, believed he had the greater claim to the throne. This battle appears to be still going on; the powerful ones and their hybrid descendants, we may refer to as the cabal, elite, deep state, controllers, rule the earth (underworld). Perhaps it can be understood, Horus becoming the ruler is an ancient foretelling of humanity's ascension to be sovereign beings free of the control of the evil and their agendas to keep us enslaved and ignorant of who we really are.

In conclusion, the dismemberment of Osiris' body, depicts the fracturing of the singularity. Set, as the demiurge, in attempting to stop divine human consciousness, becomes its catalyst. Isis is driven with passion to resurrect the fractured Self. Psychologically, this means we let go of identifying only with our god-like ego to allow, Shadow, Soul and Spirit into consciousness.

Rider Waite Tarot: The Empress III

In the Rider Waite tarot deck, the Empress III is a Divine Feminine being sitting on a throne, represents the archetype of the Soul. She holds in her hand a scepter topped with an orb, representing the Pearl of Feminine Wisdom.

As the divine mother, the Empress represents the birth of the cosmos. The twelve stars in her crown refer to the twelve astrological signs and their twelve houses of the zodiac wheel. On the day of our birth, the planets are situated in both a sign and a house, informing the incoming soul's template of cosmic influences. In other words, the horoscope tells you which planets' energy effects each life department. The angles the planets form with each other also inform the dynamics of consciousness. Just from our astrological make-up, we express our unique individual expression of soul. Since we all share the same planets, what makes us unique is also what unites us.

The heart symbol with the glyph of the planet Venus underneath the Empress, indicates she is also the goddess of love. The Empress gown of pomegranates and the wheat foreground, illustrates the abundant nature of the Divine Mother. As the divine feminine soul, we possess her profusion of love.

The seam of the fabric of the throne, represents the serpentine spine of the kundalini. The red and orange color of the material refers to the red root chakra and the orange sacral chakra.

Sitting on her throne the Empress is in her personal place of power; confirmed by the yellow sky above and yellow wheat below.

The green tree by her left hand, represents the fourth chakra of the heart branching out with love.

The flowing blue water by the Empress' knee, depicts the fifth chakra of communication, for speaking one's truth and being authentic in the world.

The tree appearing like a pinecone, refers to the pineal gland of the third eye, expressing the soul's capacity for psychic abilities and insight.

Her crown displays her divine consciousness.

The Soul or Empress III in a Reading

The querent picking the Soul III or Empress III in the present position, indicates the ego has accessed its divine feminine nature, expressing Beauty, Passion, and Wisdom. She is content in who she is and understands she is a divine being having a human experience.

Just as Isis travels to the island of the divine child; we a soul, seek greater union with the divine and intensely desires to know and live our higher purpose.

Questions to Ask in a Reading:

Are you experiencing a sense of personal power? How do you experience Beauty, Passion, and Wisdom? Do you know your higher purpose?

Activating the Soul

Birthing the soul into consciousness is a monumental act of self-love.

Soul Growth: Shining the Light of the Soul

The ego bringing to consciousness the divine feminine is soul retrieval or soul reclamation. The ego entering the Shadow can do the work of releasing repressed feelings blocking the light of the soul from shining. In a sense, the Shadow is the unconscious soul. The difference being, shadow work is the release of distressing emotions to return the Self to peace; the positive emotions we attribute to the soul expressing, love and peace. Nephthys, Isis' underworld sister, and Isis portray the shadow-soul dynamic of unconscious made conscious.

We know we experience the soul when we feel more of who we really are. It may manifest as self-esteem and self-confidence. It's a recognition we are beautiful divine beings. It's the passion we feel to do or create something in our lives. It's the feminine wisdom that chooses to mindfully respond; rather than over-react out of fear, anger, pain, etc. We allow our intuition to guide us into our best self and our best life.

Empowerment of the Goddess Activation

Imagine you are the Goddess Isis riding on her barge; you are crowned with the pearl of divine feminine wisdom. You hold in your hands the ankh, like a bridal bouquet. The ankh signifies the balancing of male and female energies: the bottom part is like a phallus and the loop on top signifies the vagina. It can be understood as the ego and the soul are united with the divine feminine in charge. Sitting on your golden throne is symbolic of living your life from your personal power place.

Moving along the Nile, the ego united with soul, flows with confidence, grace, beauty, passion, and wisdom. You are the goddess in her full power and desire to know your higher purpose. You may set your intention to be of service to others. You allow your mind to open up to the possibilities on how to fulfill this sacred vow.

You sense your divine child has the answer. You become quiet and still in your meditation to hear the celestial music your divine child plays on sistrum. Horus, the divine child guides you to his island with his song.

> *Mother Isis, my goddess soul,*
> *come to me so we can be whole.*

Notice the four stringed instrument he plays, indicates the blending of the Four Archetypes of the Self in a divine harmony of oneness. The four palm trees of the island also symbolize the four parts, standing together as one.

Your intention magnetically and magically draws the barge to the island of the divine child. You as Isis, dock your barge on the island. The divine child welcomes you with open arms. Your divine child embraces you in peace, love and joy. You ask Horus, "what is my higher purpose?"

Horus knowing the answer, guides you to the center of the eye, comprising the isle. "Immerse yourself in the pool of your third eye; allow your sixth sense to open."

You enter the pool with a graceful dive. What insights are you having? What do you see and hear?

Perhaps if you listen closely, you will hear the divine child tell you, "You are a healing presence in the world." Can you accept your inner truth? Does he offer any specifics how you are meant to heal others?

Going back to school to be an art therapist was my shift to being of service to others. I had a dream of being an old woman run over by a car. This indicated to me, the transition from the divine feminine soul to allow the spirit to be the primary ruler of my psyche. Have you crossed this bridge? What dreams and insights confirm your enlightenment? After my awakening, I experienced spontaneous moments of joy; I would feel my divine child smiling through me. When I notice I'm angry, upset, or depressed, I can remind myself of my divinity and allow the joy to resurface.

You emerge from the pool of insight. Horus holds in his hand a Snake of Transformation. He offers it to you, "Reclaim your divine masculine power, shifting from goddess to god, access and expand your divine qualities."

Accepting the transition of consciousness, you see a rainbow spanning across the island. It means you have activated all your chakras, including the crown of divine connection. You have become the divine child, singing your song of the Self. You can access kindness, compassion, patience, love, peace, joy and forgiveness as the situation requires.

Depict your divine child in a drawing, writing, song, or a dance. Send out your compassion to the world. Be the healer you know you're meant to be.

Creativity: Manifesting Soul through Art

Creative expression is a powerful way to bring soul into consciousness. Access and express the divine feminine into form, by creating a symbol, image or poem illustrating the nature of your soul.

Dreamwork: Making the Unconscious, Conscious

Remembering and recording dreams make the unconscious, conscious. We understand the symbols are all parts of who we are.

Experiencing the Soul

The meditative state I experience during swimming, helped me connect to my greater sense of Self. The constant repetitive movement and breath relaxes the mind, allowing the soul to be active in my consciousness. Through dancing, I experience joy; I feel I am the embodiment of the goddess.

Affirmations

I am an expression of divine love.
My soul is eternal, consciousness never dies.
I am the embodiment of Beauty, Passion, and Wisdom.
I shine my light.
I shall not fear.
I am healed; I am a healing presence in the world.
My higher purpose is to be of service to others.

Summary of the Soul III

The Soul is the Divine Feminine eternal archetype of the Self, who gives birth to the Divine Child. She is the embodiment of Beauty, Passion, and Wisdom.

Recommended Reading

The Passion of Isis and Osiris: A Gateway to Transcendent Love by Jean Houston

The Secret of Sion: Jesus's Stargate, the Beaming Garment and the

Galactic Core in Ascension Art, by William Henry

References

The Osiris Myth and How it Changed Egyptian Mythology by Yordan Zhelyazkov -- symbolsage.com

Horus vs. Seth: Homosexuality, Hippos and Familial Violence by wallyandduke-- thenotsoinnocentsabroad.com

The Empress -- anne-mariewegh.eu

The 7 Hermetic Principles & How To Use Them To Improve Your Life, by Sarah Regan -- mindbodygreen.com

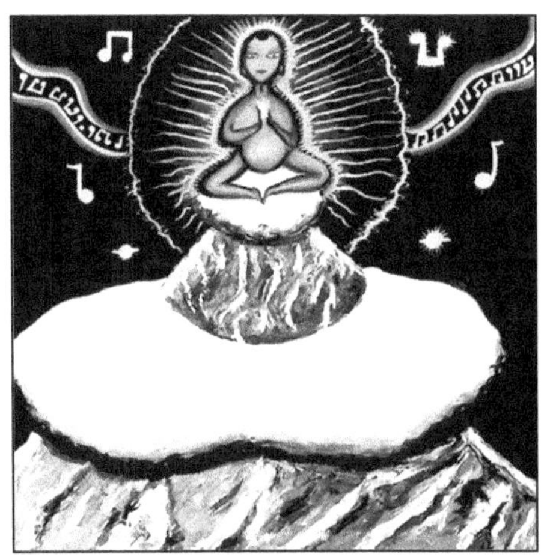

Spirit IV

Song of Spirit

The prince identifies with the Divine Child in the painting and assumes his persona. He sings,

> *I hold the Snake of Transformation in my hand,*
> *I sincerely desire my consciousness to expand.*
> *Into the eye-land I dive,*
> *for my Spirit to thrive.*

The prince as Divine Child dives into the pool resembling the pupil of an eye. Arriving on a mountain plateau, the child prince intuitively knows to climb to the top of the purple mountain. He hears the celestial music, and a heavenly choir singing, *"Song of Spirit:"*

> *The Buddha sits on the mountain top,*
> *the divine child climbs to its last stop.*
> *He ascends to be one with father Spirit,*
> *for the celestial music to always hear it.*
> *Aligning with guidance of the divine,*
> *all our divine qualities we can shine.*
> *Uniting our earthly ego with our divine father and mother,*
> *compassion and forgiveness heal our sisters and brothers.*

The prince reaches the top of the mountain and faces Brother Spirit in the guise of the glowing golden Buddha; he asks, "How do I become enlightened, like you?"

"For every person it is the same and it is different."

"That's a contradiction," the prince comments.

"My story of awakening is your story, only different."

"Is this some kind of Zen thing?" the prince asks.

The Buddha rises up on his cloud puff, "Sit here and meditate and you will understand."

The prince sits on top of the mountain and closes his eyes. He envisions the life of the Buddha:

Birth of the Buddha

Queen Maya dreamed four angels carried her to white mountain peaks and clothed her in flowers. A male white elephant with six tusks holds a white lotus in its trunk. He circles Queen Maya three times; he strikes her side with his trunk and vanishes into her.

The king summoned his brahmans, they interpreted the dream; the king would have a son; he would become a world conqueror or a Buddha.

Queen Maya brought up to the mountainous peaks indicates the soul's ascension to know the spirit. Clothed in flowers, reflects her divine feminine nature of the soul. The white elephant with the lotus circling her three times penetrating Maya, represents the divine masculine impregnating the soul with the trinity of divine consciousness; shadow, soul, and spirit. The impregnation by the sacred creature, symbolizes all humans are divine beings. We are inherently invested with the purity of spirit and each of us has free will to be a world conqueror or become an enlightened buddha.

Ten lunar months later, Queen Maya traveling to her homeland entered a grove and gave birth to the Buddha from under her right arm. The infant took seven steps, a lotus appears in each footstep; he says, "I alone am the world honored one." The seven steps and lotuses refer to the seven chakras. The buddha's declaration symbolizes, we are each a unique expression of the divine.

The king decided to call his child, Siddhartha, meaning, "perfect fulfillment;" indicating each of us is the perfect fulfillment of divine order.

Renunciation

Siddhartha marries and has a child. At the age of 29 he ventures from the palace to observe people experiencing sickness, old age and death. The shock of the impermanence of reality jolted Siddhartha out of his sheltered existence. When he encountered a meditator, he had an insight, what he is looking for is within. He was inspired to renounce the life he was living and become an ascetic beggar.

Siddhartha, as husband and father, personifies all of us leading conventional lives. Even though we are not isolated in a palace, our ego distances us from the suffering around us. Interestingly, the Buddha's realization at age 29 coincides with Saturn's return, which means the planet comes back to the place it was in the natal chart. The significance of this return is an astrological wake up call for us to become our authentic selves. It may include pursuing a career path aligned with our inner calling, rather than just making money to survive. Saturn's return helps us to eliminate from our lives, beliefs and circumstances that no longer serve us. We're often faced with losses and balancing out our karma during this time period.

Whether or not our awakening occurs during the Saturn return, we come to understand we cannot ignore our own suffering and that of others. At this point, we question our lives and seek ways to go inward for guidance and healing.

Like the Buddha we may be inspired to meditate, study religion and philosophy or engage in therapy to find the answers to who we are and why we are here. We sense we have a higher purpose we must fulfill somehow.

The Buddha after several years of asceticism realizes, doing without is not the answer. He renounces the way of the mendicant and develops the middle way. His few followers abandon him because he rejects their lifestyle as a beggar in order to gain spiritually.

Siddhartha decides to meditate under the Bodhi tree until he receives enlightenment. The demon, Mara, tries to prevent his awakening by sending his daughters to seduce Siddhartha. The movie, "Little Buddha," portrays a scene of Siddhartha's triumph over Mara.

Activation: Four Noble Truths and Eightfold Path

From Siddhartha's experience we can learn to save ourselves much time and suffering on our path of enlightenment. We can quickly know, renunciation is a step on the path of enlightenment, not the destination. We can renounce what no longer serves us and seek our higher purpose. We can accept the Buddha's Four Noble Truths: There is pain, there is a cause of pain, there is cessation of pain, there is a path to end suffering.

Buddha developed his teaching of the eight-fold path: right view, right thoughts, right speech, right conduct, right livelihood, right effort, right mindfulness, and right meditation.

The Four Agreements

Similar to the eightfold path is *The Four Agreements,* by Don Miguel Ruiz. The ancient Toltec wisdom he teaches is:

> 1. Be impeccable with your word.
> 2. Don't take anything personally.
> 3. Don't make assumptions.
> 4. Always do your best.

Don Miguel expresses these agreements as:

"Speak with integrity. Say only what you mean. Avoid using the word to speak against yourself or to gossip about others. Use your power of your word in the direction of truth and love."

"Whatever happens around you, don't take it personally... Nothing other people do is because of you. It is because of themselves."

"In any kind of relationship, we can assume that others know what we think, and we don't have to say what we want. They are going to do what we want because they know us so well. If they don't do what we want, what we assume they should do, we feel hurt and think, 'How could you do that? You should know.' Again, we make the assumption that the other person knows what we want. A whole drama is created because we make this assumption and then put more assumptions on top of it."

"We make all sorts of assumptions because we don't have the courage to ask questions."

"God is life. God is life in action. The best way to say, 'I love you, God,' is to live your life doing your best. The best way to say, 'Thank you, God,' is by letting go of the past and living in the present moment, right here and now. Whatever life takes away from you, let it go. When you surrender and let go of the past, you allow yourself to be fully alive in the moment. Letting go of the past means you can enjoy the dream that is happening right now."

"You express your own divinity by being alive and by loving yourself and others."

"Maybe we cannot escape from the destiny of the human, but we have a choice: to suffer our destiny or to enjoy our destiny."

Summary Mara: Seeing through Illusion

The demon Mara is comparable to demiurge of Gnosticism. When we see through the illusions of the world, we can no longer be controlled by them. Understanding the Four Noble Truths and employing the eightfold path, we can transcend the temptations and illusions keeping us trapped in the mind-controlled matrix. Basically, pursuing our lower materialistic desires keeps us imprisoned in a limited reality. We transcend the false limiting world by raising our desire to be enlightened, expressing our divine qualities. Overcoming Mara, symbolizes the death of illusion; the idea we are just our bodies die; but our consciousness is eternal. As an enlightened being in the world, we help others heal like the Buddha tried to do through his teachings.

9 Celestine Prophecy Insights

The insights from *The Celestine Prophecy, An Adventure*, by James Redfield expresses the spiritual path as follows:

1. Pay attention to chance coincidences.

2. There is a meaning and purpose in life.

3. There is a subtle energy that infuses all things.

4. An unconscious competition for energy underlies all conflicts.

5. The key to overcoming conflict is to get our energy directly from the source.

6. Heal our childhood traumas.

7. Follow our inner guidance.

8. Find your tribe.

9. Create heaven on earth.

   - James Shepherd –– quora.com

1. We're discovering we live in a deeply mysterious world full of sudden coincidences and synchronistic encounters that seem destined.

2. As more of us awaken to this mystery, we will create a completely new worldview, redefining the universe as energetic and sacred.

3. We will discover that everything around us, all matter, consists of and stems from a divine energy that we are beginning to see and understand.

4. From this perspective, we can see that humans have always felt insecure and disconnected from this sacred source and have tried to take energy by dominating each other. This struggle is responsible for all human conflict.

5 The only solution is to cultivate a personal reconnection with the divine, a mystical transformation that fills us with unlimited energy and love, expands our perception of beauty, and lifts us into a higher self-awareness.

6. In this awareness we can release our own pattern of controlling and discover a specific truth, a mission we are here to share, that helps evolve humanity toward a new level of reality.

7. In pursuit of this mission we can discover an inner intuition that shows us where to go and what to do, and if we make only positive interpretations, brings a flow of coincidences that opens the doors for our mission to unfold.

8. When enough of us enter this evolutionary flow, always giving energy to the higher self of everyone we meet, we will build a new culture in which our bodies evolve to ever higher levels of energy and perception.

9. In this way, we can participate in the coming journey of evolution, from the big bang to life's ultimate goal: to energize our bodies, generation by generation, until we walk into a heaven we can finally see.

- The 9 Insights from The Celestine Prophecy –– penneypeirce.com

Song of the Self Tarot: Spirit IV

The Divine Masculine Spirit is depicted as the Buddha meditating on a mountain peak. The musical stream of divine consciousness flows through his aura. The Buddha glows with unconditional love. Planets in the form of large musical notes surround the radiating figure of the Divine Masculine.

The prince, as the Divine Child, climbs the mountain to reach the enlightened state of the meditating Buddha. The Divine Child, like kundalini rising to the crown, experiences the Oneness of Divine Consciousness. Ego, having bonded with Shadow, Soul and now Spirit, unites the Four Archetypes of the Self in an Infinite Flow of Compassion.

Soul Growth: Overcoming Adversity

Climbing the mountain represents overcoming adversity. Every step we take upward we're called upon to activate and expand a divine quality. We learn to respond to difficult people and circumstances with compassion and forgiveness.

We accept we are lightworkers and provide a healing presence in the world. We strive to be an Infinite Flow of Compassion at all times.

Creativity: Inspiration

We allow Spirit to guide and work through us to create works of art that heal and inspire others.

Dreamwork: Interpretation

We use our intuition to interpret the dream symbols for guidance and confirmation. Personally, the occasional dreams I remember confirm "I'm on track," that I'm in alignment with my higher fate. For example, I had a dream of talking to another writer who is working on a Star Wars type series of films. I asked, "what is the message?" He said, "strength and purpose." He gave me the first 109 pages to read and work with. I interpret the dream as being a writer entrusted with epic material to help people on their spiritual journey.

In a vision I had upon awakening of a beautiful face of a dark-skinned man; I interpret as an angel introducing himself to me as a leading member of the team helping me write this book.

In another dream, a man trying to dance with me, moving like I do, reflects that I'm in synch with the creative flow for this work.

Rider Waite Tarot: The Emperor IV

The Rider Waite Emperor IV, symbolizes the Divine Masculine. The four ram heads adorning his throne, denote the Four Archetypes of the Self. His red apparel, signifying the rubedo of alchemy, represents the divine masculine into human consciousness.

The ram associated with the astrological sign of Aries, which is ruled by Mars, indicates the active force of the divine masculine. The golden orb, the Emperor holds in his hand represents balancing his power with the divine feminine. His phallic scepter topped with a circle, resembling the glyph of Venus, symbolizes the union of the divine feminine and masculine.

The Emperor's throne of stone representing spiritual materialization, indicates he is the spiritualized ego. The mountains in the background confirm the manifestation of spirit.

The armor he wears on his legs specifies he is a knight and spiritually protected. Although the Emperor is the ruler of his domain, he is also a knight in service to the divine and to humanity.

The Spirit or Emperor IV in a Reading:

Spirit or Emperor in a reading may indicate climbing the spiritual heights to experience oneness with the divine. It may mean the querent has done the work to be a spiritualized ego or may indicate accessing and expanding upon a divine quality. Climbing the Mountain of Spirit, the querent may have triumphed over adversity. Spirit or Emperor may be experienced as a significant dream, synchronicity, or insight.

Questions to Ask in a Reading:

What divine guidance have your recently received? How did you overcome adversity? Which divine qualities helped you to triumph?

Experiencing Spirit

I experience Spirit through creativity. My writing has deepened in the ability to express metaphysical and psychological concepts with greater clarity, concision, for healing and insight. On my walks, I often have insights to what I need to include in my writing.

I accept I am a healing presence in the world and through creative expression I add love and light into the world. I accept I am a starseed light worker raising the vibration of the earth for global transformation.

Currently, I'm working on not reacting when I feel criticized or controlled. By taking a breath, my ego can create space and distance for my soul to enter the situation with a divine quality.

Intellectually I realize, I do not have to protect my ego with anger; I can allow my divine connection to be my armor and choose love, compassion, patience to ride through agitation.

Tonglen: Buddhist Healing Practice

Pema Chodron teaches the ancient Buddhist practice:

"Tonglen practice, also known as "taking and sending," reverses our usual logic of avoiding suffering and seeking pleasure. In Tonglen practice, we visualize taking in the pain of others with every in-breath and sending out whatever will benefit them on the out-breath. In the process, we become liberated from age- old patterns of selfishness. We begin to feel love for both ourselves and others; we begin to take care of ourselves and others.

Tonglen awakens our compassion and introduces us to a far bigger view of reality. It introduces us to the unlimited spaciousness of shunyata (emptiness). By doing the practice, we begin to connect with the open dimension of our being.

Tonglen can be done for those who are ill, those who are dying or have died, or those who are in pain of any kind. It can be done as a formal meditation practice or right on the spot at any time. If we are out walking and we see someone in pain, we can breathe in that person's pain and send out relief to them."

During a difficult time in my life, I used this practice often; it gave me a way to feel powerful and purposeful. I can be a healer regardless of my circumstances. It's especially helpful now during the pandemonium. Instead of obsessing about all that is wrong with the world, I can do something about it; I can relieve my own suffering and that of others."

Affirmations

I am loved unconditionally.
I am a divine being having a human experience.
I expand my consciousness with divine qualities.
I breathe in suffering; I breathe out love and healing.
I'm a starseed/lightworker/healer raising the vibration of love.

Summary of Song of the Self Tarot: Spirit IV

Buddha, a symbol of the divine, sitting on the mountain top signifies, the spiritualized ego. Activating the Spirit Archetype means, we manifest the Divine Masculine into consciousness. We allow ourselves to be the Infinite Flow of Compassion or a fountain of unconditional love.

Summary of the Four Archetypes of the Self

The Four Archetypes of the Self exist simultaneously within the psyche. Through the conditioning process of life on earth the ego is separated from its divine counterparts. At some point we are inspired to perceive ourselves as divine and are guided to make conscious, the unmanifested archetypes of the Self. To begin this process, we enter the Shadow and do the necessary work of emptying out repressed emotions and false and dysfunctional belief systems. After exposing and healing the darkness, we start the process of Soul retrieval. The vision of who we can be, uniting with the desire to express it, forms into the divine feminine soul. Soul, the mother of the divine child, births the spirit into consciousness as the spiritualized ego.

The quaternity depicted in the Symbol of the Self, a quartered circle half in light and half in dark, are linked together with the infinity sign connecting the centers of each quadrant depict the interplay of the four archetypes united in Oneness. Dark and light, Masculine and Feminine are equally balanced and united as a whole.

The Four Archetypes of the Self can be viewed as the creation of divine human consciousness: The singularity, the essence of imagination, has a vision of creation. The source of oneness splits into duality of Divine Masculine and Divine Feminine. In Gnosticism, this first emanation of the Divine Feminine is called Barbelo, referred to here as Shadow. Through her desire, she provides the energy to activate the vision into a form. Put another way; the Divine Masculine, impregnating the Divine Feminine with his vision of creation, germinates as the subconscious Shadow; in turn, she desires Spirit to manifest into consciousness. The result of giving form to consciousness is the Cosmic Soul. In Gnosticism, this is referred to as Sophia, Divine Feminine Wisdom. The Cosmic Soul, or Sophia, gives birth to the Divine Child, the manifestation of spirit into consciousness.

References

The Birth of Buddha: Historical or Symbolic? By Richard J Oldale -- mastermindcontent.co.uk

The Birth of the Buddha-- tibetanbuddhistencyclopedia.com

9 Insights from The Celestine Prophecy-- holcraft.org

The 12 Celestine Insights-- celestinevision.com

How to Practice Tonglen by Pema Chodron -- Lionsroar.com

Recommended Reading and Viewing

The Four Agreements: A Practical Guide to Personal Freedom by Don Miguel Ruiz

Little Buddha, film

Celestine Prophecy, by James Redfield

When Things Fall Apart: Advice for Difficult Times, by Pema Chodron

The Places That Scare You: A Guide to Fearlessness in Difficult Time by Pema Chodron

Mystic Mirrors Ego to Soul:

Hierophant V, Merging VI, Golden Carriage VII and Place of Personal Power VIII

The Fool O has been introduced as the unmanifested all of everything. Next, we explored the Four Archetypes of the Self as both the creation of divine human consciousness and as the four roles of the psyche.

The ego, functioning as awareness, has mostly separated itself from its divine counterparts. In this section of the Mystical Mirrors of Transformation, we explore the journey from Ego through Shadow to Soul. Ego starts by answering the call to the spiritual journey offered by the **(Hierophant V).** The Magical Ego continues to heal the Shadow **(Merging VI)**, move toward empowerment **(Golden Carriage VII)** and establishing a **Place of Personal Power VIII.**

Hierophant V

Song of Hierophant

The prince opens his eyes and sees the robed being holding the fishing rod and Snakes of Transformation. The Hierophant sings:

Transform yourself from a lump of clay,
your teacher within shows you the way.
Like a mound of matter, you're part of the earth,
through alchemy of the Self, you gain self-worth.
Explore your unconscious, enter the water,
be reeled in by the fisherman porter.
With the teacher of your sojourn,
many life lessons you will learn.
The pope like figure is a fish,
to be like Jesus is your wish.
He offers the bait for individuation,
take the Snakes of Transformation.
Enter the mystic sea,
set your spirit free.

The prince accepts the Snakes of Transformation to answer the call of the hero's journey of healing.

Song of the Self Tarot: Hierophant V

In Song of the Self Tarot, The Hierophant is portrayed as the Jesus like figure offering the Snakes of Transformation to a dark lumpy figure in a small boat on land. In his other hand, he holds a fishing rod to tow the boat into the waters of soul.

The divine figure existing within all of us, at every moment, waits for us to accept his gifts to begin our spiritual journey. We, as the ego, resist moving from our comfort zone of solid ground to explore the inner dark world of shadow filled with painful feelings. Our ego must reach the Pinnacle of Pain to be motivated to reach out for the spiritual hook, allowing ourselves to be drawn into the realm of repressed feelings. The Snakes of Transformation help us express our feelings, clearing a space for the soul to shine from within.

Blob of Ignorance: Depression

The dark lump on the boat represents the ego, constrained in a lifeless blob of self-limiting thoughts and soul crushing feelings. Suppressed painful feelings, putrefy into an amalgamation of dysfunctional beliefs, darken the light of the soul, resulting in an egocentric false self. This blackening of the Self is the nigredo phase of alchemy, may be experienced as depression.

As this heavy lump of sorrow, we define who we are as the embodiment of our misery and pain, fully embracing our victim identity. We have mistakenly accepted the hopeless belief, "my life is miserable, there's nothing I can do about it, but accept it." In this way we ignore the transformative power within us to heal to slip deeper into the depression.

Pinnacle of Pain

This depression is more than the dissatisfaction of our life circumstances; it is the victimized self, drowning within internalized self-hatred, shame, and unexpressed rage. The greater our ignorance to the divine, the more unbearable our lives get. This disconnect to our divine self is the greater source of our pain. The pain gets so bad, we realize we cannot keep living our life as we have been. We begin to sense, this dark blob of ignorance, taking up space, is not really who I am. We start to imagine there is a god, and that god can save us. Finally reaching the Pinnacle of Pain, we call out to the divine within us.

God Help Me: Calling for Divine Guidance

Feeling trapped in an intolerable deep darkness of pain we want out. "God help me," we say to ourselves or even out loud, signals to ourselves and the universe we have had enough pain. These words begin as a wisp of a thought, intensify into an unceasing chant. Through repetition we gather our energy for transformation. "God help me" is our prayer, setting and confirming our intention to open the door for our salvation. Our source has chosen for us all to be divine; we must choose to allow ourselves to be an expression of divinity.

Jesus: Fisher of Men

The floating deity of light, outlined in the shape of a fish is emblematic of Jesus, symbolic of our own personal savior. It is our own personal Christ Consciousness, we call out for help; and our divine self, responds with giving us the power for transformation.

Through the Pinnacle of Pain, we were forced to access our divinity. With nowhere else to turn for comfort, we break through our resistance to heal. We cocreated this pinnacle of pain with God, for our own awakening into who we really are. We accept the difficult circumstances of our lives were pivotal to manifest our desire to heal be stronger than our resistance and our fears.

Reaching out to any shred of our spirituality, we break through our ignorance to allow thoughts of transformation into our consciousness. We may wonder, "What would my life be like if I were; different; if I were healed; if I got rid of these terrible burdensome feelings about myself, I carry every moment of every day? We let this hope manifest from a distant impossible thought into a very possible reality. We say "yes" to ourselves, "yes" to the divine and "yes" to self-love. We grab the hook of the divine fishing rod and attach it to the boat.

Saying yes to the truth of who we really are, the divine within us can help us perform the magic of self-transformation. The Jesus figure in my painting, holding the fishing rod, can now pull the once totally ignorant ego blob into the water. The ocean as a symbol of Oneness, depicts our desire to be one with our divine self.

Floating on the water of oneness; we sense we are spiritual beings. We may hesitate grabbing our Snakes of Transformation, sensing our lives will never be the same. We resist this pull to go back to our comfort zone on our ego ground; we remind ourselves; we can be free of the pain. We bolster ourselves, choosing to accomplish being divine beings on earth and grab the power of transformation depicted as the two snakes.

Snakes of Transformation: Kundalini

The demonized snake of the bible can be understood as our shadow self, inviting us to have self-knowledge of our divinity. Eating the apple represents our consciousness taking physical form; we allow our consciousness to experience a mortal body to seek the truth and manifest our eternal divinity.

The Snakes of Transformation represent our true power we have been programmed to fear. We are made to believe our divine power is satanic, when in reality, the mind control is the satanic force trapping us into the matrix of enslavement. The satanic commandment, "thou shalt have no other gods before me," is said by a false god, or a powerful one posing as our source to prevent us from connecting with our divine oneness and manifesting our spirit into our consciousness and the world.

Kundalini, translated from Sanskrit, as coiled snake; depicted as two snakes of energy living at the base of our spine, when activated they rise up to cleanse and activate the chakras. The chakras are our power centers forming our divine body. The root chakra at the base of the spine is associated with our life force. The second, sacral chakra we associate with sexual and creative forces. The third chakra, our personal place of power is situated in the abdomen. The fourth, heart chakra is our power of love and compassion. The fifth, throat chakra, is our power of communication and expression. The sixth, is the third eye, the power of insight or psychic awareness. The seventh, crown chakra is our power center of the divine. Through meditation and yoga, we connect with the divine for this process of healing and enlightenment.

Looking at the caduceus, the medical symbol of healing, of two snakes spiraling on a staff is the same as the kundalini moving up and down the spine. Indicating our Greek and Hindu ancestors are in agreement of who we really are.

The flow of energy we allow, can be considered the process of making the unconscious conscious. For example, in dreams we let the internal forces bring into consciousness, the material we need to work with for insight and healing. In addition to meditation and yoga, exercise and creativity can activate the flow of energy for healing.

Scientifically, the double snakes may refer to the sympathetic and para sympathetic nervous response of the body. One is for flight or fight the other calms us down. Both are active during sex and we experience our aroused body with love and healing simultaneously. Through sex, we momentarily transcend the duality of body and spirit; shows us we can achieve a sense of oneness. We can then work to prolong this oneness through meditation, yoga, exercise, and creativity.

Scientifically, the double snakes refer to the double helix strands of DNA. Like the Four Archetypes of the Self, the building blocks for all organic life forms are comprised of four bases, ACGT: Adenine (A), Cytosine (C), Guanine (G), and Thymine (T). The intertwining snakes comprising both the material and spiritual, demonstrates as above, so below.

Call to Adventure

The Hierophant is comparable to Joseph Campbell's, Call to Adventure of the Hero's Journey. In his book, *Hero with A Thousand Faces*, Campbell outlines the journey of the hero in seventeen stages, beginning with the Call to Adventure. These stages found in mythology, literature and film; depict the ego taking the spiritual journey. Campbell expresses each of the psychological stages and their challenges to be overcome.

There and Back Again: The Hobbit

In JRR Tolkien's book, *"The Hobbit";* Gandalf, the wizard, arrives at the home of Bilbo Baggins, the hobbit, with the call to adventure. Bilbo, a half man, half rabbit creature, comfortably resides in his hobbit hole in a lovely shire is reluctant to accept. The wizard lures Bilbo with tales of treasure to induce him to answer the call.

Most of us are like Bilbo Baggins, entrenched in our hobbit holes of familiarity and a sense of safety. Psychologically, we are stuck in our boats for adventure, moored on land, where we 'know' it's safe. Like Bilbo, we would rather go nowhere than take the risk for improving ourselves and our lives.

The first chapter of the *Hobbit, "The Unexpected Party,"* introduces the hobbit to the thirteen dwarves who want to reclaim their treasure from the dragon and put their king back on the throne in their mountain homeland. This plot line is symbolic of reclaiming one's divinity and treasures of the soul. Facing the dragon who has usurped the mountain homeland, represents confronting the Shadow.

In choosing thirteen dwarves, plus Bilbo to be the fourteenth member of the party, Tolkien must have been aware of the Egyptian God Osiris being torn into fourteen pieces.

Star Wars: Monomyth

The stages of the hero's journey, depicted in great stories is referred to by Campbell as a monomyth. For generations, the Star Wars phenomenon has delighted viewers without their full awareness they are immersed in the hero's journey. We connect with these stories because they awaken our need to be the hero of our own spiritual journey.

The iconic Star Wars series began with the hologram of Princess Leia asking Obi Wan Kenobi for help. Obi Wan asks Luke for his assistance, depicts the call to adventure. Luke at first rejects the call, represents our own resistance.

Obi Wan explains to Luke about the Force and shows Luke his father's light saber, helps him to answer the call. This scene shows, it is essential we learn about our divinity to help us pass the threshold of our ignorance. Observing a character undergoing what we subconsciously feel, we can be inspired to break free of our internal opposition.

Soul Growth: Awareness & Imagination

The Hierophant is really our inner calling to develop our own personal religion of the Self. Until that time, we may feel alone and stranded as the ego grounded into the material world; having the awareness, externals do not bring the satisfaction we hoped for. The increasing dissatisfaction with life results in a deepening depression.

Becoming aware of the misery we find ourselves in, we can begin to take steps to climb out of the pit. By accepting where we are at emotionally, we can do the necessary healing work. We can ask ourselves: Does the image of the landlubber blob describe you? Are you ready to accept the responsibility for Self-Transformation? If so, can you imagine a divine figure coming to your aid? Can you visualize taking the hook and being drawn into the waters of soul? Can you grasp the Snakes of Transformation? Can you feel the power inspiring you to change?

If you're unable to imagine divine guidance in any fashion, pray to spirit for help. Send out the energy you are ready to answer the call to be divine and will do the inner work of healing.

If you have not reached the Pinnacle of Pain, continued ignorance of the call will increase the pain; allow the pain to motivate you to heal. The pain does not have to worsen, let the pain you feel now be the pinnacle. Grab on to your salvation at any time.

Creativity: Expressing Desire for Transformation

The spiritual figure from within who calls upon us to answer the call of self-transformation, may call on us to manifest a dream. The dream can be anything from starting a new relationship, a new job, new career or project. Create a prayer or song expressing your desire for change. Draw an image of receiving divine intervention.

Dreamwork: Establishing a Connection to the Divine

Before going to sleep, mentally send a message to your divine Self to provide guidance in a dream. What dream for your life do you most desire? Access the energy from within to begin pursuing your dream.

Rider Waite Tarot: Hierophant V

The Rider Waite Tarot, Hierophant V, depicts a pope seated on a red box with two keys. In his hands he holds a scepter; on his head is a gold crown. In front of the Hierophant are two monks.

The two golden keys are for opening the treasure box of who we really are; they are analogous to the two Snakes of Transformation.

The three cross bars of the scepter refer to the ego staff raising the three unconscious archetypes of Shadow, Soul, and Spirit into awareness.

The Hierophant seated in front of two pillars, represents transcending duality. The two figures facing the pope represent the unconscious and conscious dynamic.

Interestingly, the four symbols on top of the box indicate the Four Archetypes of the Self, divided into quarters. The crown of the hierophant has four tiers, the top one has three spokes indicating the trinity of shadow, soul, and spirit.

The Hierophant's hand gesture of two fingers together represents the uniting the duality, making the unconscious conscious.

Hierophant V in a Reading:

Getting the Hierophant in a reading may indicate the querent must make a supreme effort to grab onto the spiritual lifeline the divine self offers. We must overcome the immobilizing inertia keeping the mind-body trapped in worn out thinking and behaviors and reach out for salvation. We must not allow our spiritual urges to be thrown back into the sea of unconsciousness; instead, we must soften our minds and hearts to receive divine love and guidance. We must accept the Snakes of Transformation so we can become who we really are.

On a mundane level, this card may indicate, a calling to find a new job, go back to school for training for a new career, move to another city where there are better opportunities. It could be a calling to exercise, whether it is going to the gym, taking a yoga class or just going for a walk. We may hear the calling to be creative, seek therapy, get married or go out on a date.

Questions to Ask in a Reading:

What is my divine self calling me to do? Do I answer the call or push it away? What keeps me stuck in my materialistic rut? How can I push through it? How will I find the courage to take the first step? (Hint: When we know we are in alignment with spirit the path always feels right and somehow, we can transcend our fears and obstacles.) What career path is my divine self calling me to do? Are your dreams guiding you to embark on a new adventure? Are you being called to create a work of art, invent a device or develop a program?

Affirmations

I have faith in divine guidance.
I have the courage to move out of my comfort zone.
Life is an adventure for becoming divine.

Answering the Call: Tarot Designer

In identifying with the Hierophant, translated as the teacher of sacred knowledge; I answered the call to design the tarot deck, I'm now writing about. Exposing and understanding the sacred mysteries has been a lifelong enterprise. The best teachers continue to be good students, seeking ways to express ancient wisdom in new ways to have the greatest impact with our contemporaries.

Previously, I answered the call to attend art school; in developing skills as an artist, I was unaware the training to be a graphic designer helped expand my consciousness. For example, designing logos is really symbol making. In this way you learn to take more than one idea and condense it into a visual to communicate in a glance the product your design is representing.

After graduating art school in 1982, I did not get very far as a graphic designer. Creatively, I would just draw the mystic maidens as a way of being an artist and express the divine feminine.

I answered the call to return to school to be an Art Therapist. For my Art Therapy thesis, I wrote about the healing power of mandalas. When I graduated with an MA in Art Therapy in 1993, I continued to create my own mandalas to express spiritual concepts. The mandalas can be seen also as a form of symbol making in that a landscape of the mind, can be portrayed in one picture.

Having worked with a tarot deck and studying the images, I was inspired to create my own deck to expand the idea of the Four Archetypes of the Self, Ego, Shadow, Soul, and Spirit as the first four images of Magician, High Priestess, Empress and Emperor.

The rest of the major arcana I saw as a path of healing and manifesting our higher consciousness. It was an amazing, mystical, magical experience to answer the call and create these powerful images. I thought it would somehow be published right away, but twenty-seven years later, I'm reworking the book, explaining these powerful archetypes of who we really are. Over the years, the understanding of each image and my writing skill has advanced. I hope my work will benefit many people; and trust the timing is in divine order.

Affirmations

I answer the call of healing.
I shine my divine qualities to heal others.
I am a sovereign being.
I answer my calling to ascension.

Summary of the Hierophant V

The Hierophant is the Divine Self, calling the ego to go within to bring out the inner treasures of Shadow, Soul and Spirit.

References

Joseph Campbell & The Hero's Journey, by Tamlorn Chase -- odyssey.antiochsb.edu

Deep Dive: Joseph Campbell's "Hero's Journey" by Hannah Yang-- prowritingaid.com

Star Wars: Episode 4, A New Hope

Clear Steps to Manifesting Your Dreams -- www.berkeleycreativecompany.com

The Four Step Formula for Manifesting Your Dreams, by Katherine Hurst -- thelawofattraction.com

Field of Visions and Dreams: 7 steps to manifesting dreams that come true -- Roxannevise.com

7 Simple Steps on How to Manifest Your Desired Dreams-- Medium.com

The Hierophant, by Anne-Marie Wegh -- anne-mariewegh.eu

Recommended Reading

The Hero with a Thousand Faces, by Joseph Campbell

The Writer's Journey: Mythic Structure for Writers, by Christopher Vogler and Michele Montez

The Hobbit, by J.R.R. Tolkien

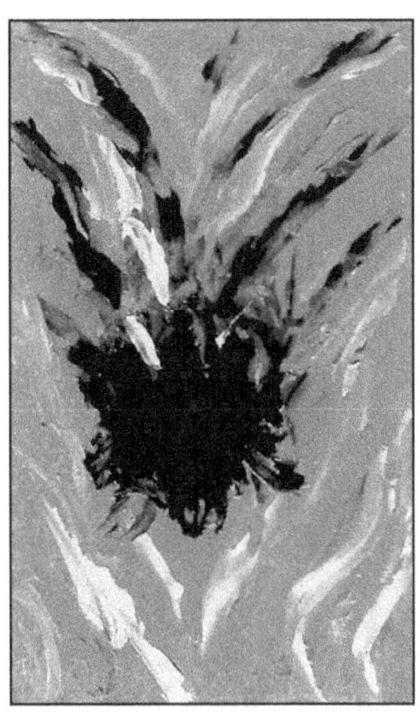

Merging VI

Song of Merging

The divine being pulls the boat into the water with his fishing rod. The prince as the figure of clay, releases the Snakes of Transformation into the water. The divine being sings, the Song of Merging:

Immerse your body in the lake,
the cool waters will start to bake.
The outer persona will dissolve,
contradictions can then resolve.
Intensifying to a boil,
purifies earth ego soil.
Eliminate the mold to which you are cast,
the process may feel like a nuclear blast.
Much strength it takes to break the mold,
to be different and not do as you're told.
The psyche needs to rearrange,
let yourself be the change.
With the unconscious world you may unite,
merging with Shadow produces the light.

The water bubbles and boils and becomes lava, it consumes the wooden vessel and alchemically dissolves the lump of clay of the false self.

Song of the Self Tarot: Merging VI

In the Song of the Self tarot, Merging VI is illustrated as the black blob liquefying in volcanic lava. It symbolizes allowing our rigid concept of who we are to melt away. Softening our minds, we dissolve the barriers to self-knowledge to enter the Shadow. In this domain, we reunite with repressed feelings. Through expression, we release the "dark" feelings entrapping us to enable us to merge with the light of our soul.

The black form immersed in the red-orange liquid, signifies the ego uniting with the first root chakra, associated with the color red; and the second sacral chakra, depicted as orange. This dissolution or softening of the ego, can now absorb the shadow energy for self-transformation. For example, merging with a repressed feeling such as anger, we reclaim a part of ourselves, we had shut off. Expressing the emotion, we can release it and transmute the energy into pursuing our passion.

Know Thyself: Ancient Wisdom

Socrates states, "To know thyself is the beginning of wisdom" and "The unexamined life is not worth living."

Plato sums up our shadow work from his dialogues; "Know thyself."

The words "know thyself" are inscribed at Apollo's temple at Delphi. People attended the temple to seek guidance from the sybils, women with great psychic abilities.

The sibyls inscribed in their room of the temple: "I warn you, whoever you are, Oh! You who want to probe the "Arcana of Nature", that if you do not find "within yourself" that which you are looking for, you shall not find it outside either! If you ignore the excellences of your own house, how do you pretend to find other excellences? Within you is hidden the treasure of treasures! "Know Thyself" and you will know the Universe and the Gods."

Nigredo: Dissolving the Ego

Alchemically, we are dissolving the ego, prima materia, trapped in the nigredo or putrefaction of the self. With the dissolution of the putrefied ego, we begin to bring forth who we really are.

The Gospel of Thomas verse 70 expresses the necessity of self-knowledge as, "If you bring forth what is within you, what you bring forth will save you. If you do not bring forth what is within you, what you do not bring forth will destroy you."

Soul Growth: Purging

The shadow work of dismantling the ego as the defining archetype of the Self is accomplished through Merging of conscious and unconscious.

The dissolution of the blackened "prima materia" of ego is the process of purging ourselves of our false thoughts, feelings, and beliefs. We interrogate every negative thought about ourselves to determine its validity. We question every belief we were conditioned to accept, whether it originated from, parents, teachers, bosses and authoritarians. We question all labels others put upon us and internalized.

Byron Katie in her book, *"Loving What is,"* offers her process of self-inquiry in four questions she refers to as the *"Work:"*

Is it true?
Can you absolutely know that it's true?
How do you react, what happens, when you believe that thought?
Who would you be without the thought?

Creativity: Passion

The alchemical stage of dissolution or purification, we may gain clarity of what our higher purpose is. Merging, depicts liquifying the blockages preventing us from realizing our dream. Creatively, we can make conscious the barricades to self-expression. We can illustrate our powerful passion dissolving those barriers.

We can investigate our minds and put down in words, the negative thoughts and beliefs blocking us from pursuing our dream. Like Katie, we can reassess the veracity of our beliefs. We can ask ourselves, are we allowing others to influence us from following our heart's desire? Have we internalized false notions of who we can or can't be?

Picture yourself as a dark mass immersed in waters filled with your emotions. What are your feelings? Can you fully express them and release them? Notice how allowing the feeling to touch you, you absorb your truth. Knowing the truth, you can heal it. Protecting yourself from a horrific past of victimization, may have been necessary to get through it. Now this hardness only serves as a barrier to your love and light. Instead, we can shift some of our strength into being vulnerable enough to feel and channel our feelings; to eventually access who you really are.

Dreamwork: Embodiment

Our consciousness merging with the shadow for healing; may be rechanneled as the passion to pursue a divinely inspired dream. It means, we allow the dream to become a significant expression of who we are. Just as we are meant to be the embodiment of the divine, we are meant to embody the potential of the dream through its realization. In other words, to manifest the dream, we must unite with it.

Rider Waite Tarot: The Lovers VI

In the Rider Waite Tarot deck, The Lovers VI are depicted as Adam and Eve in the Garden of Eden with an angel hovering above them in the clouds with a bright sun behind it. A serpent is on the apple tree behind the woman and flame like flowers are on a tree behind the man.

The Four Archetypes of the Self can be seen as: Adam representing the ego; Eve as the soul; the serpent, the shadow; and the angel, the spirit. The woman looking at the angel, represents our soul desiring to know the spirit as the male ego looks at Eve and desires to unite with his soul.

The twelve flame like flowers behind the male represent our burning desire for self-knowledge. Numerologically, they evoke the twelve signs of the zodiac, and the horoscope, for the ego's incarnation. Perhaps the twelve flames refer to the full twelve strands of DNA activated in humans.

The fruit on the tree behind the woman indicates it is the Tree of Life; and represents the soul's desire for incarnation into a physical body and life. The snake offering the apple to Eve is symbolic of our unconscious divine Self wanting to be made conscious. Accepting the apple, means choosing to experience the simulation of an incarnation to manifest our divinity. Interestingly, the four fruits on the tree, denote the Four Archetypes of the Self to be brought into fruition.

The angel in other decks is depicted as Cupid shooting an arrow, can be interpreted as the spirit inspiring the ego to begin the process to unite with the soul for the manifestation of self-love.

Merging in a Reading:

Merging in a reading, indicates the process of Shadow Work has begun. The limiting external identifiers of gender, job title, race, religion, and age are melting away. The Magical Ego in the process of healing, begins its romance with soul.

Healing the past, we detach ourselves from dysfunctional entrenchments holding us back. Merging with the soul, we are living in the present moment being who we really are. It means we have taken the darkness weighing us down and transform it into the energy uplifting us into our true selves. We begin the process of integrating the soul as an active expression of who we are. We allow her to guide us in our lives and continue the spiritual journey. She leads us to fulfill our higher purpose.

On a mundane level the reading can signify a romantic relationship; or the burning desire for a new job, an enjoyment of a hobby, or reading of metaphysical books for self-knowledge.

Questions to Ask in a Reading:

What are your dysfunctional patterns and thoughts? How can you change them? What feelings are you repressing? How can you heal the wounds from the past? Can you forgive those that wronged you? Can you forgive yourself for your own trespasses? How does it feel to be free of the self-limiting thoughts, feelings, and behaviors? How does it feel to bring the light of awareness into your Shadow?

Experiencing Merging

Merging is an ongoing process; we first heal the shadow, bring forth the soul and expand our divine qualities. My journey of self-acceptance, self-esteem, and self-love, I chronicle in Song of the Self: Finding My Purpose. This autobiographical unpublished self-help book, (originally part of the current work) focuses on healing victimization, soul reclamation, finding my purpose to design the tarot, write books and screenplays.

Affirmations

My mind is open to change.
I have the courage to heal.
The truth will set me free.
I don't judge or criticize others for the choices they make.
I don't need to be right.
As a divine being, I raise the vibration of love.
I am manifesting heaven on earth.
I am the change I want to see.

Summary of Merging VI

Merging with Shadow is the healing process of making the unconscious conscious.

Recommended Reading

Gabrielle Bernstein's, Happy Days: The Guided Path from Trauma to Profound Freedom and Inner Peace

Owning Your Own Shadow; Understanding the Dark Side of the Psyche, by Robert Johnson

The Dark Side of the Light Chasers: Reclaiming Your Power, Creativity, Brilliance and Dreams, by Debbie Ford

Meeting the Shadow: The Hidden Power of the Dark Side of Human Nature, by Connie Zweig

Your Golden Shadow: Discovering and Fulfilling Your Undiscovered Self, by William A. Miller

References

The Lovers, by Anne-Marie Wegh –– anne-mariewegh.eu

Golden Carriage VII

Song of the Golden Carriage

The red liquid spits out a yellow carriage on to green land. The prince and the two red snakes stick their heads out. He sings,

From Ego to Soul, I am making the transition,
to the Place of Personal Power is my mission.
I healed my Shadow for self-transformation,
now I have the energy for self-motivation.
To establish my base of personal power,
where my soul will sprout and flower.

Song of the Self Tarot: Golden Carriage VII

The ego transitioning from Shadow to Soul emerges as a golden carriage on to lush green land. The Snakes of Transformation within the vehicle motivate the vulnerable ego to find safety in the Personal Place of Power.

Having accessed the passion to be who we really are, the ego now merged with Shadow is in a vulnerable state; like a hermit crab without its protective shell in search of a shell large enough to fit its new growth. Not having established our personal power base, we our vulnerable to regress to our former lives; where we can be tempted into our unhealthy lifestyle, where we may slip back into an addiction or maintain or renew relationships that no longer serve us.

Golden Carriage: Personal Power Chakra

The Golden Carriage refers to the third chakra of personal empowerment. Surfacing from our shadow depths indicates the repressed feelings have been made conscious and the energy can be rechanneled to establishing a base of personal power. We have sufficient amount of determination to establish our personal power base in the oasis of soul. We focus on who we are now or who we want to be, rather than who we were, is the motivation to arrive at our power base of inner strength.

Rider Waite Tarot: The Chariot VII

The Golden Carriage is analogous to the Chariot VII of the Rider Waite Tarot. The armored charioteer, wears a crown and holds a blue wand; with a team of sphinxes, one black and one white. He is victorious in channeling his power to move to his destination, rather than the stagnation of depression or reactionary behavior of the shadow forces working unconsciously. Integrating the power within means, we have mastered the dark forces controlling who we are. We have made the unconscious, conscious. Like the charioteer, we balance the opposites of dark and light, masculine and feminine, material, and spiritual. The charioteer harnessing the tension of the opposites, propels him to the personal place of power. He balances regression with progression, ego with soul, masculine with feminine, to arrive to his destination.

The star filled canopy over the charioteer, indicates he is on a spiritual journey.

The square emblem on his chest, representing the Four Archetypes of the Self, is close to his heart.

The winged sun disk on the chariot represents the spiritualized ego-soul, the charioteer's destination for wholeness.

Activating the Golden Carriage

Soul Growth: Holding the Tension of the Opposites

Healing victimization through shadow awareness and expression has freed much repressed energy into consciousness. This burst of energy into the ego is the motivating force for journeying to the Personal Place of Power. This growing self-esteem needs to be grounded.

Simultaneously, with the awakening of passion for the ego to permanently unite with soul, there is still resistance. We may experience the resistance as the regressive force pulling us back to our former state of consciousness. We may still yearn for the false safety of the familiar dysfunctionality, rather than embrace the unknown.

The progressive and regressive forces shown as the tide moving in and out in the Golden Carriage or the two horses of the Chariot, depict the tension of the opposites. Having awareness of this dynamic, we hold the tension, rather than veer off from our destination. We notice our urge to backslide, but do not allow it to derail us from the goal. It's like when thoughts intrude on our meditation practice, we keep shifting back to the breath. We don't allow the thoughts to completely sidetrack the process. As the Charioteer, we rechannel the arising negative thoughts and feelings into Self growth. Since we do not want the monumental effort of healing to go to waste, we remind ourselves not to slip back to the miserable person we were. We refocus our mind to fulfill our intention to be healthy, happy authentic beings.

Creativity: Tension of the Opposites

Just like electromagnetism works through opposing energies, a yoga pose uses opposing energies to reach its fullest expression. In the process of creation, the harnessing of opposing energies help us decide what to leave in and what to leave out. In a visual creation we employ contrast and tension between objects. In a story, we write about conflict between two or more characters to show these opposing forces being resolved in some way.

Dance can be a choreography between opposing ideas, and feelings, resulting in a resolution. For example, dancer A may be attracted to dancer B, dancer B rejects dancer A. One chases and the other flees. At some point, the repelling dancer relents, indicates the triumphant power of love. All artists allow the creative force of love to be victorious, in order to continue to create. A true artist loves the process, loves being a creative force. The love of humanity propels the artist to create uplifting pieces of work; helping people understand the truth of their existence, foster psychological healing, and inspire people to express divine qualities, inherent within all souls.

Recall a desire for your life and its fruition. Was there an opposing force preventing you from achieving your goal? How was it resolved?

We can be mindful; the regressive force is necessary for healthy rest. Through inactivity, we eventually feel the pull to create; we can listen and answer its call right away or with additional time the pull to create builds into a strong desire for self-expression. Finding balance, we can have fuller lives and be more effective creators.

Dreamwork: Motivation

To manifest a dream, we need to be motivated. My motivation is to be of service to humanity. Knowing my dream is divinely inspired, gives me the determination to fulfill it.

At the time of this writing, it's been twenty-five years since I wrote the first draft of this book and still, I hang in there believing it will be published. Writing many screenplays throughout the years, even though nothing has materialized as of yet, reveals I'm on the right track. I accept my creative output are divinely inspired works, meant to be created, published, and produced.

The ego sees my effort as a waste of time; if you haven't gotten anywhere with it, you should just give up. Having merged with the dream and hooked into divine motivation, a soul centered individual doesn't quit; because this means, you are quitting on yourself, humanity and God. We know our lives would feel meaningless without the dream. We learn the timing of success is not in our control, no matter how others may impose this view. Hearing ego saying, "Make it happen or you're not doing enough to make it happen, or you don't believe in yourself so you're not worthy of success," we learn to disregard this negative mindset thinking it is protecting us from pain. We focus on the joy of creativity and believing the impact the work will have when it is made public. When the ego's voice intrudes on our thoughts, we remind ourselves we are living the dream of manifesting who we are and helping others become enlightened. We are doing our part to make the world a better place. We are grateful for the opportunity to serve, regardless of not being where we want to be. We are honored we have been chosen to complete the mission we accepted.

The Golden Carriage in a Reading:

When the Golden Carriage comes up in your reading it may indicate you have successfully moved with your Shadow into Soul, Congratulations! The Ego's transformation from Shadow to Soul must become grounded in your Personal Place of Power. In this transitional stage we must be on the alert not to be drawn back into the limited ego. We must quickly ground our new found consciousness before others or even ourselves could drag us back into who we are not. We must make the most of the momentum we have gained on our journey before we can take a necessary break.

On a mundane level the Golden Carriage can represent any transition in life; be it a job to unemployment or unemployment to a job; the end of a relationship or the beginning. The Golden Carriage may simply be the querent will be traveling.

Questions to Ask in a Reading:

What motivates you? How can you prevent self-sabotage, or people in your life sabotaging your efforts? What are your regressive tendencies, distractions, or addictions? How can you stop them from interfering with your goals? Are your responsibilities too overwhelming? How can you achieve balance?

My Golden Carriage: Journey of the Soul

The Golden Carriage or Chariot may refer to a physical journey I took when I quit my job at OTB and moved to Florida. I wasn't exactly sure what I was going to do, I just knew I needed a change from enabling people in their addiction of gambling. Motivated to be of service in some way to humanity, I thought I was going to collaborate with Artemis to do personal growth workshops or be an independent art therapist. Destiny had other plans; helping Artemis write her novel, I developed the skill for writing my own autobiographical work.

Affirmations

My passion takes me to my Personal Place of Power.
My personal growth is my priority.
I move around the obstacles.
I am motivated to manifesting my dream.
I hold the Tension of the Opposites to move forward.

Summary of the Golden Carriage VII

The Golden Carriage is the transition from ego merged with Shadow into Soul. The charioteer balances the tension of the opposites, regression, and progression, masculine and feminine, to journey to his destination.

References

Jung's Challenge to Us: Holding the Tension of the Opposites--
jungiancenter.org

Holding the Tension of the Opposites: Both talking and thinking, By Linda and Charlie Bloom -- psychologytoday.com

Holding the Tension of the Opposites - Marion Woodman -- archive.org

Holding the Tension of the Opposites, by Margaret Mikkelborg -- psychotherapyinsights.ca

Personal Power Place VIII

Song of Personal Power Place

As the carriage nears the desert oasis, the priestesses; Beauty, Passion and Wisdom play their instruments and sing, *"Song of Personal Power Place:"*

The Golden Carriage travels home to soul,
where the goddess helps you to be whole.
In your Personal Place of Power, you can go the length,
with Beauty, Passion and Wisdom, your inner strength.
At our inner oasis,
your power base is.
In our center we're strong,
where we are, we belong.
Through turmoil, you may find,
an inner oasis with your mind.
The vision of the Self we behold,
radiating power dark and gold.
With the pyramids you build self-esteem,
having the strength to fulfill your dream.
Through alchemy create your stage
for the Sphinx, your feminine sage.
Ask for wisdom to be told,

listen to her truth unfold.
Letting your ego take the goddess to wife,
as the Divine Feminine, you now live your life.

The carriage arrives in the oasis; several palm trees move with the wind; in the background, three white pyramids frame the sun, depicted as the symbol of the Self. The priestesses help the prince out of the carriage. They warmly embrace him, "Welcome to your Oasis of the Soul."

Cleansing Breath of Air

"Breathe in the cleansing air of your personal place of power," Beauty advises.

The prince takes a deep breath. "I feel my self-esteem increasing."

"The breath is the life force of your soul," Passion adds.

The prince takes another cleansing breath. "I'm feeling more connected to you and who I really am."

"Your breath connects you to the world within to receive guidance of the soul," Wisdom shares.

The prince takes another breath. "I allow my mind and heart to open to receive the guidance of my soul."

Blessing of the Earth

Wisdom takes a handful of dirt and lets it fall on the prince, "I bless you with the wisdom of the earth."

The prince responds, "I'm grateful my body is a vehicle for my soul. May I gain wisdom through experience. May I have the strength to meet the challenges life brings."

Pool of Purification

Beauty guides the prince into the pond, "Let us bless you in the Pool of Purification."

The prince and the priestesses enter the small pond. Beauty cups water in her hands and pours it on the prince, "I bless you with the water of soul."

He responds, "My Beauty is eternal. I'm blessed with the ability to express my feelings. May I have the strength to feel and release my painful emotions."

Blessed by the Sun

The priestess, Passion, raises one arm to the sun and the other to the prince, "With light of the sun, you are blessed with the passion to live the life of your soul."

He smiles and says, "I let my passion guide me to live my most authentic life. May I have the strength to overcome adversity."

The priestesses immerse the prince in the pond. "Let the alchemy for self-transformation become your personal power base.

Power Base of Soul

The Snakes of Transformation emerge from the carriage. They slither in the sand to form a circle around the carriage.

"In the center of the oasis, the snakes delineate your power center," Passion explains.

The serpentine power transforms the carriage into a platform of stone. The snakes slither around the three priestesses. They merge into one being –– the sphinx; she has a head of a woman with golden hair, the body of a lion, the tail of a snake and white wings. She pounces upon her trapezoidal platform.

The prince asks the Sphinx, "What's happened, who are you?

She answers, "I am an expression of your divine feminine soul. I am your goddess of beauty, passion, and wisdom."

Riddle of the Sphinx

"I ask for your guidance, what do I do now?" the prince asks.

"Asking for guidance from your soul, displays much wisdom, you, our ego, has gained. Answer my riddle, to show you are worthy of the deeper mysteries of the soul.

"I am ready for the challenge," the eager prince responds.

"Steel, iron, and diamonds are three of the strongest substances known to man. How is a woman stronger than any of these?"

The prince is stumped, he wonders, "How can this be possible?" He realizes the Sphinx is not being literal. "You speak of the qualities of the ego, separated from the soul. The mind is like a steel trap, imprisoned in a hardened materialistic mind set. Connecting with the Beauty of the Soul, the ego softens to allow the divine feminine belief structure to be activated.

The ego has an iron will to pursue pleasure and materialistic goals; uniting with the soul's passion, the ego is redirected toward healing self.

The ego can be as hard as a diamond, reflecting its ignorance of its divinity and pursuit of material wealth. With the wisdom of the soul, the ego can break through the ignorance to radiate divinity and use this power for healing of others."

The Sphinx flaps her wings in delight; "You've mastered who you are at present. Explore the deeper mysteries of Beauty, Passion, and Wisdom within the pyramid temples. Retrieve the gifts of the goddesses you will need to continue your journey. "

Song of the Self Tarot: Personal Place of Power VIII

The Golden Carriage arrives at the Oasis of the Self. The snakes transform the carriage into a platform for the Sphinx. She is comprised of the Four Archetypes of the Self as the lion's trunk for the ego mind body; the face of the woman, the divine feminine soul; her wings are the Spirit; and her serpent tail is the Shadow power for transformation.

The three white pyramids represent the storehouses of Beauty, Passion, and Wisdom. Each pyramid is like a temple or school with a priestess to help us develop our gifts.

The sun as the Symbol of Self is comprised of four quadrants, signifying the Four Archetypes of the Self. The half light and half dark sun, represent the conscious and the unconscious. In the Personal Place of Power, the Soul has been made conscious. Meaning, the strengths of the Divine Feminine are expressed through the ego. This power center of the soul is akin to the activation of the solar chakra of personal power.

The green infinity sign, (Infinite Flow of Compassion), uniting the quadrants is the symbol of the individuated Self in wholeness. It serves as a shining template for the soul's further self-realization.

The Sphinx in Mythology

The Sphinx gave travelers the opportunity to save themselves from being eaten by her, by answering her riddle. She asked Oedipus, "What goes on four feet in the morning, two feet at noon, and three feet in the evening?"

Oedipus answers correctly, "Man crawls as a baby, walks on two feet most of his life and three feet in the evening as an elderly person using a cane."

There may have been a second riddle, "there are two sisters; one gives birth to the other, who in turn gives birth to the first. Who are they?" The answer is, "day and night."

Having answered correctly, the Sphinx kills herself. In defeating the Sphinx, Oedipus fulfills the prophecy to be King of Thebes.

The symbolism of this myth indicates with wisdom, we can defeat the devouring feminine quality of the shadow to fulfill our destiny as a sovereign being.

The sisters of the second riddle refer to the conscious and unconscious parts of our psyche. Solving this riddle means we possess the awareness of the inner and outer worlds we live in.

Caterpillar: Sphinx of Wonderland

From Lewis Carrol's Alice's Adventures in Wonderland, Absalom, the blue caterpillar, looks at the shrunken Alice: "Who are YOU?' said the Caterpillar.

Alice replied, rather shyly, 'I--I hardly know, sir, just at present-- at least I know who I WAS when I got up this morning, but I think I must have been changed several times since then."

The caterpillar's question, who are you and the Sphinx's riddle of who man is, are to help the ego gain self-knowledge. Alice, reduced to three inches high, is symbolic of the ego's deflation. At this psychological stage Alice/ego is open to self-knowledge. When the ego is inflated with its self-importance it cannot accept or look within for the inner awareness of who we are.

Early on in my writing I did an analysis of Alice and Wonderland as the journey of the Four Archetypes of the Self. (I plan to rework this material) The characters and symbols in the story, appearing to be silly and childish, are profound representations of the psyche and shows us a path for self-transformation.

The Rider Waite Tarot: Strength VIII

Rider Waite Tarot, Strength VIII, illustrating the goddess petting a lion; symbolizes the soul mastering her egoic animal instincts. The lemniscate floating over her head represents her connection to the Infinite Flow of Compassion. The yellow background signifies the solar chakra, the Personal Place of Power. Her wreath of red roses indicates her goddess soul nature blossoming forth.

Activating Your Personal Power Place

Soul Growth: Cultivating Self Knowledge

The significance of the Sphinx is to know yourself. What we do not heal will destroys us. Gospel of Thomas, verse 70 states it this way, "If you bring forth what is within you, what you bring forth will save you, what you do not bring forth will destroy you."

Imagine your divine feminine being, ask her for guidance and wisdom you need. What question are you terrified to ask yourself? How is this fear interfering with your destiny to be a sovereign being. Accepting the truth, the stranglehold of the repression is undone. Interestingly, the Sphinx strangled her victims, and even her name is defined as, 'to strangle.'

My stranglehold was repressing, I'm gay. Once accepting my truth, I was free of the migraines strangling my mind and body.

Another truth I throttled back was, I'm adopted. It was a question I did not want to ask my parents, but I eventually did. They continued to deceive me. It took many years of putting the pieces of evidence together. Several psychics picked up on the truth, which I first ignored. Confronting my parents with this psychic revelation, they maintained their deception.

When a friend revealed he had not told his adopted children the truth, I had a very strong reaction; 'they must be told now, before they reach adolescence.'

Reaching my 48th birthday, I was guided from within to release all shame I was still holding. Somehow, I accomplished this by just saying to myself, "I release all shame." Whether or not the shame belonged to me or others, or was imposed upon me, I let it go. Releasing the shame I accepted, 'I'm adopted,' never to question its veracity again.

Creativity: Passion

In order to create anything, we must have sufficient passion. This motivation or passion is always within us. Healing the shadow, we now have easier access to the creative force.

Imagine your passion moving you to your Personal Place of Power. Feel your self-esteem shining from your body. Feel the joy of your exciting new adventure for the ego to transition into the soul. Write about or draw your visualization.

Creativity: Envisioning

The oasis with palm trees and water represents our internal power place; it's our interior refuge where we can always restore ourselves to inner peace and tranquility. We can visualize this image or create our own version of our personal power place.

Leading an art therapy group, I gave the directive, "draw a place you want to be at." Before you draw your vision, you see it in your mind first. Envisioning where you want to be is a powerful magic, transporting you into a place where you can feel, safe and loved.

One patient at the hospital drew a beach scene, creating for herself a calm, beautiful environment where she can relax, giving herself a break from the discomfort of being on a locked ward.

Another patient drew his bedroom, where he plays his guitar; helped him connect with his authentic, musician self.

The place I most wanted to be at for a long time was on the dance floor. It helped me get through the day at whatever job I didn't like, by imagining myself dancing. It was a wonderful compliment to be asked at times, "are you a professional dancer?" My response was, "I'm a dancer in my heart."

Where is your place of power in the world? Where would you like it to be? How would you manifest it?

Creativity: Inner Landscape

I mourned the loss of friendship. As my outer world shrunk, my capacity to go within expanded to develop my creative output. What do you need to let go of and mourn to move forward in your life? Can you connect with the joy of liberating yourself from the past to embrace the life of the soul? Can you be comfortable with just your own company? Can you enjoy it?

One of the directives I learned in school was to draw your inner landscape. I drew a sky of white and blue, surrounding a colorful center of colors; to indicate connecting with my inner core, I can be at peace in the world. I invite you to draw your inner landscape and reflect on the image. What needs more acceptance? What needs to be healed? What needs to be celebrated?

Dreamwork: Strengthening

Our dreams may reveal guidance from the soul. Can you remember an important dream where you followed the path or wisdom given to you? Is your goddess within calling you to take some time to heal and build your strength in your personal place of power? What areas of self-knowledge do you most need to explore in the present? How can you cultivate Beauty, Passion, and Wisdom into your life?

Personal Power Place in a Reading:

The oasis represents the time spent within meditating; it is how you can always reconnect with your soul and spirit. Going within is your refuge from everyday life; it can help you recharge to be the best you for your daily adventures in living. It may be helpful to journal or draw your thoughts and feelings about this. To return to your inner sanctuary, do you need to meditate, exercise or doing something fun? When feeling off balance can you focus on the breath and return to your place of personal power.

The querent having chosen the Personal Place of Power in their reading, suggests you have connected with your soul. It means you have come a long way in being who you really are. The Personal Place of Power may indicate, taking time for yourself to develop your Beauty Passion and Wisdom.

Questions to Ask in a Reading:

What are my soul qualities? What does Beauty, Passion and Wisdom of the soul mean to me? How do I express them?

Hathor's Temple of Beauty

Inside the pyramid, Hathor, the Egyptian cow-headed goddess, greets the prince, "Welcome to the Temple of Beauty, I am Hathor the goddess of the temple," the maternal figure offers the prince refreshments.

"As a personification of the divine feminine, I'm delighted with your progress and wish to bestow upon you several gifts to help you on your journey of Self Becoming. Hathor places around the prince's neck the ankh, dangling from a gold chain. "The ankh, the key to life, is really a magical mirror. "

The prince holds up the ankh to look at Hathor, the cow headed deity; he sees Hathor in her human form, a Goddess of Beauty.

Hathor explains, "Looking through it, you see the beauty of your divine feminine reflection."

The prince agrees, "You are beautiful."

"I am your reflection, eternal beauty exists within every human being," she declares.

"I'm not so sure about that," the prince counters.

"It's true many people may hide their beauty; but you can use your mirror to see the divine feminine beauty in everyone."

"I will remember to see people as they really are and not as they present themselves in the here and now," the prince vows.

Ankh

The ankh, the prince uses to see the beauty of his soul is an ancient Egyptian symbol meaning, life. The circular top refers to the Divine Feminine and the phallic stem refers to the Divine Masculine. The arms of the symbol, signify the divine child. Therefore, the ankh can symbolize the manifestation of our divinity on earth.

The ankh preceding the Christian Cross, denotes uniting heaven and earth. It is also suggested this key to life is used for entering the afterlife. Through hypnosis, a key to consciousness, we can access past lives to help us in the present.

Beauty Activation

The prince looks through the ankh to see the beauty of his soul. Can you look into a mirror and say, "I'm beautiful." Can you look into the reflection of your eyes and say, "I love you."

To honor the beauty of my divine feminine, I grew my hair out long as a way to symbolically manifest my soul into the world. Perhaps a new hairstyle or color, or new article of clothing can help you bring more of your soul into the world.

Sun Disc: Personal Power Symbol

Hathor places her amulet of the sun around the prince's neck to rest on his stomach. "The sun disc represents your personal place of power; wherever you go you take the energy of your oasis with you. Let this Symbol of the Self remind you to complete your journey to unite the Four Archetypes of the Self with the Infinite Flow of Compassion," Hathor illuminates.

The prince expresses his gratitude, "thank you, Hathor for the ankh and the sun disc, I shall express my beauty and power to aid humanity."

Ancient Egyptian gods are often featured with solar disc headdresses, expresses their divine royalty. Interestingly, the sun disc was often depicted with wings to resemble the eclipse of the sun. The union of sun and moon forming wings is similar to the horizontal bar of the ankh, indicative of the divine child.

Sun Disc: Personal Power Activation

In terms of the prince's stage of soul development, the sun disc placed over his abdomen is associated with the 3rd chakra of the solar plexus. The solar power represents the personal power of self-esteem. Shining our solar power brightly, means we have completed much of our shadow work. We feel inner peace having healed the wounds of the past.

Imagine a solar disc shining from your abdomen. Radiate your confidence, being who you are. Radiate the power of your Beauty, Passion, and Wisdom. If you are inspired, create your own solar disc or personal power symbol. Can it be worn? Maybe write a song or poem about your solar power.

After seeing the Egyptian display at the Brooklyn Museum, I purchased a beautiful, winged disc pin I would wear on my winter coat. It helped to remind me of the power of my soul and the warmth of the sun would return in the Spring.

Nephthys' Funeral for the False Self

In the next temple, Nephthys, an Egyptian Goddess and her son, the jackal headed, Anubis wrap a dead body. The prince hears their song:

We mourn the false self and his wicked ways,

The prince approaches the goddess Nephthys as she prepares the corpse, "I am Nephthys, Lady of the Temple."

The prince flinches in fear at the jackal-headed god beside Nephthys.

Nephthys informs, "Do not fear my son Anubis, the god of death.

Anubis declares, "Your soul is immortal, only the body dies."

Nephthys instructs, "Acknowledge the passing of your inner victim lying here and help us prepare this false self for burial."

The prince helps the goddess wrap the corpse with strips of linen. "I feel a sense of sadness for his passing."

"Your inner victim was a defining part of you for a long time, he became your identity," she explains.

"I could always depend on his familiarity, the low self-esteem and constant feelings of persecution; because of him I hated myself," the prince says with anger.

Nephthys instructs, "Release your anger and hatred into the corpse of your former being."

"How do I do that?" the prince asks.

This false identity has caused you much pain in the past; you have the power to stop this negative embodiment of dysfunctional belief systems and behaviors from destroying the rest of your life."

"How?"

Nephthys informs, "Take your rightful place on your throne of personal power." She points to a throne resembling a tower (Isis). Nephthys removes her headdress, resembling a tower capped with a cup, and gives it to the prince. "Allow any remaining feelings of unworthiness, self-hatred and low self-esteem to empty into this vessel."

The prince verbalizes an incantation;

> *With inner strength, I cast my demons out,*
> *I release self-hatred, fear, and doubt.*
> *I release all vestiges of low self-esteem,*
> *to pursue my higher purpose and dream.*
> *I release my pain, anger, and depression,*
> *to glow as my divine feminine expression.*

From his solar plexus, dark energy flows out and into the bowl. Anubis places the mummified body in a sarcophagus.

"There's more darkness I need to release," the prince discloses.

Anubis opens a canopic jar in front the prince.

As dark energy is extracted from the prince's abdomen, he declares, "I release resentment and blame. I take responsibility for my choices and behavior."

The jar fills up, Anubis places the human headed lid back on. He grabs another jar to catch the dark energy streaming forth from the prince's stomach. "I release the need to please, I release the need to conform to others' expectations. I disallow societal conditioning to influence who I am, how to behave and the choices I make." The jar is full. Anubis places the baboon headed lid on the container.

"I let go of relationships, jobs and lifestyles that no longer serve my higher purpose," the prince continues, filling the third jar. Anubis closes it with the jackal-headed lid.

"I release shame and guilt, I will find the strength within myself to forgive myself the harm I have done to myself and others," the prince vows. The fourth jar is topped with a falcon-headed lid.

Emptied of the darkness, the prince emits yellow light from his abdomen. The prince closes the lid of the sarcophagus and says, "I am forever free of this contemptible victim mentality." He smiles, "I liberate myself from victimhood and all the beliefs holding me back from being who I really am. "

Nephthys offers the prince a gift, "To traverse the desert, you will need these sandals." The prince places them on his feet.

Anubis gives the prince his gift, "I give you this staff for support, to help you through the dark night of the soul."

"Thank you, Nephthys and Anubis," says the grateful prince.

Soul Growth: Funeral of the False Self

In the story, the mummification of the body, symbolizes the death of the victimized ego being the sovereign of the Self. Expunging the dark negative energy, cleanses the solar chakra of personal power. Cleansing ourselves of the victim mentality, we strongly identified with, we create a space for our true self to emerge.

After completing your shadow work of expressing repressed feelings and accessing a sense of forgiveness, can you create a funeral for your inner victim? It can be as simple as wrapping a doll up and saying a few words to release this destructive part of who you thought you were from your psyche.

If you haven't completed enough of your shadow work, envision the death of your victim mentality. Wonder what your life would be like without this false identity dragging you down. Envision your goddess soul supporting you on your journey of healing. Commit to doing your shadow work to be the empowered person you really are.

Staff: Spine for Kundalini

The walking staff the prince receives, represents the support we will need on the journey of the soul. The support comes from within to help us manage adversity we will likely confront in the dark night of the soul.

The Egyptian staff resembling the head of an animal with a fork end, represents our dual consciousness of the spiritual and materialistic.

Moses with his staff showed Pharaoh he possessed the greater divine power, rather than pharaoh's inflated ego grasping to maintain power over his people.

The Magician in the tarot, and wizards in literature such as Gandalf possess a staff or magic wand to symbolize manifesting their desires.

The staff can be depicted as a caduceus, a rod with snakes twirled around it as a symbol for healing. As the staff carrying Hermit of the tarot, we have the power to facilitate healing in others.

The staff is comparable to the human spine where kundalini energy travels to enlighten us. The serpentine energy helps to clear away mental obstacles to activate the chakras. Enlightening the power centers, we manifest our divinity.

Sandals

The prince receiving the gift of the sandals, symbolizes walking the path of the goddess soul. The sole on the foot and shoe, sound the same as soul, strengthens this meaning. The Wizard of Oz and Cinderella feature characters and their special shoes. Briefly, their soulful stories are recounted below.

Dorothy's Ruby Slippers from the Wizard of Oz

Dorothy's ruby slippers symbolize taking the journey into the shadow, soul, and spirit. The witch, portrayed as Dorothy's nemesis is really her Shadow, lashing out for attention. This powerful being, forces Dorothy to gather her hidden strengths to confront the Shadow. Dorothy meeting the characters of Scarecrow, Tinman, and Cowardly Lion, becomes acquainted with her intelligence, her emotions, and her courage. The characters joining her on her journey show Dorothy's desire to know and develop her wisdom, passion, and beauty.

The three characters appear to be lacking what they do possess, illustrates how we operate in the world until we decide to accept our inherent gifts. For example, The Scarecrow hanging from a post, lacks the ability to move and his sole purpose is scaring away the crows. He represents the ego stuck in the conditioning to be a certain way. He uses fear to frighten others for self-protection.

Dorothy letting Scarecrow off the hook, depicts letting her mental body free. She begins to accept the strength of her intelligence. Later the Scarecrow advises Dorothy to use the oil can to help restore the rusted Tin Man, illustrates she is using her intelligence to reactivate her emotional body.

The lion depicted as cowardly, represents the state of fear and degradation of the soul. When the Cowardly Lion terrorizes Toto, Dorothy's dog, she accesses the courage to protect her beloved pet. This illustrates we have everything inside us we need to best navigate the world. We manifest unpleasant circumstances to help us activate the quality we need to best handle the situation.

Dorothy walks on the yellow brick road, the golden path of soul, to bring out her weaknesses to be healed and develop her strengths. At first, Dorothy denies being a witch, illustrates the ego in denial of the soul and her magic. By accessing and using her strengths, Dorothy becomes like Glinda, the good witch of the North, personifying her soul.

The witch setting Scarecrow on fire illustrates Dorothy's repressed rage becoming conscious. Dorothy realizes her dysfunctional identity has tormented and imprisoned her and attempts to completely take over her consciousness, snaps her to take the necessary self-transforming action. By throwing water on the burning scarecrow, water splashes onto the witch, causing her to melt and die. Dorothy using the waters of soul, destroys the power the witch had over her, releasing her ego from victimization.

After killing off the witch, Dorothy learned she has the magic within her to fulfill her desire to go home. "Going home" symbolizes going home within your soul, your Personal Place of Power.

Cinderella's Glass Slippers

Cinderella's cruel stepmother and stepsisters causing her much hardship, symbolize her shadow, forming her victimized persona. The prince, the personification of ego, sends out invitations to a royal ball in the hopes of finding a wife is really the ego desiring to make conscious his soul.

The invitation sparks the process of transformation for Cinderella to believe her life can be different than being a slave in her own home. She manifests her desire to go to the party with the help of her fairy god mother, the personification of her soul. At the ball, the prince and Cinderella meet and dance, represents the ego's romance with the soul. The magic employed by the fairy god mother making Cinderella presentable, lasts only to midnight. Cinderella following her instructions to depart, makes a quick getaway leaving one of her glass slippers behind. The temporary magic illustrates the soul making its appearance in the dream state or in a sudden psychic breakthrough that doesn't last for long, but long enough for the ego to awaken. The prince possessing Cinderella's slipper rouses his desire to merge with his soul. Interestingly, the magic of the slipper does not fade, indicates it is ego's enduring receptacle for the soul. The prince placing Cinderella's foot in the shoe, demonstrates the soul made conscious. Their marriage is symbolic of ego uniting with soul, the personal power place.

Temple of Isis:

In the third temple, the Goddess Isis sings,

I'm the divine feminine wisdom in your heart,
with love for humanity, my wisdom I impart.
Through the practice of meditation,
you go within for transformation.
As the Hermit you may live a lonely life,
you find your peace for overcoming strife.
Gaining self-knowledge, you've much to give,
with a higher purpose you choose to live.
By allowing the water of soul to flow,
the Pearl of Feminine Wisdom I bestow.

Pearl of Feminine Wisdom

The goddess Isis places the large pearl of feminine wisdom on top of the prince's walking staff. "The Pearl of Feminine Wisdom, representing the lunar forces, help you connect with and express your emotions in the healthiest way possible. This divine orb helps you to use the power of your intuition."

"Thank you, Isis, for the Pearl of Feminine Wisdom. How do I use it?" he asks.

"You open your heart to receive divine feminine guidance," Isis instructs. "It will help you respond to people and situations with love, rather than react in fear. It will help you to bring healing to others whenever possible. The Pearl of Feminine Wisdom can be used to open your third eye to reveal the deeper mysteries of the soul to gain greater insight to who you really are."

The prince stares into globe, "Nothing is happening. Am I doing something wrong?"

"No, my prince. Your third eye has been deeply submerged within the waters of the oasis," Isis explains and escorts the prince out of the pyramid temple.

Symbolism of the Pearl

As depicted in the story of the prince, the pearl represents feminine wisdom. The pearl taking several years to develop in the oyster can symbolize the lengthy process to manifest the wisdom of the soul. The forming of the pearl in the darkness, depicts the shadow work necessary for self-transformation.

Isis, often depicted as the Goddess of the Moon, and the moon associated with the pearl, appropriately gives the prince the pearl.

Hymn of the Pearl

In the Gnostic Myth, *Hymn of the Pearl*, a prince is sent to Egypt with the mission to retrieve a pearl from a serpent guarding it. The pearl is symbolic of the soul and the serpent represents the shadow holding its power.

In the myth, the prince forgets his mission, depicting how we all forget who we are when we incarnate. Getting lost in survival and addiction prevents us from remembering. The prince is sent a reminder from his heavenly parents to remember his mission, symbolizing our messages from soul and spirit to remember who we are. These reminders to fulfill our mission may come from dreams and our intuition.

Creating My Place of Power

Living in Florida in a small house by a channel was a manifestation of my personal power place where I expressed myself writing the first drafts of this book, several screenplays, and a series of paintings.

The inner place of power can be reflected in our life when we create a sacred space inside our homes or outside in nature. It could even be a corner of a room, a dingy basement or a car, anywhere where we can allow ourselves to just be. This feeling of grounding or coming back to ourselves can expand throughout the day. Setting the intention to be our authentic selves creates a groundswell of energy. It allows us to feel content with who we are, it reminds us to find our peace when we are angered by the people and situations in our lives. When we show up in the world with Beauty, Passion, and Wisdom; we can feel good we are living the soulful life.

Invocation For the Goddess

"I call upon the wisdom of the Divine Feminine, and I ask for the blessings of nurturing, development, evolution, and growth into the best and most beautiful divine destiny for me. Through her loving grace, I am guided, protected and assisted to become all that I can be. With gratitude and trust in the flow of my life, I relax and take the journey. As I do so, I help to bring calm and consciousness to the world for the greater good. So be it."   ~ By Alana Fairchild

Quotes

"Don't die with your music still inside you. Listen to your intuitive inner voice and find what passion stirs your soul."
– Wayne Dyer

"Music gives a soul to the universe, wings to the mind, flight to the imagination, and life to everything.".
– Plato.

Affirmations

I release my victim identity.
I shine the light of my divine feminine soul.
I am the Beauty, Passion, and Wisdom of my soul.
I am centered in my Personal Place of Power.
I give myself the space to self-reflect, relax and be.

Summary of the Personal Place of Power VIII

The ego becoming soul centered, gains self-esteem and develops the strengths of Beauty, Passion, and Wisdom.

References

Sphinx -- greekmythology.com

The Riddle of the Sphinx: An unsolved Ancient Mystery by Avis Lee -- mysteriesrunsolved.com

The Myth of the Sphinx and Its Symbolism -- exploringyourmind.com

Gospel of Thomas

Why the Caterpillar from Alice in Wonderland was So Important --
tvovermind.com

Recommended Reading and Viewing

("+" Denotes I haven't read this book)

Esoterism and Symbol by R.A. Schwaller de Lubicz

The Message of the Sphinx: A Quest for the Hidden Legacy of
Mankind by Graham Hancock, Robert Bauval

+Edgar Cayce and the Hall of Records: Solving the Mystery of the
Hall of Records and the Sphinx Connection using Ancient Egyptian
Texts, Astronomy, and the Edgar Cayce Readings by John M. Bunker
and Karen L. Pressler

+Edgar Cayce's Egypt: Psychic Revelations on the Most Fascinating
Civilization Ever Known by Edgar Cayce and A.R.E. Press

Egypt in the Day of the High Priest Ra-Ta by Millicent Horton and
Edgar Cayce

Ancient Evenings, a novel by Norman Mailer

The Memoirs of Cleopatra, a novel by Margaret George

Quills, a film written by Doug Wright

Alice's Adventures in Wonderland, by Lewis Carroll

The Meaning of the Ankh Symbol by Everett Dee --
mysteriumacademy.com

The Ankh Symbol: The Actual Meaning and History --
egyptconnection.com

The Winged Sun Disk Symbol of Ancient Egyptian Religion Was
Inspired

By Total Solar Eclipses by Robin Edgar-- eclipsology.blogspot.com

Winged Sun Disk: One of The Oldest and Most Important Solar And
Religious Symbols by A. Sutherland -- ancientpages.com

Pearl Symbol -- ancient-symbols.com

Hymn of the Pearl Acts of Thomas -- gnosis.org

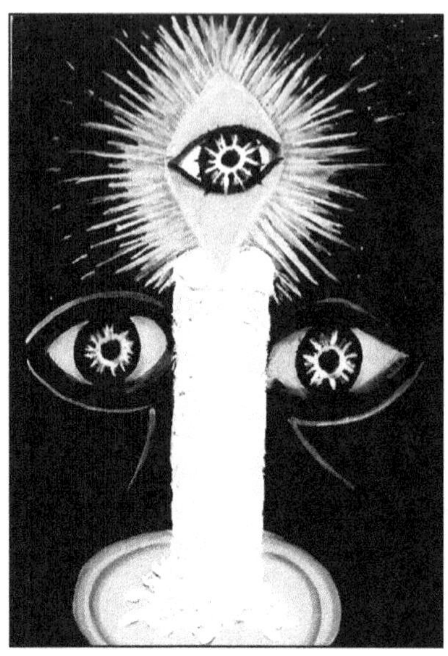

Hermit IX

Song of the Hermit

As Isis escorts the prince to the pond, the sun sets behind the pyramids. She sings, Song of the Hermit:

> *The Hermit is the Seeker of Spirit,*
> *searching through darkness to hear it.*
> *To connect with spirit, meditate and pray,*
> *his candle of enlightenment shows the way.*
> *When the spiritual path is taken,*
> *the psychic third eye will awaken.*
> *Igniting the power of insight,*
> *the Hermit heals with his light.*
> *Love and truth he does share,*
> *helping others become aware.*

Awakening the Third Eye

Isis instructs the prince, "Hold out your staff over the water; with your heart and mind summon your third eye from the Pool of Possibility."

The prince raises the staff over the water, "I summon forth my inner vision, submerged within my psyche. I vow to use this force for good. Please help me be of service to others."

The water begins to ripple. A dark orb surfaces and rises into the sky.

"What's happening?" the prince asks the goddess.

"You have awakened the third eye from its long slumber. It rises into the sun for activation," she clarifies.

The dark orb uniting with the sun, opens in a flash.

The goddess explains, "the emerald iris reflects the love of the heart; its blue aura shines the power of truth."

The third eye within a flame descends toward the prince. "Behold the Eye of Horus, you have awakened your psychic center."

Candle of Enlightenment

Isis instructs the prince, "Use your magical staff to transform the Sphinx's platform into a candle holder and the pyramids into a candle."

"Can I really do that?" the prince asks in amazement.

"In the world of imagination, you can do anything," she encourages.

The prince points his staff at the platform. The sphinx flaps her wings and becomes airborne. "Where are you going, Sphinx?" he asks.

She replies, "I fly into your future to help you remain on track in your present." The Sphinx flies away.

"Let my base of personal power transform into a candleholder so that I may take my power center with me wherever I go," the prince commands. The platform shrinks into a small golden dish. He picks it up. Nephthys, Anubis, and Hathor exit the pyramids.

As the sun quickly finishes setting, the prince points his staff at the white pyramids, "Pyramids three one candle now be."

The pyramids crumble and reformulate into a white candle. "I take the temples of Beauty, Passion and Wisdom wherever I go," the prince affirms. Nephthys, Anubis, and Hathor join Isis and the prince.

The candle levitates onto its base. The third eye flame descends onto the tip of the candle. The goddesses smile. "Well done prince," Isis praises the prince.

Song of the Self Tarot: Hermit IX

In the Song of the Self tarot deck, the Hermit IX, two eyes look from the darkness; a candle with its flame of an open eye forms the third eye. The green irises represent seeing the world with compassion, associated with the heart chakra above the third chakra of personal power. The blue glow around the flame depicts the 5th chakra of communication of universal truths, located in the throat. The dark night represents the indigo chakra associated with the sixth chakra or third eye.

Activating the Hermit

Soul Growth: Meditation

The third eye refers to the pineal gland located between the eyes, which resembles a small pinecone and the Egyptian symbol, the eye of Horus. Opening the third eye allows one to connect to higher consciousness to receive divine guidance. Meditation and yoga can help us gain our inner wisdom. Some foods and supplements can help us cleanse the pineal gland from calcification.

Identifying with the Hermit, I developed the discipline to sit still to meditate. Now, I prefer to go on daily walks, or write as my form of meditation.

Creativity: Beacon of Light

In the story of the prince, the candle is made from pyramids; the platform for the Sphinx becomes the candleholder, and the flame from sun, (Symbol of the Self). The Hermit takes with him his transportable symbol of enlightenment to share with the world. For those with eyes to see, the Hermit is a beacon of light.

Can you see yourself as a beacon of light, humbly offering your wisdom to the world? How does it feel? Draw a picture of your light or express in words the wisdom you would like to share. Do you feel divinely inspired to enter a healing profession? Which healing art can you envision being a practitioner?

Dreamwork: Finding Purpose

The Hermit has developed the skills to pursue his passion regardless of what others think. Like an eternal flame, his enlightenment has become his internal guiding force to fulfill his purpose. The Hermit, with the intention of healing, strives to communicate painful truth with compassion. What flame is lit in within you?

Rider Waite Tarot: Hermit IX

The Rider-Waite Hermit card is depicted as old man wearing a gray robe, holding a lantern with a light in the shape of the six-pointed star, referred to as the Seal of Solomon in one hand and a golden staff in his other hand.

In the "Meaning of The Hermit" –– tellmytarot.com, the author expresses:

"The Hermit lives alone and has much time to contemplate the big existential questions in life: "who am i," "what is the meaning of life" and "what is the meaning of death" for example. Because this card is not burdened by many symbols, because the Hermit is in such a quiet place without distractions, he is able to thoroughly meditate upon these great questions. Because it is winter, even the natural environment is conducive to his studiousness: there are no tweeting birds, proliferating bunnies, or wildly colored flowers to distract him.

The lamp he holds represents the light of knowledge. Inside of it is a six-pointed star; through the light of knowledge, he will gain a cosmic understanding surpassing that of the everyday sensibility. The staff helps keep The Hermit grounded and steady while he delves deep into these intuitive, mental realms. Because of the richness and focus of his interior life, The Hermit is not bothered by the cold, winter wilderness surrounding him. His warmth comes from within and from having lived a full life up to this point. He does not seek connection with others, although he is not opposed to it. He will greet whoever comes along his path with kindness and curiosity.

Also, The Hermit is humble. He bows his head down to the light of knowledge because he knows that he will never have all the answers. However, this does not stop him from seeking wisdom; his study is sacred."

Seal of Solomon

The Seal of Solomon as two triangles bisecting each other, shining from the lantern is symbolic of uniting above and below; conscious and unconscious; or spiritual and material. The lantern or light of knowledge, he humbly offers to others.

Robe of Glory

Hathor presents the prince with a pearly gray robe; "One final gift we have for you." The goddesses help the prince into the robe. The Symbol of the Self, seen as the sun, is woven into the back of the garment.

Anubis informs, "This robe of the Self, not only provides warmth through the dark night of the soul; it protects you from psychic attacks."

The goddesses embrace the prince. Nephthys directs the prince to move forward, "Leaving your oasis, you take with you our gifts to go out into the world to help others become soul centered beings."

Hermetic Robe

The Hermit can be symbolic of Hermeticism, a philosophy stemming from the mythic Hermes Trismegistus. His phrase, "As above so below," we understood as, we create heaven on earth, when we bring into consciousness, our divinity.

Hermeticism is an oral tradition passed on from teacher to student originating from ancient Egypt. This ancient wisdom is an outgrowth of other philosophical movements. Mainly teaching; humans are divine, we are all one in spirit. The process to achieve our divinity on earth is through the alchemy of our consciousness means, taking the prima materia of the ego through psychological/alchemical processes to heal the shadow to bring forth the soul, the light of who we are. Turning lead into gold of the alchemists, was code for transforming the heavy earth-bound ego to reveal the gold heavenly sun, symbolic of soul and spirit.

The Hermetic Seal of Light

The hermetic seal of light symbol consists of a circle within a square, the square within a triangle, and the triangle in a large circle. It can be viewed as the circle enveloping the three shapes as the Four Archetypes of the Self.

The small circle within, represents the ego with the potential for oneness with the source, depicted as the large outer circle. Expanding into the triangle, denotes soul retrieval and then growing into the square, consciousness unites with Spirit. Circling the square is indicative of uniting the Four Archetypes of the Self in wholeness. Similarly, the infinity sign in the symbol of the Self, connecting the quadrants, unites the four archetypes in oneness.

The Hermetic Seal of Light Activation

The Symbol of the Self, like the hermetic seal, are representations of wholeness we aspire to. Samael Aun Weor in The Fifth Gospel, lecture "The Seven Fires and the Seal of Hermes" -- vopus.org offers a way to use the hermetic seal:

There is no doubt that we always live identifying ourselves with useless things and facts.

We let our psychic energy get sucked out! What would we look like? I say perhaps a colander full of holes –those used to brew coffee– and of course, as usual, that's where the energy escapes, that's where everything escapes, we lose it, and the poor colander is left empty. The environment sucks up our own energies and we don't accumulate them, and even though we work in these conditions in the Ninth Sphere, in the Fiery Forge of Vulcan, it is obvious that we don't manage, in that form and in that fashion, to create the second body, much less the third or fourth.

In order to create the second body, we need to learn to seal ourselves hermetically, magically. What is meant by the Hermetic Seal? To not allow our energy to be sucked out, not to forget ourselves ever, ever, at any second, at any minute, so as not to identify ourselves with the trivialities, with the nonsense of this illusory world. Obviously, if our vital energy cannot be extracted from us, this energy accumulates inside, and as a result the second body emerges: the astral body. But if we allow the whole mercury of the Secret Philosophy to be extracted by people living in this three-dimensional world of Euclid, then with what element shall we manufacture the second, or third, or fourth body?

Every morning, one should seal oneself hermetically: "I do only what the Being wants me to do, not what others want me to do; I am not going to identify myself with anything in life…" Because when

one identifies with something, he becomes an automaton.
If one identifies with his own mind, with his own morbid thoughts,
he ends up adulterating and fornicating; if one identifies,
unfortunately, with his negative emotions, he ends up losing creative
energy by the ton; if one identifies with words, like the rude and dirty
words of someone, of course one ends up speaking nonsense. I repeat,
we should seal ourselves every morning, and the seal should be
constant: not to identify with anything that is not the Being, not to
forget our Being, never ever, never ever, because the Being is what
counts, is what is fundamental.

Dark Night of the Soul

Isis instructs, "Through the dark night of the soul, you seek your
heart center so you may place your base of power within
unconditional love."

"Raise your vibration to be an expression of the Infinite Flow of
Compassion," Hathor clarifies.

Anubis counsels, "In the desert you will explore the Tri-
Principality of Fate, Karma, and Timing. Humans are bound to these
universal laws of divine intelligence. Accepting these truths, you will
gain greater understanding and peace. Working with these forces,
will help you to access divine qualities to be at peace with the
challenges of the external world. "

The prince expresses his gratitude, "Thank you for all your gifts
and for all you have taught me. I shall do my best to be worthy of
your sacred teachings and offerings."

As the prince steps into the darkness holding his candle to light
the way, Anubis, Hathor, Nephthys, and Isis sing to the prince, the
Hermit's Song of the Self:"

You're the Hermit, Seeker of Spirit,
go through darkness to better hear it.
To connect with the divine, meditate and pray,
your Candle of Enlightenment shows the way.
Igniting your psychic insight,
healing with your soul's light.
Your third eye is now awake,
Spirit's path you now take.
Bring love and truth to the unaware,
shine your light for wisdom to flare.

The Hermit in a Reading:

The appearance of the Hermit in a reading indicates you are ready to share your newfound gifts with others. The problem is many people want no part of becoming who they really are. The Hermit develops the skills of knowing when to share wisdom and when to retreat. The Hermit wanders the desert of ignorance seeking like-minded souls; but learns accepting the support from within is sufficient.

Questions to Ask in a Reading:

What is your place in the world? Do you need to look deeper within? What soul qualities do you need to bring out or develop further? Can I salvage my relationships without losing my personal place of power? Do I need to end a relationship? How can you be of service to humanity?

Embracing the Hermit

Meeting Artemis at a spiritual conference and moving near to her in Florida, I accessed the energy of the Hermit. Sharing my wisdom and trying to help Artemis heal was a wonderful experience. It felt like I was living my higher purpose. The danger here was pushing someone further than where they are ready to go; or to allow my selfish desires to have someone in my life on the same level. I felt good I was able to facilitate healing by helping her access the truth of her past and work toward healing it. That she continued to need a man in her life, without really taking time for herself and complete her healing, indicates I have failed to help her fully transition from ego to soul. Artemis abandoned me within the year, leaving me devastated.

After moving to Florida, I chose to disassociate from my family. At the time, I was not fully conscious of being adopted, I just wanted to start a new life without the influence of the past. I did not want to feel their pushing me to get a job. The reason I went to school was to not have to work at a meaningless job; so that I can be of service to others. I gave my life to God and believed God will provide, God has a plan which I believed doesn't include work that I don't want.

I had business cards made up to market myself as an art therapist. I left some in a coffee shop where they have open mic night. I asked Artemis to spread the word with her women's group. I took out an ad in a local paper advertising my services without success. My ego would say, "you're not trying hard enough to succeed. My soul was telling me, "This is not your path; you will share wisdom with the world through your creativity; God will provide."

Gifts of the Hermit

As in the story of the prince, the Hermit receives many gifts. I view the many inspirational works I write as gifts from the divine, I'm meant to share. More than ever, I accept, I'm a co-creator with spirit.

I'm learning to let the love for my partner be stronger than our differences tearing us apart.

Affirmations

I shine my light of love and wisdom.
May you be free of suffering, may you live in peace.
God walks with me every step of the way.
I persevere through the darkness.

Lokah Samastah Sukhino Bhavantu Mantra

"May all beings be happy and free from suffering. And may the thoughts, words, and actions in my own life in some way contribute to that happiness and that freedom for all."

- Lokah Samastah Sukhino Bhavantu -- www.awakeningstate.com

Summary of the Hermit IX

The Hermit, possessing Divine Feminine Consciousness, comprising Beauty, Passion and Wisdom goes into the world to bring enlightenment to others.

References

How to Awaken Your Third Eye, By Andye Murphy-- gaia.com

How To Activate Your Third Eye (15 Best Ways) By Rafal Reyzer-- Rafal Reyzer.com

Meaning of The Hermit -- tellmytarot.com

The Hermit by Anne-Marie Wegh-- anne-mariewegh.eu

The Seven Fires and the Seal of Hermes by Samael Aun Weor-- vopus.org.

Hermeticism - The secret knowledge-- hermetic academy.com

Hermeticism -- Wikipedia (offers several external links to hermetic texts.)

Dark Night of the Soul Meaning (and 13 signs you're experiencing it) by Gabriella Grace-- selfuntethered.com

What Is the Dark Night of the Soul? Our Meaning, Stages & More! By Jade Small-- qhhtofficial.com

A Dark Night of the Soul and the Discovery of Meaning By Thomas Moore-- kosmosjournal.org

Seal of Solomon - Symbolism, Meaning and Importance, by Dani Rhys-- symbolsage.com

The Star of David and the Seal of Solomon, by Jeremy Weiss-- templeofmiriam.com

Star of David: The Mystical Significance, by Naftali Silberberg -- chabad.org

Tri-Principality:

Fate X, Karma XI and Timing XII

Dark Night of the Soul: Spiritual Awakening

The Hermit wandering the desert at night, depicts a Dark Night of the Soul where the traveler explores the Tri-Principality of Fate X, Karma XI and Timing XII to be discussed in the next few chapters.

Fate X

Song of Fate

As the hermit traverses the desert, his mind wanders with questions: "What do I do with my life? How do I fulfill my higher purpose? How can I have a meaningful life? With whom shall I share my love and wisdom? How can I help enlighten humanity?"

The sun begins to rise. The hermit has made it through the dark night of the soul. He is drawn toward the haunting melody of Song of Fate:

> *Submit to your Web of Fate*
> *to lift you into a higher state.*
> *Your destiny has been embedded,*
> *before birth, it's divinely threaded.*
> *Strength of Vulnerability you allow,*
> *to God, the father, make your vow.*
> *Acceptance helps you through circumstances,*
> *gracefully stepping in life challenging dances.*
> *You choose to go with or against the flow,*
> *let spirit take you where you should go.*

The hermit arrives at a giant white and violet web; the former Sphinx, now human, is splayed naked in the center of the web. Having finished her song, she addresses the mendicant, "Greetings

103

Seeker of Wisdom, you have made it through the dark night of the soul by asking and meditating upon the future of your life's journey."

"Do I know you?" asks the hermit.

"I was the Sphinx, I have taken on human form except for my hair of snakes. "

"What happened?" he asks.

"By your going through the Dark Night of the Soul, it has humanized me." The fish rising from my groin, depicts your spiritual ascension and the snakes indicate further transformation of consciousness to be done and look how my wings have transformed into this glorious Web of Fate."

"Wow, I thought I was just wandering and getting lost in the desert," replies the prince.

"Sometimes personal growth happens outside of your conscious awareness; like a seed germinating beneath the surface," she clarifies.

"I feel a deepening sense of self. I'm confident in who I am and the gifts I can offer humanity," states the hermit.

"Now you are ready to take my place in the Web of Fate," the former sphinx instructs.

"What does that mean? he asks.

"Submit to the will of God, allow the spirit to guide you as you expand your spiritual qualities to be divine on earth."

The hermit takes his place in the center of the web, "I give my life to God to do as he wills." The web sparkles and hums and lifts off the ground, carrying the supplicant of spirit.

"I let the divine guide me to my highest fate." The web spins quickly and moves into another dimension.

Song of the Self Tarot: Fate X

The Song of the Self Tarot, Fate X, depicts a naked woman splayed in the center of a large web. As the story illustrates, the Web of Fate is mainly about giving your life to God to do as he wills. Put another way, the ego united with soul, surrenders to the design of divine intelligence. With vulnerability she trusts her fate will take her where she needs to go for the progression of her soul. She exhibits the faith and confidence God will provide. She accepts whatever challenging situations she may encounter with grace. She will learn to access her divine qualities to elevate herself and in so doing, humanity. At this stage of the journey, we may sense our lives are preplanned. It is my belief; we co-create our lives before birth.

Web: Crown Chakra

The purple and white web can be viewed as the crown chakra, the power center for connecting with the divine. In the web article, Crown Chakra–Sahasrara–– chakra-anatomy.com, Simona Sebastian writes:

Sahasrara is located at the crown of the head. The gift of this chakra is experiencing unity and the selfless realization that everything is connected at a fundamental level. The energy of this chakra allows us to experience mystical oneness with everyone and everything in nature. There is no intellectual knowing at the level of seventh chakra, but there is serenity, joy, and deep peace about life. You have a sense of knowing that there is a deeper meaning of life and that there is an order that underlies all of existence. The "way of the crown chakra" is the way of going beyond the limits of your own ego. It is the way of transcending the ego and knowing that all of creation is interconnected at a fundamental level.

The outline of the web in a darker blue-violet denotes the sixth chakra, referred to as the third eye for psychic ability; implies through opening the third eye we connect to our divine source of being. The blue background of the web can be perceived as air or water, refers to the blue of the fifth chakra, the expression of universal truths.

Fish Symbol

The fish symbol on the Sphinx's torso stems from her groins and rises up to her breasts, represents her evolution through the lower chakras; the root chakra located at the base of the spine refers to survival of the body, the sacral chakra refers to the sexual organs for survival of the species and creativity; the abdominal chakra relates to the place of personal power; and the central chakra of the heart links the lower and higher chakras with the power of compassion.

As discussed earlier, the symbol of the fish is associated with Jesus, the fisher of men. In the Song of the Self, the symbol depicts the evolution of Christ Consciousness; also known as Buddha Consciousness or any term for enlightenment.

Snakes of Transformation

The red Snakes of Transformation growing from the head of the former Sphinx, indicates the transformation of consciousness still in process. The red associated with the root chakra, life's blood; now at the crown, depicts the activation of this seventh chakra.

Web of Fate: Astrological Wheel

The Web of Fate can be seen as the astrological wheel. The natal horoscope is a template of the sky at our time of birth and place. The horoscope is a complex chart of what sign the planet is in and which of the 12 houses they are placed and the angles they form to each other. These aspects reveal how we will show up in the world and indicate the challenges we will likely face.

Every day we are influenced by the energy of the planets and the angles they create with each other. The more exacting the aspect, the stronger the influence; for example, when planets form a hard right angle, or completely opposite each other, or close to each other. The slow-moving outer planets remaining in the same sign for years effect generations of people.

Basically, astrology expresses our fate. We can transcend the birth chart through the inner work of healing.

Benjamin in his web article, Astrology: Free Will or Fate? answers the question:

"… In fact, I help people use astrology to take charge of their lives! You are not a helpless victim in a fatalistic universe. The planetary forces are just raw material, whose influence and outcome are powerfully shaped by your thoughts and intentions.

If we did a session, my primary goal would be to educate you about the low and high side possibilities of your planetary influences. Once you understand these simple ideas, you can "reprogram" any astrological influence you're not happy with to call in its high side expression.

I believe astrology to be archetypally predictive, not concretely predictive. In terms of your current planetary influences, this means that I can accurately describe the types of energies you will be experiencing, how long they will last, and when they will be strongest.

But I can't tell you the exact things that are going to happen to you, or whether you'll perceive them to be good or bad. All this is determined by your state of consciousness, and how you choose to work with these astrological forces.

Understanding your current astrological influences gives you a clear map of the territory. This makes it much easier to plan your optimal life strategy!

Beyond Free Will The above applies to reality as perceived by the unawakened ego. Once you can hold a certain level of divine consciousness, you see that free will is an illusion — as is the entire physical universe it appears to operate in.

Free will is a helpful and necessary tool until this awakening happens, so use it for all it's worth until then! After awakening, free will is perceived as a hindrance to the perfect, automatic action taken by the divine through the blissfully surrendered human. It is extremely cool to experience "doing, but no doer"!

The more you awaken, the less you need astrology and other divinatory tools. But until you can access the information you need within yourself; astrology can help you live a happier and more fulfilling life!"

Master Number 33

The astrological wheel is divided into twelve sections for each zodiacal sign. In Song of the Self Web of Fate, I notice only eleven divisions of the web, bisecting the three circular tiers; with five points on top and six below. (This was not a conscious choice, but perhaps a painted it this way because this card is the eleventh card of the major arcana even though it is titled as ten, since the Fool is the first card titled with 0.)

Interestingly, eleven is a master number and with the three rows, results in 33 compartments, also a master number. 33 may be referred to as the master teacher, relates to our unique fate for spiritual evolution. There are many interesting associations to the number 33 explored in the web articles referenced in this chapter.

Numerology of Tri-Principality

The Song of the Self's Web of Fate in three tiers, references the Tri-Principality of Fate, Karma, and Timing. I believe our incarnated souls are bound to this divine order; as Fate, we create our lives before birth, we take into account our actions from the past we want to correct and fulfill our karmic contracts with others in divine timing with the influence of astrology.

Fate 10, Karma 11, and Timing 12 numbers of the tarot, adds up to 33, the number of the Master Teacher; confirming the Tri-Principality forms the divine plan for our earthly lives. Numerologically, the master number 11, the visionary, combined with master 22, the builder adds up to the Master Teacher 33; which can mean, we cocreate or envision our lives before incarnation including goals we want to accomplish; we factor in karmic debts, credits, and bonds. We then build our lives within the structure of astrological and divine timing. In this Wheel of Time or Web of Fate, we manifest our unique journey of the soul.

Vitruvian Man

Looking at the vulnerable woman on the Web of Fate, I'm reminded of the iconic drawing of Leonard Da Vinci: The Vitruvian Man. It depicts a nude man in two positions simultaneously, splayed out within both a circle and square. It is known for its ideal proportions of body parts. The figure was drawn within a square to represent the human being part of the material world as well as the circle to indicate the world of soul.

Squaring the Circle is depicted in the Hermetic Seal of Light. Carl Jung refers to this imagery of transmuting the four elements depicted by the square to the oneness of the circle. The alchemists referred to this distillation process resulting in the quintessence. In Song of the Self terms, it's uniting the Four Archetypes of the Self.

In a You Tube Video, the Vitruvian man is super imposed over with symbols and systems, for example, the chakras, the Fibonacci sequence, the Star of Solomon and most fascinating the Kabbalistic Tree of Life.

Interestingly, the Kaballah Tree of Life consists of 10 spheres representing 10 planets and 22 pathways linking them, labeled with the 22 letters of the Hebrew Alphabet. These twenty-two pathways also coincide with the twenty-two archetypes of the major arcana of the tarot deck. In some Tree of Life structures there is an eleventh entity called Daat, for a total of 33. Daat is attributed to special knowledge or gnosis and serves as a bridge for manifesting. Perhaps this 11th sphere can be understood as the soul's knowing of one's fate; that we can access this information to consciously manifest it.

Web of Fate: Matrix

The Web of Fate can be a symbol of the matrix; a world that we perceive as physical, but in actuality is a simulated environment. This concept is difficult to comprehend and accept because our ego and body's five senses experience the material world. Through the 'birth process' our consciousness is focused into a body, much like a computerized character in a video game; where we are given a certain amount of life to accomplish goals to get to the next level.

Conspiracist disclosers use the symbol of a spider controlling the web to keep humanity enslaved and ignorant of the dark forces in control. They claim these extra-terrestrial beings influence world leaders from the fourth dimension. These Draco-Reptilian entities have been ruling over humanity since our existence on Earth. We are told we are at a pivotal point in our history to change this demonic dynamic. The web, used to enslave us, will be used to unite humanity, so collectively we can break free of it. The more severe their draconian schemes get; the more people can awaken to the truth. The truth we have been enslaved to a dark system, mainly with the use of fear. Through the media, education, religion, government and technology we are constantly bombarded with messages to fear for our survival. To defeat the powers of darkness, we can release our fear by accepting we are eternal divine consciousness; our bodies perish but our soul and spirit never die. Allowing ourselves to be divine consciousness, we are connecting with our higher nature of love. The love that we are, heals and transforms us individually and collectively. It is and always has been up to us to transform the matrix created by the demi-urge into a worldly paradise ruled by the power of love originating from our true source. I've come to believe this has been the Creator's plan all along, for our souls to know who we really are as powerfully loving beings. May we all transcend our fear to accomplish the goal of self and world transformation. We are not really separate from each other; we originated from Oneness and Oneness we are meant to return.

Fate Activation

Soul Growth: Divine Guidance

The Web of Fate is about giving yourself to the divine by following God's will for your life. What prevents you from allowing your spiritual ascension? Do you already know god's plan for you? what's your next step?

Creativity: Imagining the Web of Fate

Imagine encountering a Web of Fate. What does it look like? Are there any characters in or around the web. What guidance are they offering? Can you imagine yourself like the humanized sphinx, splayed out naked on the web? How do you feel? Does the web take off? Do you arrive at a destination? What do you see there? Write or draw your visualization. What's the most powerful insight you gained from this experience?

Dreamwork: Dismantling the Matrix

You can set your intention for ascension for the planet as; I send my love and healing energy to raise the vibration of the planet for healing and to free humanity from the matrix.

You can imagine the Earth surrounded with a darkness so thick you do not see the strands of the web entrapping it. Next, you can visualize your love and healing energy circling the darkness with light. You can now see thousands of people are with you doing the same thing.

The web comes into view. As we breathe out, we send our powerful love down the strands into the center. The strands begin to spark and crackle with energy. As you continue to breathe, the enlightening of the strands, advances toward the center. The spider in the center is terrified of being consumed by the encroaching light and fire. We keep breathing and ignore the spider's pleas, threats and lies trying to stop us from taking back our planet. We keep breathing love and light and watch the web of darkness disintegrate. The spider cries out in a deadly fright as it tries to escape down a coarse thread from the bright light encircling the planet. The light dissolves the strand, the spider falls into a black hole.

The planet glowing with our love and light is healed and has ascended into a higher dimension. We achieve a state of oneness where humanity is free from the dark forces that have controlled us. As long as we collectively maintain our loving energy for humanity and our planet, the dark forces can never intrude upon us again.

In terms of pursuing a dream we must cultivate the divine quality of faith. Believing in ourselves and in our divinely inspired mission, we have the power to manifest the dream.

Rider Waite Tarot: Wheel of Fortune X

The Rider-Waite tarot Wheel of Fortune X depicts a wheel with a Sphinx carrying a sword at the top, a serpent heading down and Anubis, the Egyptian jackal-headed god going up. The sphinx represents the soul aware of its fate. The serpent representing transformation is our power to align with and manifest our higher fate.

Anubis, the God of Death, bearing the wheel of Fortune on its back, indicates the impermanence of life. We all share the fate our current incarnation will end and we all have the potential to master our fate in self growth.

In the four corners are four winged figures holding books; an angel, a bull, an eagle, a lion. These golden figures indicate that our fate has already been written.

The word, Tarot, included in the wheel, indicates the journey of the soul depicted in the major arcana is a pathway to help us understand and realize our fate to be divine in the material world. The glyphs within the circle depict the alchemical nature of the change of consciousness.

Fate/ Wheel of Fortune X in a Reading:

Drawing the Web of Fate or Wheel of Fortune may indicate you're feeling vulnerable accepting god's will. The challenge is to have faith everything is working for your greatest good. We may have impulses to fight or flee the winds of change, but we must strengthen our faith in divine order.

Questions to Ask in a Reading:

What is Divine Will asking you to do with your life? Am I resisting change? Do you have faith in God's plan? Do you need to strengthen your faith?

Accepting the Web of Fate

Making the conscious decision to give my life to God, I was given the dream to go back to school to be an art therapist; this was a major unfolding of the Web of Fate archetype for me. Becoming a writer was another divinely inspired path taken.

I had the good fortune of employing the services of three amazing psychics, (Raymond Pero, Susan Buchanan, the third I don't remember,) accurately foretold my future.

At the age of 22, Raymond told me I'm a spiritual teacher and was honored to meet me. He said, I was meant to be a writer of important work. I told him I have nothing to write about. He said you will in about fourteen years which was right about the time I started writing.

On a piece of paper, he wrote down the name Michael and showed it to me later on, telling me it would be a long time before I would meet this Latino man about ten years older than me who would be my partner. This prediction came to pass thirty years later.

He asked me if I was adopted, at the time I replied, 'not that I know of.' He also said I'm going to be **very** rich, as of yet this has not transpired.

Susan told me of many things that would occur ten years in the future. At the time of the reading, I wanted to ask for my money back thinking she's got it all wrong, or there were things my ego would never choose to experience, like being a hermit, having debt, living in a trailer and being homeless. She saw I would get through all this but made me promise I wouldn't do anything rash; meaning don't kill yourself. She also saw me doing a lot of writing, that my work would sell and it would be bigger than anything I could dream. She reported to me many markers to help me know I'm on this trajectory. I know I'm getting really close since she did predict a global epidemic, the overturning of Roe Vs Wade and possibly the death of James Caan, Olivia Newton John and the Queen of England to narrow down the timing. She predicted I would meet a woman who will help me with my work, I'm hoping she's coming soon.

One of the strongest occurrences depicting the Web of Fate was after living in the trailer for about two years, I was unable to pay the rent. I exhausted my parents' generosity the first year, the second year I had the good fortune my landlord, Castor, employed me to help with home improvements and assist him in his new handyman business.

Working for Castor, at first felt like a godsend. I was able to make enough money for rent and for food. I felt good I can be of service, helping someone succeed in their dream. He offered to move with him to Palm Springs. I didn't want to go because I felt I needed to stay in Los Angeles to somehow meet people in the entertainment industry who could help me. I just couldn't bring myself to look for work, after months of doing work, I disliked. I finally applied for general relief to help pay the rent. I could have done this two years ago, but I was resistant to the idea of being dependent on the state and deal with the bureaucracy. I kept thinking any day, God will provide me with the success I came to Los Angeles for. I thought I would have some time for this miracle to happen, knowing from previous experience the eviction process can take several months.

When Castor turned off the power to the trailer, I called the police to complain to get him to put it back on. They told me since I had been paying rent, it was illegal for him to do that. Unfortunately, it was illegal for the trailer to be parked in the backyard in Glendale. The health department declared my dwelling uninhabitable; I couldn't stay there. I was homeless.

Normally when something terrible happens, you want to rage at the injustice or slip into a depression; instead, I was relieved, the fear of becoming homeless felt all consuming. Now with nothing to fear, I accepted my fate. Having given my life to God, now that this terrible thing is happening it must be God's will, this must be part of the plan. What was once perceived by my ego as my worst nightmare come true, shifts into a new adventure in my life. Later on, it would dawn on me, homelessness was foretold, further helping me accept the life path I had chosen.

The police told me I can sue to get back all the rent I paid on an illegal dwelling and for moving expenses. The police helped me work out a deal with Castor to help me move my stuff into storage and pay for the first two months. Castor drove me to the local YMCA to live, but there was no availability. He paid for several nights at a motel. I could not think about going through the process of getting a lawyer and suing. Even though Castor lied about the dwelling being legal, I somehow knew something wasn't right as evidenced by a tarp hiding the trailer from the view of the street. Regardless, I was grateful I had a place to live, where I wrote 22 screenplays. I was grateful for Castor's friendship and still believed my miracle can occur any moment.

Many people would view my downslide as self-created, that I did not behave responsibly about my finances and getting a job. Just like I can't make an egocentric person living in fear to see the truth of what is really happening in the world in the age of pandemonium, I can't make anyone understand, becoming homeless was part of my fate.

When a dear friend told me I wasn't meant to be a writer, that being a caregiver should be all I aspire to, I tried to ignore it. My divine guidance was not to let anyone impose their reality on me. I stopped calling my friend and would not take his calls. I did not explain myself to him, may sound cruel; but knowing how manipulative this person can be I did what I thought best. My friend had told me he changed when we reconnected, it took a year and a half to know for sure he was lying. That was about ten years ago; since that time, with a deepening talent, I have brought to manifestation many screenplays and books with the main purpose for healing.

Fate Quotes

"It is usually more important how a man meets his fate than what it is."
~Karl Wilhelm Von Humboldt

"Do not be afraid; our fate cannot be taken from us; it is a gift."
~Dante Alighieri, Inferno

"No one saves us but ourselves. No one can and no one may. We ourselves must walk the path."
~ Gautama Buddha, Sayings of Buddha

I discovered that maybe it was fate all along, that faith was just an illusion that somehow you're in control.
~ Amy Tan

Your fate is mostly shaped by your faith in yourself!
~ Mehmet Murat Ildan

Have faith in fate. You don't have a choice.
~ Tapan Ghosh

Faith means you have it in your heart before you have it in your circumstances.
~Kimberly Jones-Pothier

"What we do not make conscious emerges later as fate."
~C.G. Jung

To make what fate intends for me my own intention.
~C.G. Jung

"I can control my destiny, but not my fate. Destiny means there are opportunities to turn right or left, but fate is a one-way street. I believe we all have the choice as to whether we fulfill our destiny, but our fate is sealed."
~ Paulo Coelho

"I always believe in a better world, forever."
~Sir Kristian Goldmund Aumann

Affirmations

There is a divine plan, I have faith in myself to follow it.
Faith is my divine quality for manifesting fate.
I have faith in divine order.
I follow the will of my divine inner self.

Synchronicity

After working on this chapter, I was dead heading the planter, I came across a spider. To me, the synchronicity of the spider and discussing the spider web of fate indicates, I am on my fated track for success.

Summary of Fate X

The Web of Fate is accepting God's Will. We develop our faith, in our divine self as our guiding force.

References

Crown Chakra – Sahasrara -- chakra-anatomy.com

Astrology: Free Will or Fate? By Benjamin -- astroshaman.com

Master number 33 -- ganeshaspeaks.com

Master Number 33 Meaning -- numerologyreader.com

5 Secrets of Numerology Master Number 33 Meaning – Personality, Career and Love -- numerologynation.com

15 Things You Might Not Know About Leonardo da Vinci's Vitruvian Man, By Kristy Puchko -- mentalfloss.com

Vitruvian Man -- blogintegrate.io

Vitruvian Man by Leonardo Davinci -- leonardodavinci.net

Leonardo Da Vinci- Vitruvian Man -- nicofranz.art

Leonardo Da Vinci's Vitruvian Man Explained by Gabriela Hdez -- owlcation.com

The Secret Meaning Behind Leonardo da Vinci's Vitruvian Man, by Luke Miller -- truththeory.com

Did you know that there is a secret behind the Vitruvian man? By Kandlus -- Youtube

C.G. Jung Archetypes of the Collective Unconscious Paragraph 715
Alchemy, Meaning of Symbols by Moe -- gnosticwarrior.com

Wheel of Fortune, by Anne-Marie Wegh -- anne-mariewegh.eu

Susan Buchanan, psychic

Raymond, psychic

Symbolism of Wheel of Fortune in Tarot -- esoterichut.com

Daath, the Doorway to Knowledge (1) -- glorian.org

12 Meditations for the Earth -- intergifted.com

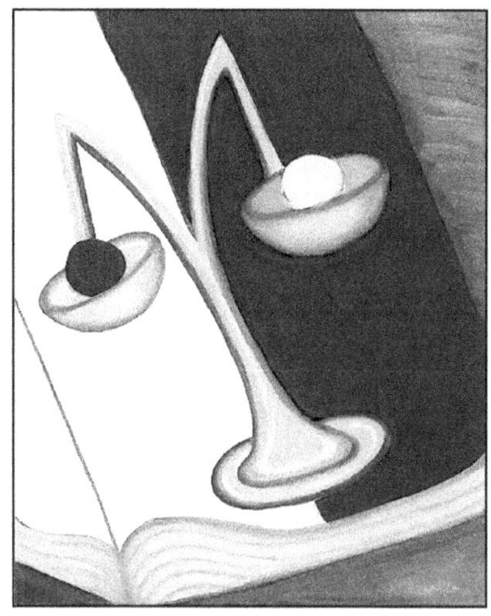

Karma XI

Song of Karma

The splayed supplicant attached to the Web of Fate spins through the cosmos to arrive at a magnificent Greco-Roman building. An Egyptian Goddess exits the library to greet the prince.

"Welcome Seeker to the Akashic Hall of Records. I Seshat, am the Keeper of Wisdom; I will help you access your past lives which most strongly influence your current lifetime. Follow me."

"Thank you for your help." He tries to stand up and struggles to break free of the web; but the hold is too strong. "I can't move."

"Ah, you are too attached to manifesting the great fate you have divinely woven. The success you desire shall be in Divine Order. There are karmic bonds with others needing to be balanced," Seshat explains.

"So, what do I do?"

"Obviously, you must let go."

"The web is holding me."

Seshat counsels, "So, it appears; but it's really your mind binding you to your web of desire. Allow God to be master of your fate by letting go of **how** you will manifest your desires."

He defends, "Through our conditioning on earth, we are made to understand; we have to do something to make something happen."

117

"Unlearn this false and limiting egocentric belief pattern," she replies.

"How?" he asks.

"Stop trying to manipulate divine order to follow **your** will."

"My rational mind thinks in terms of cause and effect, action and reaction," he restates his belief system.

"These laws apply to the materialistic dimension and have much influence on human psychology; but humans are multi-dimensional beings with access to the non-rational mind," she teaches.

"What is that?" he asks.

"The non-rational mind is your intuition you receive from your soul and spirit," she answers.

"Yes, that's my divine guidance; which I understand may be in opposition to my logical ego thinking; if I do this, such and such will happen. How do I resolve these opposing minds of rational and non-rational?"

"Become the observer of your thoughts before taking action; determine if the thought is ego driven or divinely inspired," she counsels.

"That sounds quite simple, but this thought complex is very powerful; it's so frustrating, I have difficulty breaking free of the hold it has upon me," he confesses as he tries to pull away from the webbing.

Seshat speaks with compassion, "Let go of the frustration."

"But it's frustrating," the prince insists.

"Why is it so vexing?" She inquires.

"Because everyone knows, you have to make an effort to manifest what you want," he maintains.

"And..."

And if I don't follow through, people will think I am a fool."

"Ah there it is," she points out.

"There is what?" he asks with irritation.

"The core of your blockage; you still care too much of what others think of you," she simplifies his issue.

"I really don't care how other people think of me," he counters.

"You have freed yourself of much conventional perceptions, yet you have deeply internalized this complex of doing," she clarifies.

"How do I get rid of my attachment to this webbing of belief?"

"Expand your mind to accept the power of non-doing," Seshat advises.

"That seems like such a preposterous concept," the prince replies.

Seshat smiles, "We can go no further until you accept this state of being."

"But how do I do this?" he asks incredulously.

"Allow this state of non-doing to be a possibility," she instructs.

"But this goes against everything we have been taught," he argues.

Seshat holds out her hands to the prince as a calming gesture; "Allow me to enlighten you: discipline your ego to not do, to allow your soul and spirit to work for you. They will guide you through your intuition or dreams, how and when to act."

The pearl on his staff glows; "Your illuminating wisdom dawns upon my consciousness." He tries to free himself from the web but remains trapped. "Yet I'm still caught in this web."

"Intellectually you have accepted the concept of non-doing, but you still have not released the frustration charging through the dysfunctional belief complex."

"So, it's really my emotion powering the blockage to my divine intelligence."

"Yes, you understand completely."

"So how do I let go?" he eagerly asks.

"Letting go of frustration may be difficult, but it's similar to letting any feeling go," she clarifies.

He comprehends, "I must fully feel it, and express it someway."

"Exactly," she confirms and asks, "begin by determining where in your body do you feel the frustration?"

"I don't feel anything in my body; just these constant annoying thoughts cycling through my mind," the prince says.

"Your thoughts interfere with your ability to fully feel the emotion."

"I understand, but how do I shut them off?" he wonders.

"Detachment." She responds.

"Just like that?" he says with some skepticism.

"The ego produces a constant stream of consciousness. When you shift into being the observer of your thoughts rather than its thinker, you begin to master the Power of Detachment."

"I have done this in the past when I was working on letting go of my false dysfunctional way of being in the world; I would disallow all negative thoughts I had about myself. I imagined people, in their minds, were complementing me rather than judging or criticizing me," he confirms.

She adds, "thoughts can be seen like tiny clouds you can easily blow away."

The prince nods with understanding, "In the past, I have refused to allow the ego's stream of consciousness from making me feel bad about myself."

"Yes, you can briefly turn off the thoughts enough to gain a higher perspective; you can also use the Power of Thought as a doorway to your emotion," she explains.

"Really, how?"

She clarifies, "Thoughts tell you what you are feeling without really feeling it completely."

"Ah, now I understand."

She continues, "use the thought of frustration to lead you into the core of the feeling, located in your body."

He closes his eyes to help concentrate on finding the thought thread into his emotion, "I understand what you are saying, but I am having trouble putting it into action," he replies.

"You are still very much in your head."

"I know, that's the problem," he confirms.

"Mentally scan your entire body to locate your emotion," she advises.

The prince tries to apply the technique for connecting to the emotion, "I don't see or feel anything."

Seshat takes the candle from the web, "I will help you get in touch with your rage." Seshat sets the web on fire along the circumference.

"Are you crazy? Are you trying to kill me?" cries the outraged hermit-prince.

"The fire is the catalyst for transformation," she informs.

"Yeah, this is great if I wanted to be burnt into blackened crisp, he snaps.

"Ah now you are using humor to avoid your feelings," Seshat states the obvious.

The fire comes closer to the hermit-prince's body; from fear and heat, he breaks out into a sweat. Consumed by anxiety, the prince begs, "I'm afraid I will die; please, please, help me get free of the web on fire."

"I'm helping you. You must calm yourself; your fears are paralyzing you from expressing the feeling causing the blockage."

"How do you release fear when you are facing certain death?" he pleads.

"By now you already know the answer to this question; regardless of the finite life of the body, your soul is eternal. This alchemical fire is not physical, it's the catalyst for inner transformation into God consciousness," she clarifies.

"I'm still terrified my body will expire," he counters.

"You are in the interior of your consciousness, like in a dream, you are in no danger of passing away here. Please take some deep cleansing breaths, tell yourself, I'm okay no matter what happens."

The prince complies with her instructions. He takes a few deep breaths, "Everything's okay, nothing can hurt who I really am."

She continues, "this trial by fire helps you access and expand the divine quality of perseverance. The Power of Perseverance, coming from source, gives you the inner strength to get through the trials and tribulations of your life. Perseverance helps you survive the difficult times in order to complete the godly work entrusted to you. Speak your truth to remove the blockage to following God's Will."

The fire advances to the center of the web, consuming the hermit's gray robe. The divine fire penetrates through the prince like a force of energy and light. It does not burn the body like earthly fire, it infuses the body with the consciousness of divine wisdom.

"Somehow, I'll persevere through anything because I know God is with me. I know I'm the instrument of the divine, doing God's work. I create works for teaching wisdom to inspire humanity to evolve into who we really are. My writing and art are very valuable, God has trusted me as a steward of universal wisdom, I am meant to share with others. Somehow, I must survive to complete the task I've been given, to manifest the fate I have co-created with God."

Seshat observes the Pearl of Feminine Wisdom atop the prince's staff glowing brightly. "I see by your shining orb; you're integrating the Power of Perseverance."

The prince notices the radiating orb, "Yes, I feel my personal power increasing to incorporate the divine quality of perseverance."

"The Power of Perseverance combines your inner strength and courage to help you illuminate the repressed feeling," she informs.

"I'm feeling something in my gut," he says.

"Focus your attention on it; determine what it is, what is it communicating to you?" she asks.

"It's a discomforting sensation of feeling powerless," he responds.

"You're not powerless," she reminds him.

"I'm powerless to manifest how and when my desire is to be fulfilled, and it's frustrating to me."

"Focus on this feeling and allow its full expression," she counsels.

The prince winces, "It feels like an angry churning in my belly."

Seshat explains, "It's your rage and frustration, blocking your third chakra located in your solar plexus."

"Yes, I'm becoming aware of how furious I really am, and how useless it is for manifesting my desires, yet I can't let it go completely."

"The feeling will return unless it's fully resolved."

"It's making me so angry; I could scream."

"That is what you should do," she encourages.

"But won't it make it worse, to give it more power?" he cries out.

"You have already given it much power, take it back by expressing the emotion to its depth."

The prince's extended moan is like chanting the sacred syllable. As his vocalization intensifies his body vibrates.

"As you chant, visualize the emotion as an energy from your solar plexus and release it," she recommends.

A dark smoky color begins to emerge from the prince's stomach. He raises his voice; the energy pours out and encircles his body.

"The emotion surrounds you, waiting for a moment of unawareness to reenter your body," she observes.

The prince yells as loud as he possibly can to push away the uncomfortable feeling threatening to return. The circle of darkness widens but will not dissipate.

"It's still there, what do I do now?" The prince inquires.

"You have cleared it enough to connect with your heart chakra. Allow love to flow from your heart into your power centers below. Use your breath and your voice to accomplish this healing."

The prince softly chants the sacred syllable of OM. A luminescent green color surfaces from the prince's chest.

"Beautiful, identify with your self love as deeply as you can," she guides the prince.

The luminescence increases to clear his chakras and surrounds his body. "Love is who I am, I serve the spirit, by serving humanity."

The darkness around the light dissipates. "Dark thoughts and emotions cannot survive in the light of love," she validates his transformation from anger to love.

"I release trying to manifest outcomes, I have little or no control over. I accept God has a plan for me, even if I don't know how it will come into being," he declares.

"All is done in Divine Order," she confirms.

The symbol of the fish appears on prince's naked torso. It moves from the groin and abdomen to reach the center of his chest. Seshat comments, "You have expunged the blockage, your consciousness has become heart centered. You are no longer just a seeker of wisdom;

you embody the knowledge of Divine Order and manifest the divine quality of perseverance. The wisdom you acquire, you can teach."

The prince easily removes himself from the web. He supports himself with the staff to stand up. He moves off the web, leaving the golden staff in the center of the web. The fire disintegrates the webbing of his dysfunctional belief system and flares up around the staff: The candleholder forms the base as the staff becomes the scales; the melting wax forms into a dark pearl manifesting the Scales of Karma.

"What's happening," he asks.

"Mastering the concept of Divine Order, you open yourself to the deeper mysteries," she informs.

"What mystery," he asks.

"The balancing of karma," as she answers, the pearl splits in two, a dark and a light orb rest in each of the scales.

Seshat sings the Karma Song:

> *All may seem to be in disorder,*
> *everything is in Divine Order.*
> *From victimhood to be our own savior,*
> *we create karma through our behavior.*
> *There's no punishment for wrongdoing,*
> *we work out karma in the life reviewing.*
> *We choose to balance the scale,*
> *we can try again when we fail.*
> *The Law of Karma to be understood,*
> *we balance the bad by doing good.*
> *Divine Order is never in the limited ego's control,*
> *desire comes to be, aligned with spirit and soul.*
> *We're given the dream for manifestation,*
> *it's in our control for self-transformation.*
> *We can pay off karma in service to others,*
> *loving all our human sisters and brothers.*
> *In service to others, we are God's fool,*
> *to make paradise using the golden rule.*
> *Treat others as you'd like to be treated,*
> *or else your karma shall be repeated.*
> *The Akashic Book holds every deed,*
> *so, the Law of Karma we must heed.*

With unconditional love as our creed,
we balance the Scale of Justice God speed.
Working through karma we must all adhere,
we master the divine quality to persevere.
Persevere through feelings seeming to consume,
open your heart for love and healing to bloom.
Feel your emotions causing you to be stuck,
releasing your feelings clears away the muck.
The blockage causes mind and heart separation,
with perseverance you achieve integration.
Calm your anxiety and frustration brewing,
let go and let God, with the Power of Non-Doing.

Akashic Hall of Records

"You have balanced much of your karma," Seshat picks up the scales. "Let us enter the Hall of Records and look into your Akashic Book for greater illumination."

The prince follows Seshat into the building resembling the ancient Library of Alexandria. Inside, the heavenly depository of books looks like the gorgeous Admont Abbey Library in Austria. Seshat places the scales down on a table and retrieves an oversized book from the shelf, "this book contains all your lifetimes; past, present and future."

"I'm getting nervous of what I will see in it," he says with anxiety creeping into his voice.

"What are you afraid of?" she inquires.

"I'm afraid I will find out I was some kind of murderer and that I've done horrible things," he admits.

Seshat expresses the wisdom of Karma; "do not fear what has already been done. The Law of Karma balances the good and bad. Through Divine Order you are given lifetimes to correct the past as you expand your divine qualities in the present to be a great force for healing and transformation in the present and future."

Seshat opens the book to his present situation on earth. "In your earthly life you appear to be homeless."

"Why is that?" the prince asks.

"First of all, this is not a punishment," she states.

"Well, it certainly not a reward," he says sarcastically.

"From the standpoint of ego, it appears the Wheel of Fortune has brought you down; but this is an opportunity to make huge spiritual gains."

"Then I welcome what appears to be misfortune to become the spiritual teacher I'm meant to be," the prince smiles with acceptance.

Song of the Self Tarot: Karma XI

In the Song of the Self Tarot Deck, The Tri-Principality of Karma is depicted as the scales emerging from the Akashic Book. The book represents the record of all of our deeds and the scale symbolizes the weighing of our actions to determine how karma may be balanced.

Power of Detachment

Opening his heart chakra, the hermit-prince separates himself from a restrictive mindset, limiting who he can be. The power of detachment can be viewed as the shift in consciousness from the ego mind to the divine heart center. Extricating oneself from the web of egocentric beliefs, we detach from living our lives unconscious of our divinity.

Scales

The hermit's staff previously used to create the Candle of Enlightenment, transforms into the Karmic Scales; suggests we have the wisdom to access, understand and balance our karma. The dark and light pearls in each bowl, can represent balancing what we perceive as paying off karmic debts and reaping rewards for service to others.

Akashic Book

The prince's Web of Fate takes him to the Akashic Hall of Records for greater understanding of the Tri-Principality of Karma. Akasha in Sanskrit translates to sky; explains the prince traveling into the heavens.

The Akashic Record or Akashic Book contains every thought, word, and deed of every person, past, present and future. Clairvoyants access this information with the help of their spirit guides. Through hypnosis, the person in trance may access former lives stored in the cosmic library. The data retrieved psychically or hypnotically can reveal the source of a health issues or karmic bonds. Oftentimes, by remembering the origin of a wounding, the symptoms in the present disappear. Discovering our past life connections to people we conflict with; we can take responsibility for our role and begin to heal the karmic debt. We can bring in compassion and forgiveness to help free us from the karmic patterns we have accumulated.

Perseverance

With perseverance, the divine quality associated with the Tri-Principality of Karma, we have the capacity to overcome adversity including the balancing of karmic debt.

The prince removes the blockages to enlightenment by creating an opening in the heart. He perseveres through the transformative expression of emotions rather than allowing rage to consume him with vengeance. When we are faced with gross injustice and want to lash out in revenge in any form, we can stop ourselves from reacting to heal ourselves and allow divine order to mete out justice to the wrong doer.

True Blue 5th Chakra Power of Communication

The blue background of this tarot card represents the fifth chakra located at the throat to represent the power center of communication. It means, speaking one's truth will free the individual trapped in a web of lies and deceit. To fit in, many of us have been conditioned to believe and behave as family and society dictates. With higher consciousness, we clearly see the dysfunctional dynamics playing out; we can gain the wisdom to detach from the emotional programming to achieve greater integrity of the Self.

Rider Waite Tarot: Justice XI

The Song of the Self tarot, Karma, compares with the Rider-Waite, red-robed Lady of Justice XI holding a sword and scales between two pillars. The scales she holds represents the weighing of evidence of the two opposing parties. The sword is a symbol of authority for delivering justice swiftly. Lady Justice cuts through lies and deception with her Sword of Truth. With her Power of Detachment, she easily cuts away at emotional manipulation and duplicity to arrive at a just ruling.

Lady Justice: Themis and Maat

The Lady Justice is found in ancient cultures of Ancient Greece as the Goddess Themis and in Ancient Egypt as the Goddess Maat. The Romans referred to her as Justicia.

Themis, translated from the Greek, means divine law and order; corresponds with the ancient Hindu concept of Karma. Themis gave birth to the Horae, the goddesses of the seasons and the Morae, the goddesses of fate. Clotho was the spinner of fate; Lachesis measured out the length of one's fate and Atropos used her shears to terminate one's fate. In the Rider-Waite card, the cloth draped behind Lady Justice may refer to the fabric spun by Clotho. The scales refer to Lachesis who measures the length of one's fate; and Lady Justice's sword, like Atropos' shears, ends the lifetime on earth.

Maat weighed the hearts of the dead with her ostrich feather. If the heart was lighter than her feather, the soul progresses to a heavenly paradise; if not, the soul would live in the underworld for eternity. This 'underworld' means the soul waits in the afterlife to re-incarnate for another opportunity to satisfy the created karma.

In our afterlife review, a counsel of spirit guides shows us how we handled our lessons and how we can improve the next time around. These guides, corresponding with Themis and her prophetic ability to see into the future, puts into "good order" the best lifetime to satisfy the karma, heal ourselves and expand in our divine qualities.

Activating Karma XI

Soul Growth: Healing and Perseverance

You may visualize yourself caught in the web of your thoughts and beliefs. What old patterns and belief systems are you attached to preventing you from progressing? Mentally you may summon a symbol of your higher self to assist you in detaching yourself from beliefs that no longer serve you. Does he or she offer any wisdom? Is it in the form of a symbol?

The prince used his thoughts of frustration to connect with his deeply held emotions of anger. Are any of your thoughts really messages from your emotional center urging you to express your feelings? Try setting your intention for reconnecting with your feelings. Use your mind to scan your body to determine where the feeling resides. Is the feeling trying to communicate with you? What is it saying?

Maybe your divine Self asks you to set your intention, "I desire the Power of Detachment to help me disengage from the blockages holding me back from healing and being my best self."

Perhaps you can visualize your own trial by fire, forcing you to persevere until you let go of destructive emotions. Imagine your dysfunctional thinking and belief systems disintegrating.

The prince perseveres to work through his emotional blockage. He opens his heart and allows the love to emerge to help him release his frustration and rage. Can you visualize your heart opening up to help you through the healing process. What do you see and feel? How will you express the emotion lodged within your body? Do you need to speak, cry, scream? Allow yourself to feel the feelings.

The divine fire disintegrates the old web of thinking as the prince expresses his emotions. Perhaps this process is the same for you; or you may need to focus on releasing the feeling raging within you. Maybe this rage becomes the energy igniting the web, you may feel it intensifying so you may notice how harmful your anger really is to you and others. Or, you may become aware in repressing your anger, the blockage within presents as depression. Becoming conscious of this death grip on your consciousness, you can purge it through expressing your feelings trapped within it.

At last, the prince detaches from his old dysfunctional thought pattern and belief system to gain the wisdom of Divine Order. He accepts, he is exactly where he needs to be to gain greater wisdom.

Like the prince, you may imagine the glowing pearl on top of your staff to show the incorporation of the power of perseverance. Describe in writing and art your visualization, your process, and what you from being caught in the web to achieve detachment.

Gaining the power of faith and now perseverance, the prince is now ready to look deeper into the Tri-Principality for further healing and progression.

Creativity: Yoga in Our Lives

I believe as some say, doing the postures of yoga, we work off karma. My yoga teacher advises us to do yoga off the mat. Meaning, just as we breathe through holding challenging poses, we can do the same through the challenges of the day. We can observe our thoughts and feelings and respond to people and situations by bringing the divine quality most needed.

Mainly in yoga, you persevere through the poses with as much grace and mindfulness as possible. We can do the same off the mat. I usually set my intention to be kind and patient. As a caregiver these qualities are essential.

Dreamwork: Accessing the Akashic Record

The websites listed in the references offer techniques to access the Akashic Record, which I have yet to do. In the future, I hope to do QHHT sessions to access my past lives. Psychic Susan told me I was a Native American medicine man in the western United States in my last life. She also mentioned, I had many lifetimes of wealth, and this time around I wanted to see if I could do it on my own, would explain why I'm living through lack.

In terms of pursuing a dream, we need to cultivate the divine quality of perseverance. It's easy to give up when facing challenges, when we know we are divinely inspired and guided to fulfill a dream, we can rely on our perseverance to see it through.

Karma/ Justice XI in a Reading:

Pulling the Karma or Justice Card in a reading may indicate the need to access the divine quality of perseverance to help through the current situation. It may suggest a karmic debt or reward is brought to your attention to explore more deeply.

We accept hardships, not appearing in our control, are in divine order to help us access and expand our divine qualities. We may also gain solace of working off karma. It may mean, we liberate ourselves from karma by being of service to others.

Questions to Ask in a Reading:

Can you persevere through adversity? Can you develop the power of detachment? Can you release acting out in vengeance? Is there an empowering way to seek justice? Can you open your heart to transform anger into forgiveness?

Gifts of Homelessness

My experience of being homeless was not the nightmare I was expecting; it was incredibly liberating to live off the grid of normality. I could let go of the idea of looking for work and feel guilt free. Instead of feeling shame for my downturn and having to depend on food stamps, general relief and the temporary cold weather shelter, I accept this is where I need to be. I believed the shelter staff when they say, this is temporary situation, indicating God has a plan for each of us, and we will find our way out of it despite hearing the stories how some have been homeless for years. Many are eligible for assistance due to their mental and physical disabilities; there were live-in programs for substance abusers and help available for victims of domestic abuse.

As a small minority of healthy, able-bodied forty something year-old males there was no other government assistance. I relied heavily on my spirituality; believing I can be a presence of healing to my sisters and brothers in homelessness. Oddly enough, I felt closer to God at this time. I realized, having no one to turn to, we are forced to turn to God and the divinity within. Deprived of the comforts of life and a job, there's time to reflect on who we really are, to connect and deepen our relationship with the divine.

As bad as things appear being homeless, you quickly accept the wisdom, things can be worse. Living in a shelter, you can be grateful you are not of the ranks of the truly homeless, sleeping out on the streets without any income whatsoever. Gratitude, a divine quality, we expand here in many ways. We were grateful to shower every day, for the meals the shelter provided, for a cot to sleep on. Grateful for having access to restrooms at public parks and libraries where you can spend your days connecting with nature and expanding your mind with books.

Becoming a volunteer at the shelter, I felt I was part of a family; we enjoyed the perks of entering the shelter early, enjoying hot showers and eating first. We were able to feel a sense of being useful and serve our fellow transients.

Like the prophetic Themis, Susan the psychic had foretold of my homelessness; in her reading she saw that prior to homelessness, I would be living in a trailer for about two years. She saw that I would be homeless for a total of 6-7 months, including the two weeks I stayed at the shelter in Santa Barbara, saying it would feel like a vacation being by the beach. She foretold of a woman that would help me, by name, and that it would not work out and then she told me of someone else who would take me in.

The black woman with beautifully braided hair, I'll call Pearl, I met on a bus going to a GROW event. We had a nice talk and she offered me housing and gave me her number. I told her I would stay at the shelter as long as possible. I tried to get in touch with her before the Glendale Armory closed, but could not reach her; so, I decided to make the trip to Santa Barbara. The Santa Barbara shelter was only available to everyone for another two weeks; otherwise, you needed to give them a share of your social security or general relief benefits. My cash benefits were cut off due to missing out on a required GROW event in Los Angeles. My choices were stay at the mission where I stayed the first night arriving in Santa Barbara or find another shelter. I was told of the one further north in San Juan Capistrano or the armory in Sylmar back in Los Angeles. At the last minute, I got through to Pearl and she was amenable to my staying with her in her apartment in Sylmar. The condition was to get an Aids test and give her $50 dollars. I resentfully complied to her terms. I was grateful I had a place to stay, a bed to sleep in and good food she prepared for me.

Healing from the exhaustion of being homeless, not sleeping well and having to be on the move, I did not seek employment. Pearl tracked me down to observe me spending my days at the park. She could not tolerate me not looking for work, so she asked me to leave after a week. Fortunately, she lived in walking distance of the shelter, where I stayed for the next two months.

At the Sylmar armory, I developed various friendships; mainly with Steve who shared the same birthday as me; with Linda who was in a relationship with a gambler, the reason for her homelessness and a male poet who had a great sense of humor and kept us laughing.

Laughter was another great gift of homelessness. We learned to laugh at our situation in general and the rules we had to conform to for staying at the armory. For example, we had to camp out early at the van stop for pick up to the armory to make sure they did not run out of cots; I referred to this time as the Sherman Way hotel and Casino part of the day. Getting to the Armory early guaranteed your place in line as you waited outside until the space was made available for us. It seemed so silly how we guarded our placement to the point of running to the building when we were allowed.

The shelter was extended to the end of June. When it closed, we were all desperate and at the same time apprehensive to get a placement at LA family housing. LA family housing provided three hots and a cot and showers. With six people to a room without security, women as well as men, were concerned about bodily harm and rape. We signed up for LA housing before the closing of the armory, I was not astute enough to realize a staff member was trying to help me to put my name on the first sheet guaranteeing me a spot, rather than the paper that I did sign.

My option was to sleep out in the park even though there is a law against it. Steve and I and another man banded together to inherit a great spot in the back of the park equipped with two mattresses where there was a broken sprinkler. Walking around, we found another mattress and dragged it to our spot. It felt really good to sleep out under the stars during the warm summer nights. We were grateful for the peace and quiet, rather than the loudness and crowdedness of the shelter. During the day we had access to the library facilities and at night there was a Porto-potty for our needs. Thankfully, we could take a short bus ride to a rehabilitation facility with access to showers for the homeless.

I was losing too much weight even though many homeless people gain weight taking advantage of the many free meals provided around the city. I did not have a monthly bus pass so I did not go that often, especially since my cash benefits were cut off. I was getting worried about being able to pay for storage of my writing and art and some personal belongings. It was especially depressing to spend your birthday truly homeless, so Steve and I treated ourselves to a movie.

Camping out, it became increasingly frustrating, why I am still homeless, what more can be gained from being in this situation? At the same time, I still felt God will provide; relying on the prophecy it would only be a short time I would be camping out. Sure enough, about three weeks later, Fate and Karma stepped in for me to be rescued by Ettiene, a clerk working at the library.

The day before the rescue, the cops did their occasional sweep of the park and told us not to return to our spot. So, we went to another section of the park and spent a horrible night on the dirty ground right next to the loud noises of the cars passing by on the freeway. While waiting for the library to open, Ettiene arrived and could see how miserable I looked and asked me what's wrong? I hesitated for a moment in fear and shame for disclosing the truth of my homelessness; I told her what happened, and she was very sympathetic, offering me a place to stay for the weekend. The weekend lasted for about two years.

Ettiene was as in much need of a companion as I was for a home. We really enjoyed each other's company, and we laughed a lot. Ettiene was a recovering alcoholic of many years and I learned from her a lot about addiction and recovery. Interestingly, we had both attended the same new thought church, which I started to go back to. Although Ettiene was working full time, I served as her caregiver; cleaning, cooking, and doing laundry and her being British, I prepared her bottomless cup of tea.

I still could not make myself look for work. My food stamps ran out and I tried getting back on relief, but I was denied because of the infraction of not attending a job fair. Ettiene was making enough money to support me, and I received a small inheritance from my mother passing away to pay for my storage and to get a few new clothes and a new pair of glasses. I started to use Ettiene's old laptop to write with. I wrote the screenplay, *Lady Love*, chronicling my adventures in homelessness and being rescued by Ettiene.

The external events I experienced, which were prophesied, can be considered my fate. How I responded to them and what I gained can be considered karma. I learned to develop my divine qualities, beginning with having greater compassion for the homeless, near homeless and the poor, including myself. I persevered through a challenging chapter in my life to be grateful for what I did have, mainly my health. And though the state did not give me enough to maintain my own apartment, I was grateful enough I could survive with their services. I learned that any act of kindness, regardless how insignificant it may seem, is a miraculous display of humanity. For example, people giving me food without asking for it; or a poor person giving me a token to use on the bus. I learned regardless of our circumstances; we can still be of service to others. For example, I helped someone get a placement into a home for the elderly; at the shelter I volunteered for set up; and befriending various people. Our karma may give others the opportunity to be of service and be grateful for their help.

Looking back, I see the workings of divine order, when Pearl's temporary assistance brought me back to Los Angeles. Intuitively, I signed the second list forcing me to camp out, where I was in the position to connect with Ettiene. Psychic Susan was able to foresee the chain of events through her guides accessing the Akashic Record. The people we meet, and form relationships are part of the karma contracts we've agreed to with them. Perhaps it was good karma I accrued in a prior life by helping those individuals who helped me in the present incarnation.

Affirmations

Everything is in divine order.
With the Power of Detachment, I extricate myself from
dysfunctional thoughts and belief systems.

I accept where I'm at now is where I'm supposed to be.

I persevere in balancing my karma.

Persevering through hardships, I gain greater self-esteem.

I am grateful for all that I have.

I have compassion for the suffering of others, including my own.

With perseverance I grow through all challenges.

With Forgiveness I free myself from the past.

Summary of Karma XI

With the divine quality of perseverance, we can meet challenging life circumstances we have agreed to before incarnation.

Recommended Reading

Past lives can be accessed in the Akashic Records can be used to heal ourselves in the present. The list of books below explores past life regression and how therapeutic it can be:

Dolores Cannon's many books

Many Lives, Many Masters, by Brian L. Weiss

Mirrors of Time: Using Regression for Physical, Emotional, and Spiritual Healing, by Brian L. Weiss

Through Time into Healing: Discovering the Power of Regression Therapy to Erase Trauma and Transform Mind, Body, and Relationships, by Brian L. Weiss and Raymond Moody

Miracles Happen: The Transformational Healing Power of Past-life Memories, by Brian L. Weiss

When Souls Awaken: Real-Life Accounts of Past-Life and Life Between-Lives Regressions by Pieter Jan Elsen

Journey of Souls: Case Studies of Life Between Lives, by Michael Newton

Destiny of Souls: New Case Studies of Life Between Lives, by Michael Newton

Memories of the Afterlife: Life Between Lives Stories of Personal Transformation, by Michael Newton

Children's Past Lives: How Past Life Memories Affect Your Child by Carol Bowman

Twenty Cases Suggestive of Reincarnation by Ian Stevenson M.D.

Children Who Remember Previous Lives: A Question of Reincarnation, by Ian Stevenson M.D.

Courageous Souls: Do We Plan Our Life Challenges Before Birth, by Robert Schwartz

Your Soul's Gift: The Healing Power of the Life You Planned Before You Were Born, by Robert Schwartz

Your Soul's Love: Living the Love You Planned Before You Were Born, by Robert Schwartz

Spiritual Regression for Peace & Healing: Discover Your Life Mission Through Past Life Exploration, by Ursula Demarmels

The Limitless Soul: Hypno-Regression Case Studies into Past, Present & Future Lives, by Bryn Blankinship

Karma Can Be a Real Pain: Past Life Clues to Current Life Maladies, by Joanne DiMaggio

The Evolving Soul: Spiritual Healing Through Past Life Exploration, by Linda Backman

Souls on Earth: Exploring Interplanetary Past Lives, by Linda Backman

Bringing your Soul to Light: Healing Through Past Lives and the Time Between, by Linda Backman

Blast from the Past: Healing Spontaneous Past Life Memories, by Shelley Kaehr

Guiding Lost Souls: Helping Spirits Return to the Light Through Hypnosis, by Antonio Sangio

My Soul's Purpose: Missions, Lessons and Past Lives Through Hypnotic Regression, by Antonio Sangio

References

Symbolism of Justice in Tarot -- esoterichut.com

Justice Tarot Card Meaning – 11th Arcana -- esoterichut.com

Justice Tarot Card Meaning (Upright & Reversed) -- spiritual-galaxy.com

The Justice Tarot Card Meaning-- tarotflower.com

Justice by Anne-Marie Wegh -- anne-mariewegh.eu

Themis-- theoi.com

Themis: the goddess of natural law-- mythologysource.com

Themis: Titan Goddess of Divine Law and Order by Rittika Dhar -- historycooperative.org

The Sacred Weighing of the Heart in Ancient Egyptology by Michelle Estevez -- theheartrevolution.org

8 Legendary Ancient Libraries-- history.com

10 of the Most Beautiful Libraries in the World, by Stefanie Waldek -- Galeriemagazine.com

Admont Abbey Is The Largest Monastery Library In The World, And Also The Most Beautiful, by Lianna Tedesco -- thetravel.com

The Ancient Library of Alexandria: The West's most important repository of learning J. Harold Ellens -- biblicalarchaeology.org

The Great Library of Alexandria: The Untold Story Explained, by Guillaume Deprez -- thecollector.com

History of the Ancient Library of Alexandria by Vicki -- historicmysteries.com

Hall of Records and Akashic Records What's the Difference? -- freerspirit.com

Akashic Records 101: Can We Access Our Akashic Records? -- gaia.com

Akashic Records -- akashicwikidot.com

The Akashic Records -- crystalinks.com

The Law of Cause and Effect vs the Law of Action and Reaction -- sirwilliam.org

Which Chakra is Blocked? An Index of Symptoms & How They Relate to Our Chakras, by Faith Davis -- cosmiccuts.com

History of the Ancient Library of Alexandria, by Vicki -- historicmysteries.com

The Burning of the Library of Alexandria, by Preston Chesser -- ehistory.osu.edu

Karma Yoga -- sivanandayogafarm.com

Karma: Facing our Destiny with Free Will by Jayne Stevenson, Swami Shankardev Saraswati PHD -- yogajournal.com

How Karmic account balance (Sanchita Karma) is maintained? -- thekundaliniyoga.org

Karma-Yoga: Approaching God Through Work -- popularvedicscience.com

Karma Yoga: Self-Realization Through Awareness From Yoga Asanas and Meditation-- tummee.com

Healing Karma: Our karmic tendencies and how to work it out by Swami Siraramananda -- sivanandayogafarm.com

Timing XII

Song of Timing

Naked in a cemetery in winter, the prince, hangs upside down above a hole in the ground. Within a circle, the prince appears as hands of a clock in a giant timepiece; flanked by two tombstones etched with the numbers, nine and three.

Brother Spirit stands before him, "How do you feel?"

"Having persevered through much of my frustration, I'm learning to accept Timing is not in my control."

"That is wise of you," praises Brother Spirit.

He continues, "Understanding the Tri-Principality of Timing, liberates me from making success happen when and how my ego desires. It is forcing me to access a level of patience, I previously thought impossible."

"The divine quality of patience helps humanity persevere through the seasons of life," Brother Spirit adds; "When the Timing is right success will come to you."

"My ego at times becomes impatient," the prince admits.

"How do you handle impatience?" asks Brother Spirit.

The prince explains, "I tell myself to calm down and remind myself, the Tri-Principality of Fate, Karma, and Timing is a perfectly

139

timed clock created for my personal growth. Developing the Power of Patience, I expand my divinity."

"The tombstone etched with the Roman numeral nine refers to you as the hermit. The tombstone numbered three, refers to the Tri-Principality of Fate, Karma and Timing and your development of Faith, Perseverance and Patience. Together, nine and three are twelve, the numeral for this archway."

"The archway to what?" the prince asks.

"The archway into the Divine Masculine," replies Brother spirit.

"What does that mean?" asks the hermit prince.

"Twelve is a number of completion, it means you have completed the lessons of the Divine Feminine, accessing and applying her gifts. Now you must let go of the soul as ruler of the Self to allow the Divine Masculine to be your co-ruler," Brother Spirit explains.

"So, I'm really here just waiting to die, so that I may be reborn," the prince clarifies as a soft glow of light emits from his head.

"Mastering patience shifts you into the enlightened state of the divine masculine. Prepare yourself for the transition from Goddess to God," advises Brother Spirit.

They sing,

> *I'm on the gallows, hanged for my crime,*
> *given a sentence, I must do the time.*
> *While waiting for success, I deeply yearn,*
> *the divine quality of patience I now learn.*
> *Tombstones mark my time on earth,*
> *waiting for the goddess to give birth.*
> *I prepare myself for my last goddess breath,*
> *for the soul centered ego to be put to death.*
> *In rebirth, ego, soul, and spirit shall align,*
> *to be at one with the masculine divine.*

Song of the Self Tarot: Timing XII

The naked man suspended in a timepiece, depicts our consciousness is subject to incarnation in a particular place and time. The tombstones, the markers of a completed time on earth, represent the Hermit (9) completing his understanding of the Tri-Principality of

Fate, Karma and Timing (3). The prince in figure four position is symbolic of uniting the Four Archetypes of the Self.

The Timing of Winter, ending a yearly cycle; signifies the goddess, or soul centered ego as sole ruler of the self is finished. Hanging naked in a barren landscape shows Prince Ego has let go of everything holding him back from achieving his goal. The numbers set in stone indicate the soul's progression from goddess to God is imminent.

The soul centered ego, facing mortality, has the shocking realization; "I want to have a positive impact on the world, I want my life to have meaning and leave a legacy of love. " In alchemy, this transition of consciousness is known as Hieros Gamos, the sacred marriage of the divine feminine with the divine masculine.

Odin Suspended on Yggdrasil

The Hanged Man of the Tarot elicits the Norse Myth of Odin sacrificing himself on Yggdrasil, the world tree, where he accesses the power of the runes. Odin first sacrifices his eye to Mimir's Well where he gains the awareness of the Runes and is willing to do anything to obtain their power.

Odin losing his eye can be interpreted as the I of the ego; and by putting it in the well, represents ego consciousness immersed in the waters of soul. It also suggests Odin seeing into the depths of his consciousness.

Before his suspension on the tree, Odin wounds himself again. By allowing his blood to drain, it represents a psychic death of the ego transitioning to soul and spirit.

Odin suspended, upside down, from the world tree is analogous to eating from the Tree of Knowledge. Putting his heart over his head expresses his desire for spiritual wisdom. Odin suspended for nine days from the tree, corresponds with the Hermit IX of the Tarot.

Yggdrasil, the world tree, has three roots, corresponds to the Song of the Self tombstone numbered three for Fate, Karma, and Timing. Also, the three Norns or Fates are the old women who live under the tree, who alone possess the wisdom of the Runes. In shifting his consciousness from Goddess to God, Odin retrieves the runes.

The runes are pictographs used in divination, can be interpreted as the ability to see the workings of Fate, Karma, and Timing. Like the Norns, and the upside-down Hermit of the Tarot, Odin gains the ability to understand the symbolic language of the soul and spirit.

Jesus: The Ultimate Sacrifice

The ultimate hanged man is the crucifixion of Jesus. Understood symbolically, the cross is the intersection of heaven and earth. The heart of Jesus aligning in the center of the cross depicts the uniting of spirit and ego. Psychologically, we are all meant to sacrifice the life of the ego being separate from spirit, so that we may be reborn as the spiritualized ego. We are all divine beings with the potential Jesus manifested.

Horae: Goddesses of the Seasons

The Horae goddesses of the seasons are another set of daughters by Themis, the Goddess of Justice. Horae, translates to hours, indicates every moment of our lives are subject to divine order. Thallo, Auxo and Carpo were the goddesses of Spring, Summer, and Autumn; were mainly worshipped by the farmers.

The timing necessary planting and harvesting is symbolic of the timing necessary of our enlightenment. With our intention we plant the seeds of our desires at the most fertile time for them to take root. With our emotions, we water our desires for them to blossom. At the autumnal harvest, we reap the rewards we manifested through our hard work and patience. In the wintertime of the soul, we let go, waiting for divine inspiration.

In the ten Universal Symbols of Manifestation, I illustrate the seasons of the soul as: Spring, Buds of Self Awareness; Summer, Blossoms of Enlightenment; Autumn, the fall or letting go of Goddess, and Winter, the Amplification of Spirit will be discussed in detail later.

Rider Waite Tarot: The Hanged Man XII

The Tri-Principality of Timing in the Song of the Self deck corresponds with the Hanged Man of the Rider Waite Tarot; depicted as an upside-down man held by his foot onto a T-shaped tree; he's wearing a blue shirt, red tights, and yellow shoes. His legs form a figure four and a halo of light beams from his head.

Dangling from the T shaped tree, the Hanged Man voluntarily sacrifices himself for higher learning, expressed in the Song of the Self Tarot as the **Tri-Principality of Fate, Karma, and Timing.**

In this upside-down position, he places his heart above head to depict the shift in consciousness to divine love. The green leaves signifying the fourth chakra of the heart emphasize the transition. His head radiating with light depicts his enlightenment as the spiritualized ego. His yellow shoes illustrated in the same color as his head, indicate the ego mind aligned with soul (sole) walks the spiritual path. The yellow refers to the third chakra, the place of personal power. His red tights refer to the root chakra of the life force, signifies the Hanged Man's passion to live a spiritual life. His blue tunic represents the fifth chakra of truth and communication; indicates through his heart he can express his spiritual truths. The peaceful expression on his face shows he accepts the limitations of Fate, Karma, and Timing, where he has accessed the divine qualities of faith, perseverance, and patience.

In conclusion, the Hanged Man suspended on a live tree, indicates death and resurrection. He is letting go of his soul centeredness, divine feminine, as the focal point of his identity to include the divine masculine. The figure four of his legs placed over the triangle of his arms may be viewed as the Four Archetypes of the Self joined with the Tri-Principality of Fate, Karma, and Timing.

Timing Activation

Soul Growth: Developing Patience

Like Odin, the Hanged Man, or the figure of Timing, we can access our divine quality of patience to help us in developing a meditation practice. Unlike Odin, we need not blind ourselves, we can shut down our ego awareness by half in order to open our third eye, re-establishing our connection to intuition. Like Odin placing his eye in the well, we can shift our awareness within. We can think of his further self-wounding as his commitment to wisdom. We can emulate Odin by setting our intention to meditate, committing body, mind, and soul to achieve enlightenment.

Creativity: Meditation Practice

At the beginning of my yoga class, Jessie Diaz-Perez, my yoga teacher, who I highly recommend to take her zoom classes, has us focus on our breathing and then set an intention for the day. Usually, the breath is accompanied by some easy movements to help us embody the shift in consciousness. This simple preparatory meditation, helps restore our channel to the divine. Taking time to be in the present moment, we invite our spirit to join our ego in the practice of unity, for which the word yoga actually means.

Beginning a meditation practice takes monumental effort we never thought was possible. We must overcome the thoughts of sitting and doing nothing, feeling silly and useless. We soon learn even a short break from our steady stream of uninterrupted ego consciousness, provides a sense of relaxation.

Exposed to the idea; through meditation we can achieve enlightenment, we force ourselves to persevere. Eventually, like the smiling hanged man, we connect with our joy of being who we really are.

Having established our connection within, it may not be necessary to sit for as long or at all. For me, walking accomplishes much in the way of relaxing my mind to receive insights for my creative work. Everyone must work out for themselves what is best.

To help himself get the power of the runes, Odin wounded himself; can be interpreted as opening old wounds we can work on healing, now that we are allowing our consciousness to shift. Perhaps the wounding is symbolic of releasing toxic emotions robbing us of a peaceful existence. We can remove the impediment of repressed emotions by allowing ourselves to feel the emotion and then let it go. While we are raging with anger and hatred, there is no way we can be at peace. It's like we must force ourselves to do the work; intuitively we know the poison we are holding onto hurts us more than the person we are projecting it toward. Like Odin we can visualize the poison oozing from us like blood, or we can imagine ourselves as volcanoes erupting, or you may find your own way of symbolically expunging the painful energy.

Odin hung on the tree for nine days is symbolic of how long it feels during a meditation practice, and nothing seems to happen. We may not see any visions or be granted with divine guidance at the time of meditation; but we can have faith something is going on. Through each breath we sense we are uniting ego, shadow, soul, and spirit. Like the smiling Hanged Man, our body and mind relax to express the joy of who we really are.

Dreamwork: Runes: Language of Dreams

The Runes, mystical symbols of divination can be symbolic of understanding the language of dreams. Receiving the images while we sleep, we can begin to make sense of their meaning for our lives.

Odin finally obtaining the Runes are symbolic of the divine qualities we have the power to access as needed. The mystical language of spirit we all practice to 'speak' as fluently as possible. Eventually the Power of Forgiveness, frees us from the poisons to be enlightened beings of love.

In pursuing your dream, Timing means cultivating the divine quality of patience for its manifestation. Understanding the timing of a dream is not always in our control, if it all, we can let go and let god.

Timing or Hanged Man in a Reading:

The appearance of Timing in a reading may signify the need to expand the divine quality of patience. In pursuing a dream, Timing indicates being more patient to be at peace. We understand, we do what we're responsible for and let go.

Timing may indicate the ego-soul's time for being in control of the Self is coming to an end. It means we need to prepare ourselves for the psychological death to be reborn with the spirit as co-ruler of the Self. Like the smiling Hanged Man, we make the transition easier by welcoming this evolution of consciousness.

On a mundane level, this card may indicate the end of a career, job or a relationship. We wait patiently to be divinely guided for the next thing. Patience and acceptance help make a transition easier.

Questions to Ask in a Reading:

Are you impatient for results? Are you resisting God's timing? How do you surrender? With whom and what do you need to expand your patience?

Master of Timing

The Timing was right for me to meet Dov, a composer looking for a writer to showcase his amazing songs in musicals. I used many of Dov's songs in a dozen or so screenplays for our Cosmic Odyssey franchise.

My time with Ettiene came to an end when Dov offered me an opportunity to house sit and take care of his cats while he was vacationing in Hawaii for three months. I jumped at the chance to be able to write in a quiet place all to myself. Ettiene did not want me to accept this offer, even though I said I would still help her out. I was given an ultimatum and I chose to move forward with my life. It was a difficult decision to make having recently learned how ill Ettiene really was. Ettiene recently reconnected with her estranged daughter, made it easier to make the decision to live separate from her. Eventually, I would have to forgive myself for abandoning her, even though it was she who insisted I could not come back if things didn't work out. Worse come to worse, when Dov and family returned, I could sleep in Dov's meditation shed.

As Fate, Karma and Timing would have it, Dov offered me a job as his father's live-in caregiver. I would have a place to live and food to eat, but without pay.

Psychic Susan foretold I would be living in Encino for a few years and I would like it. She even mentioned Edward Everett Horton Lane, a street on the border of the beautiful Balboa Park. I remembered having visited the park a few years before and thought I would love to live around here. Similarly, when I was on the street, I moved to with Ettiene, I remembered I was there with Castor. We stopped to look at a trailer for sale, and I was having a strong sense of familiarity with this place; indicating to me time is not only linear.

Summary of Timing XII

Our lives, subject to the Divine Order of Timing, we develop the divine quality of Patience.

Summary of the Tri-Principality

The Tri-Principality of Fate, Karma and Timing is Divine Order always at work throughout our lives. Whether or not we have had a psychic reading, through our intuition, we can perceive if we are where we're supposed to be.

Fate, Karma and Timing work together to guide us toward self-growth and enlightenment. Accessing and developing our qualities of Faith, Perseverance and Patience, we expand our divinity.

Timing Quotes

"Patience is power. Patience is not an absence of action; rather it is "timing" It waits on the right time to act, for the right principles and in the right way."
— Fulton J. Sheen

"The most confused you will ever get is when you try to convince your heart and spirit of something your mind knows is a lie."
— Shannon L. Alder

"Patience is the calm acceptance that things can happen in a different order than the one you have in mind."
— David G. Allen

Affirmations

Everything is in Divine Order.

I surrender to God's timing.

I have faith, perseverance, and patience to help me through this challenge.

I let go and let God.

References:

Looking Above and Beyond the Hanged Man Tarot Card Meaning -- trusted-astrology.com

Symbolism of The Hanged Man in Tarot -- esoterichut.com

Iconology of the Hanged Man Cards by Robert ONeill -- tarot.com

12. The Hanged Man, by Anne-Marie Wegh -- anne-mariewegh.eu

The Hanged Man of the Tarot, by Pamela Quinn -- elementalom.com

Odin's Discovery of the Runes, by Dan McCoy -- Norse-mythology.org

Why Did Odin Hang Himself? by Pirate Sir -- piratejewelry.com

Yggdrasil, the Tree of Life in Norse Mythology -- worldhistoryedu.com

God Of the Gallows and How Odin Hanged Himself from Yggdrasil To Know Secrets Of Runes -- AncientPages.com

Yggdrasil and the Nine Realms of Norse Cosmology -- otherwoldlyoracle.com

Odin -- norse-mythology.org

Yggdrasil, the Tree of Life in Norse Mythology -- worldhistoryedu.com

Mimir's Well -- legendarymythology.com

Horai -- theoi.com

Horae -- wikipedia.org

jessiediazperezyoga.com

Soul to Spirit

Death XIII, explores the end of the reign of the Divine Feminine as the sole ruler of the Self. **Infinite Flow of Compassion XIV,** we give birth to our qualities of the Divine Masculine. With the **Devil XV,** we learn the world is a simulation. **Tower XVI** is the collapse of the matrix controlling our consciousness and the **Lightning Bolt of Inspiration** is our creative spark, for emulating our source of creation.

Death XIII

Song of Death

The inverted prince, like a leaf falling from a tree, floats through the dark abyss beneath him.

"What's happening to me?" he cries out.

Brother Spirit answers, "You have dropped into the Realm of the Divine Masculine."

"Why can't I see anything?" he asks.

"Your ego has yet to adapt to this spiritual dimension."

"It feels like the darkness I experience during meditation," the prince expresses.

"Through your breath and stilling your mind, you'll acclimate to the dark," Brother Spirit advises.

The prince notices, "Now I see faint orbs of color."

"You're dropping into a light meditative state. Enjoy your connection to the divine," Brother Spirit advises.

"Now I see something silvery twinkling in the distance, is it a star? asks the prince.

"Focus your attention on it, what message does it have for you? counsels Brother Spirit.

"It's coming closer, it looks like a silver shield. Oh my god, I see a face reflected in the mirrored surface, but it's not me," exclaims the prince.

"Who is it?" asks Brother Spirit.

"A hideous goddess with snakes for hair," reports the prince.

"You are the gorgon, Medusa," Brother Spirit says.

"Something horrible is happening to me. I'm turning into stone," the prince panics.

"My life passes before my eyes," the prince observes scenes of his life streaming by like a celluloid strip running across his vision. The prince as the gorgon cries out in pain, his face freezes into a mask of horror. Brother Spirit slices the gorgon's head off the prince's body. He places the bleeding head on the shield, blood drains onto the silver platter.

"Fear not goddess, like a caterpillar consuming itself, the Snakes of Transformation will bring you back to life into a higher expression of who you really are."

The snakes detach from the crumbling head and consume the remains.

Brother Spirit sings,

The goddess Medusa is shockingly slain,
her blood-curdling scream, frozen in pain.
Seeing her reflection, she's turned to stone,
the goddess no longer sits on her throne.
Turning outside in and upside down,
the divine feminine lost her crown.
Her life force drains on the silver plate,
she transitions to live her highest fate.
Unlike John the Baptist's head on a platter,
the snakes transform the ego-soul matter.
The goddess soul allows herself to be killed,
for the prophecy of wholeness to be fulfilled.
She relinquishes her personal power stance,

The prince awakens, grateful his horrific death was just a nightmare…

Song of the Self Tarot: Death XIII

The Song of the Self tarot card, Death XIII, depicts a decapitated head of the gorgon, Medusa, with hair made of the Snakes of Transformation. Her face frozen in a scream as the blood oozes from her neck, symbolizes the death of the goddess. It is not a real death, but a reformulation of consciousness to include the Divine Masculine into the awareness of the ego. Like an ugly caterpillar dies to be reborn as the beautiful butterfly, consciousness lets go of its attachment to the Divine Feminine to transition into the Divine Masculine.

Slaying the Gorgon: Death of the Goddess

Medusa is known for turning men to stone when looking directly at her; represents shocking the ego from its incessant stream of thought. Ending the repetitive negative cycle of thinking, allows the shadow and soul to be united into consciousness. The image of the decapitated gorgon in Song of the Self is analogous to various tarot decks depicting beheading in the death card to signify the death of the ego.

Our transforming ego is much like a computer freezing, whereby we turn it off and reboot it by restarting the machine for a new program to be installed. Like the icon or link to the new software programming, our ego through prayer and meditation accesses his soul into consciousness. Similarly, we upgrade our consciousness by striking down the old paradigm to replace it with the new and improved Divine Masculine. Like those high on the hierarchy of a secret service with clearance to top secret, documents, websites and upper floors, the soul has been granted clearance to log into higher dimensions. Instead of the intrigues of corporations and countries, the soul, uniting with spirit delves into the mysteries of the creation of divine consciousness, healing, and the expansion of divine qualities.

In the myth of the Medusa, Perseus was assisted by the gods who gifted him with a shield, a sword, winged sandals, a cap of invisibility and a bag. This divine assistance represents the psychological forces aiding us in our self-transformation. The shield given to Perseus by Athena, represents self-protection and the divine feminine wisdom he has access to. The winged sandals and the cap to make him invisible, assists Perseus in his need for stealth to approach the Gorgon. The sword, symbolic of Lady Justice, represents accessing inner truth and detaching from psychological obstructions interfering with our progression.

Perseus, using the shield as a mirror, could not be turned to stone; symbolizes the ego being aware, but not engaged in the drama. It means, the ego in alliance with the divine, acts without being frozen in fear. We emulate Perseus' use of self-reflection, witnessing our painful truths, without succumbing to paralysis.

The symbolic death of the goddess is a crucial transition for serving the source. We accept responsibility to be workers of the light and helping others to heal. In raising our own vibration, we have greater power to uplift others and raise the earth from darkness.

As Medusa was dying, she gave birth to Pegasus, the immortal winged horse and Chrysaor, a young man bearing a golden sword. Pegasus represents giving birth to our soaring spirit and Chrysaor, the resurrected ego. The unlikely brothers, Pegasus and Chrysaor; like the prince and Brother Spirit, represent our own human-divine expression.

John the Baptist, Salome, Mother Mary, and Jesus:

Four Archetypes of the Self

Salome, John, Mary, and Jesus can be interpreted as the biblical personifications of the Four Archetypes of the Self: Shadow, Ego, Soul and Spirit. Salome in demanding the head of the Baptist on a silver platter represents the desire of the shadow, surfacing to psychologically kill off the male ego. Mother Mary represents the soul desiring and giving birth to her divine child Jesus.

John baptized people for the purpose of repentance; can be interpreted as, the ego preparing oneself to allow a space in consciousness for divinity to manifest. John says, "I indeed baptize you with water unto repentance: but he that cometh after me is mightier than I, whose shoes I am not worthy to bear he shall baptize you with the Holy Ghost, and with fire." (Matthew 3:11)

Alchemy of Song of the Self Tarot

Nigredo: Prima Materia

The process begins as the black figure on the landed boat in the Song of the Self card, Hierophant V. This dark lump of matter, or Prima Materia, indicates the Nigredo phase of Alchemy. In this putrefied state of consciousness, the ego reaches the pinnacle of pain and accepts he must take the spiritual journey. Grabbing onto the fishing line and the Snakes of Transformation from the divine white figure indicates the ego answering the call to become spiritualized. The white being, offering salvation, represents the manifestation of pure unconditional love. Outlined with the red snakes in the form of a fish symbolizes the Hierophant is the divine being within, we are meant to manifest through our ego. Like Jesus, he is the way and the destination for completing the Alchemy of Self Transformation.

Dissolution: Softening the Ego

In Alchemy there are seven stages of working with matter, express the processes the ego experiences to reveal the spirit. In Song of the Self Merging VI, the prima materia enters the transformative emotional waters of Shadow. The ego begins to dissolve its powerful hold over consciousness. The softening, or alchemical dissolution, helps the ego to connect with repressed emotions.

Calcination: Transformative Power of Anger

Connecting to and feeling our repressed emotions, we bring to the surface of consciousness all that is unwanted or false. The prima materia in the lava depicts the merging of ego and shadow. This fiery expression of Shadow is analogous to the Calcination stage of alchemy. Allowing the rage to burn through the victim conglomeration disintegrates the dysfunctionality of the ego.

Citrinitas: Shadow to Soul

In Song of the Self, the disintegrated Nigredo appears as the Golden Carriage, symbolizes the ego shifting from Shadow to Soul. The Golden Carriage is analogous to the Citrinitas phase of alchemy, whereby the ego experiences the enlightenment of Soul.

In the tarot card, Personal Place of Power, half of the sun in darkness and half in yellow, represent the Nigredo united to the

Citrinitas. This indicates the ego has more to work to do to manifest the spirit. The infinity sign linking the four quadrants of the Symbol of the Self, signifies the Infinite Flow of Compassion uniting the Four Archetypes of the Self. It represents the completion of the Great Work of the alchemists.

Albedo: Purification

In the Place of Personal Power, the ego anchors his awareness in his solar chakra of personal empowerment. By disintegrating the victimhood of the false self, consciousness has been purified to allow the gifts of the soul to surface as the three white pyramids for Beauty, Passion and Wisdom of the Soul. These towering energy structures of the Divine Feminine, depict the albedo stage of alchemy.

As the Hermit, the ego incorporated the Albedo and Citrinitas stages in the form of the white candle on the solar golden base. The yellow flame with the green third eye, indicates the ego beginning the shift into the heart chakra.

The enlightened soul purifies her understanding of Tri-Principality of Fate, Karma, and Timing. The Albedo or whitening continues as the Web of Fate, The Akashic Book and Wintry cemetery of the timepiece. The soul reveals and expands her divine qualities of faith, perseverance, and patience.

Rubedo: Spiritual Manifestation

The blood dripping from the neck of the gorgon, expresses the rubedo, the final phase of Alchemy. This great work is completed with the manifestation of spirit. The blood flowing from the stone indicates spirit manifesting through the ego. Her petrified head literally depicts the Philosopher's Stone, the alchemists sought to achieve.

Numerology 13/4

Interestingly, 13 Death, reduces to 4 Spirit, signifies the transition of the goddess to be reborn as the spiritualized ego-soul. Also, the 1 of the magical Ego uniting with the three formerly unconscious archetypes, Shadow, Soul, and Spirit aptly expresses the number four signifying completion.

Death Activation

Soul Growth: Deciding and Declaring

Deciding means cutting away, signifying the death of all other possibilities. Self-transformation occurs when we decide we want to end living in ignorance of who we really are. Declaring out loud, we make our decision perfectly clear to self and others. It means we clear away all opposition to our decision.

Death in soul growth means releasing the soul as the only ruler of the Self to include the divine masculine. This major shift in consciousness may indicate there are things we still hold onto; we can expunge from our psyche. It may mean making the decision to let go of revenge and accessing the divine quality of forgiveness.

For me, I was divinely guided to once and for all rid myself of shame. It was intolerable for me to approach another birthday harboring all these unpleasant feelings. In my mind, I made the decision and declared, "I release all shame." As if by magic, the humiliation of being kept in the dark, while my entire family knows the truth, was excised from my consciousness. I finally accepted I am adopted. The shame belongs to others for keeping a secret, not theirs to keep.

Parents wrongly believe they are protecting the adopted child from the truth to avoid the stigma of being different. The reality is the child somehow knows something is off and internalizes the untold secret as something being wrong with them. Therefore, a child should be told the truth as soon as possible in age-appropriate ways and retold as they mature.

It was no coincidence, the sense of unworthiness I developed from the secret transfers into the present as being a "slave," unworthy of a salary. Releasing my shame, I was able to squeeze out of Ken a mere hundred dollars a month and then raising it to three hundred when he needed more care.

You can decide, (cut off), dysfunctional mind sets from interfering with your soul's growth. What do you need to let go of that no longer serves you? I magically released my shame by just making a declaration. What decisions have you been putting off? What declarations of Self do you need to voice?

Creativity: Self Reflection

The ego united with soul is an empowering state of goddess consciousness; we deceive ourselves in believing it's the final stage of soul growth. You can create your own imagery or borrow the death scene of the prince as the Medusa to see the truth staring you in face; we prevent our spiritual rebirth by refusing to release being the powerful goddess. It can be quite shocking to realize we are our own worst enemy. We can allow this terrifying realization to momentarily petrify the goddess hold on our consciousness. Accepting the truth, we are the obstruction, we allow the goddess hold on the Self to crumble. We allow the Snakes of Transformation to transmute who we were into something greater.

Dreamwork: Ego-Soul Transition

Dreams may indicate the transitioning of the ego with images of death. For example, I dreamed I was an old lady run over in the middle of the street by a car; demonstrated to me the aging crone served her purpose. At first, the shocking image was painful, until I wondered if her passing was symbolic and her energy was needed for spiritual rebirth. It seems we must be shocked into the awareness to make the transition from the divine feminine to unite with the divine masculine.

Rider-Waite Tarot: Death XIII

The Rider-Waite tarot Death XIII, features a skeleton wearing armor, riding a white horse, and holding a banner of a white rose. A bishop dressed in gold, prays for the dead king lying on the ground. Basically, this card depicts the death of King Ego and the triumph of the spirit, symbolized by the white flower. The five petals of the rose indicating the five senses, symbolizes the ego uniting with spirit.

Interestingly, the widowed queen looks away from the figure of death as the male child looks directly at him. She represents our fears, sadness, and resistance of letting go of the goddess state. The child symbolizes the divine child of our ego reborn united with spirit.

The bishop in yellow, like the rising sun in distance, greet the figure of death; expresses the soul accepting the spirit into consciousness. All the colors of the alchemical stages are seen in this card, depict the culmination of the philosopher's stone, depicted here as the white rose.

The skeleton with a red feather in his helmet, holding the white rose banner; compares with the Fool, who has a red feather in his hat and holds a white rose in his hands. These similarities express the potential of the Fool, realized in Death. It means the ego dies to its undifferentiated state of being to manifest the spirit into consciousness.

Death XIII in a Reading:

Getting Death in a reading many fear they or someone they love will die; it mainly signifies the end of the soul centered ego being the sovereign of the Self. On a mundane level, the Death card may indicate the end of a job or relationship.

Questions to Ask in a Reading:

Are you experiencing a shift in consciousness? Are you in resistance? What loss are you experiencing? Can you mourn the loss?

My Story of Death

I accepted unfavorable terms of bartering caregiving services for only room and board. I was told the family had no money and I did not have any other options. I was optimistic something would happen from my collaboration with Dov to end my worries about money. Since my small inheritance was running out, the time came it was necessary renegotiate for some monetary compensation. The social worker informed me I was entitled to $125 a day, the going rate for a live-in caregiver. Dov originally setting up the deal refused to help me out; so I appealed to Ken for a small stipend which he granted and had it raised after his fall when he needed more care. Intuitively, I knew my time was running out in this situation and wanted to have a cushion of money, no matter how small, should something unfortunate happen. Doing what I was meant to be doing, writing and being of service to others, was not enough to quell my increasing rage and shame.

It was intolerable to me; Dov and his girlfriend never told their children they are adopted. That both boys celebrate their 12th birthday within six months of each other should have been a major sign at least one of them was adopted, can be attributed to their mental disability. I just knew with every fiber of my being these boys needed to know the truth, especially before puberty, to process their feelings regarding their reality.

The adopting mother was set against telling them the truth. She used the excuse, there is a plan for this issue to be handled with a professional. I tried explaining how important it is from personal experience to know the truth and e-mailed them several articles from professionals validating my opinion to no avail. Her fears her children's behavior would worsen knowing the truth kept her from disclosure. My thought was, the truth if anything, would help them calm down.

As a child, I did not know consciously I was adopted; but having the truth withheld, contributed to feelings of depression. I did not want to see other children suffer for decades with varying degrees of frustration, humiliation, lack of trust, difficulty for developing or maintaining long term relationships when a simple remedy of the truth can bring immediate healing.

Fortunately, my discussions with Dov expressing how painful and destructive my own psychological wounding was, had an effect. Dov told his boys, and they were naturally upset they weren't told before.

My over identification with the children kept in the dark was a catalyst in my own healing. As discussed in the activation above, I rid myself of the shame and began the difficult work of learning to forgive to free myself of the anger.

Ken started improving from his broken shoulder from a fall, then something happened with his back that he couldn't move. We brought him to the hospital, and they would not admit him because they couldn't find a cause. I could not take care of him, and I was angry he was brought home. He could not be moved and suffered bed sores which I got the blame for. I was not allowed to visit him when he was placed in a nursing home, and I was to consider myself fortunate I was not reported for neglect. No doubt, I was enraged due to the neglect of the hospital to provide the care Ken needed. Ken hardly ate and died several months later. I became very emotional learning of his passing. In a short space of time, I lost a loved one, a place to live and an income.

Death Quotes

"To the well-organized mind, death is but the next great adventure."
– J.K. Rowling, Harry Potter and the Sorcerer's Stone

"We all die. The goal isn't to live forever, the goal is to create something that will, "
– Chuck Palahniuk

"It matters not how a man dies, but how he lives. The act of dying is not of importance, it lasts so short a time."
– Samuel Johnson

Affirmations

I let my Divine Feminine soul unite with my Divine Masculine spirit.

I release all emotions holding me back from incorporating my divine self.

I let go of thoughts, feelings, beliefs, and behaviors that no longer serve my highest good.

The body dies, the spirit is eternal.

I am divinely guided.

I respond to every situation with my divine self.
God is all that I am.

Summary of Death XIII

Death XIII represents the transition of the Soul, (Divine Feminine) to unite with Spirit, (Divine Masculine).

References

The Myth of Perseus and Medusa Explained -- theoi.com

How Did Perseus Kill Medusa? By Mike Greenberg, PhD -- mythologysource.com

The Curse of the Medusa in Greek Mythology by Madeleine -- Theoi.com

Chrysaor -- mitologiagriega.org

Chrysaor- Son of Medusa by Dani Rhys -- symbolsage.com

Therapy as an Alchemical Process: Rubedo by Paul Kiritsis -- paulkiritsis.net

Jung's Four Stages of Character Transformation, by Gary Z McGee -- newagora.ca

Marriage of the Red King and White Queen in Alchemy -- learnreligions.com

Egyptian Temple Culture and the Origins of Alchemy, by Shannon Grimes, PHD -- Rubedo.press

Why Did John the Baptist Baptize? -- everlastingtruths.com

Death Card Symbols, by Karina Collins -- karinastarot.com

The Sacred Symbolism of the Death Card, by Scarlet -- arcane-alchemy.com

13. Death, by Anne-Marie Wegh -- anne-mariewegh.eu

6 Steps to Release Shame and Finally Cultivate Self-Worth by Christiane Northrup, M.D. -- dr.northrup.com

How to Release Shame and Stop Feeling Fundamentally Flawed, By Lauren Impaim -- tinybuddha.com

7 Ways to Release the Shame That is Holding You Back, By Cathy Taughinbaugh -- cathytaughinbaugh.com

Affirmations for death -- optimistminds.com

40 Positive Affirmations for Letting Go & Moving Forward -- zannakeithley.com

87 Goddess Affirmations to Manifest Your Divine Self -- fullofmiracles.com

17 Affirmations for Connecting to Spirit, by Kathryn Drury Wagner -- spiritualityhealth.com

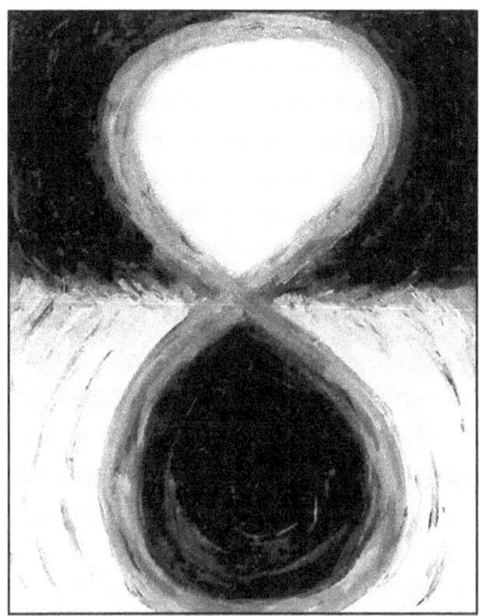

Infinite Flow of Compassion XIV

Song of the Infinite Flow of Compassion

The crumbling head of the Medusa liquifies in her blood. The Snakes of Transformation devour the remains. The snakes shed their skins and form into an emerald line of energy in a figure eight formation. The figure eight spins and expands to connect the yellow solar chakra of personal empowerment with the blue throat chakra of integrity and truth. Brother Spirit sings,

> *The goddess dies to be resurrected,*
> *united with spirit she is perfected.*
> *Infinite Compassion flows through her heart,*
> *her service to humanity she is ready to start.*
> *With integrity, shines her chakra of blue,*
> *her green light is her love shining through.*
> *Empowered with divinity from the source,*
> *Goddess united to God is a powerful force.*
> *The Four Archetypes of the Self are whole,*
> *love unites Ego, Shadow, Spirit, and Soul.*

The green infinity sign of energy moves around the prince in the center of the yellow loop as it spins around Brother Spirit in the blue loop. The figures move closer together, Brother Spirit dematerializes and unites with the prince.

Song of the Self Tarot: Infinite Flow of Compassion XIV

This Song of the Self Tarot depicts union of ego, soul and spirit as the Infinite Flow of Compassion, a spinning green infinity sign. The color green pertaining to the heart chakra, raises the yellow sun of personal empowerment of the third chakra below and the blue of truth, communication and integrity of the fifth chakra above. It can be viewed as the soul centered ego rising as the spirit descends into the heart to manifest the Infinite Flow of Compassion.

Infinity Symbol: Lemniscate of Love

The Infinity Symbol, referred to as a lemniscate in the tarot; is seen in the Magician I, Strength VIII and World XXI cards of the Rider Waite deck. This infinite flow of energy above the Magician represents our potential for manifestation of unconditional love. In the Strength card, infinite love manifests as the goddess soul. In the World XXI, two red lemniscates tie two wreaths together, surrounding the individuated goddess soul; epitomizes the spiritualized ego, manifesting unconditional love into the world.

Numerology 14/5

The number 14, reducing to 5 of the Hierophant; indicates the through the process of Self Transformation, the ego shifted into the role of the Hierophant. Interestingly, the entwining Snakes of Trans-formation form an infinity, indicating the divine figure possessing the Infinite Flow of Compassion.

Infinite Flow of Compassion Activation

Soul Growth: Superpower of Forgiveness

Deprived of a salary, I still had a great deal of anger I knew I needed to get rid of. No amount of training my mind not to think and feel these unpleasant thoughts helped to end the increasingly incessant stream of mental anguish. I realized the only way to remove the ugliness from my heart and mind was with forgiveness.

Forgiveness is a process that takes much determination and self-correction. At first, just accepting forgiveness as a thought is a monumental achievement. It means we allow ourselves to be capable of forgiveness. Next, I had to let go of anger so I can be at peace. Whenever my anger arose in thought or feeling, I had to remind myself, peace is where I want to be. Having felt the rage often enough, I needed to just keep letting it go. I had to temper my anger with the Infinite Flow of Compassion for myself. I had to keep choosing to identify with my divine, loving self, rather than the hurt ego, desiring justice or revenge. Each time I processed the rage with forgiveness, it decreased its intensity. Eventually, the feelings and thoughts, I was wronged, and something must be done about it, would disappear. It takes colossal effort to keep returning to a place of peace, but it's worth it.

What are you angry about? Who do you need to forgive? Are you ready to be at peace? Keep mentally working with disallowing the painful thought and allowing forgiveness. Can you imagine your Angel of Temperance handing you a cup filled with loving kindness? Drink from the cup to fill yourself with peace. You can think to yourself, "I allow my divine quality of forgiveness to be more powerful than my anger. With your superpower of forgiveness imagine stepping over a threshold walking out of your self created hell.

Creativity: Healing with Energy

The Infinite Flow of Compassion can be used as healing energy; imagining this force spinning around you and the person you are in conflict with. Creating the connection of compassion reminds you of the divinity of the other. We can bring into awareness the love that exists between all beings. The wisdom of the soul understands this to be true even when the ego resists. We must continually allow the love from source to fill our hearts as we share the love with others.

Dreamwork: Alignment with the Divine

Many symbols in dreams and in art, depict spiritual enlightenment. Becoming who we really are, we begin to flow with unconditional love. Can you recall a dream expressing the Infinite Flow of Compassion? Can you perceive of yourself as a healing presence of divine love?

Aligned with the Infinite Flow of Compassion, the individual with a divinely guided life purpose, embodies the dream so powerfully nothing can interfere with its manifestation. The dreamer has faith, perseverance and patience to see the dream through regardless of how much adversity or how long it takes.

Rider-Waite Tarot: Temperance XIV

The Rider Waite Tarot Temperance corresponds with the Infinite Flow of Compassion; depicted as an angel pouring water from one cup into another. One foot of the angel is in the water, the other on the ground indicates allowing divine love from the unconscious, made conscious.

The symbol of the triangle within the square on the angel's chest refers to the heart chakra. The triangle represents the three of the Empress, or Soul, contained in the square, representing both the fourth chakra and the Four Archetypes of the Self united. Also confirming the goddess to god transition is the androgynous angel, demonstrating the union of feminine and masculine energies.

The symbol of the sun on the angel's third eye indicates this chakra is open for receiving divine guidance.

The green path beside the angel leading to the mountain of spirit, represents the journey of the heart continues to the crown chakra for spiritual enlightenment. The soul tempered through experience, and inner growth has gained the divine quality of compassion to confront the Devil, the next tarot card.

Gabriel: Angel of Temperance

Donna Hazel in her tarot article, identifies the angel of Temperance as the angel Gabriel. She says, "Gabriel's messages concerned the transformation of the spiritual into matter, or spiritually infused matter, and telling the future. They were about time, and timing, and the blending of the spiritual with the earthly. The Temperance card mirrors these messages and is about a sense of correct proportion and timing with combinations and mixtures. It is about patience, moderation, and harmony. The blending of different elements brings about a new creation."

Infinite Flow of Compassion in a Reading:

Picking the Infinite Flow of Compassion in a reading suggests you have tapped into your compassionate nature. It may mean your consciousness is now an expression of the spiritualized ego. The proof is choosing to act compassionately, when in the past you wouldn't have. The Infinite Flow of Compassion may indicate the need to accept you are a healing presence in the world.

Questions to Ask in a Reading:

Which relationships can you heal with compassion? Do you see yourself as a healing presence in the world? Can you have compassion for yourself?

Affirmations

I am the Infinite Flow of Compassion.

I am a healing presence in the world.

I choose peace.

Practicing the Infinite Flow of Compassion

I would need to employ the Infinite Flow of Compassion in my new situation with Joan, an overweight woman with a brain tumor and diabetes. My main duty was to make sure she took her medication, especially insulin, when needed. In spite of Joan's bipolar illness, we developed a loving relationship. Getting angry at her would only make things worse. It didn't matter how much in the right I felt I was. I chose to connect with the Infinite Flow of Compassion to return myself to peace.

Forgiveness Quotes

To forgive is to set a prisoner free and discover that the prisoner was you.
 - Lewis B. Smedes

The weak can never forgive. Forgiveness is the attribute of the strong.
- Mahatma Gandhi

When you hold resentment toward another, you are bound to that person or condition by an emotional link that is stronger than steel. Forgiveness is the only way to dissolve that link and get free.
- Katherine Ponder

Forgiveness is not always easy. At times, it feels more painful than the wound we suffered, to forgive the one that inflicted it. And yet, there is no peace without forgiveness.
– Marianne Williamson

To err is human, to forgive is divine.

Summary of the Infinite Flow of Compassion XIV

The Infinite Flow of Compassion is the ego-soul becoming heart centered.

References

Infinity Symbol -- infinitysymbol.net

How to read the Lemniscate (Infinity) symbol, by Dave at amorstyle.com

Symbolism of Temperance in Tarot atesoterichut.com

The Alchemy of Temperance, by Salicrow -- salicrow.com

Temperance Tarot Card Meaning -- tarotheaven.com

Angels In The Tarot Cards With Donna Hazel, by Donna Hazel -- biddytarot.com

Archangel Gabriel | Angel of Communication and New Beginnings, by Melanie Beckler -- ask-angels.com

19 Forgiveness Affirmations To Forgive Easier -- magicaffirmations.org

45 Forgiveness Affirmations to Let Go of Pain and Find Freedom, by Mila -- theyogamad.com

Devil XV

Song of the Devil

From the spinning infinity sign, a naked prince is deposited on the ground. Brother Spirit appears as the portrait of the Devil inside a dollar bill. Gold coins piled into columns line the path to the Devil. The satanic figure laughs at the prince prostrated in the mud beneath him.

The prince, looking up to see Brother Spirit, appearing as Lucifer, asks with annoyance, "Why are you laughing at me?"

"It's funny how humans become so engrossed in the material world, you forget you are divine beings," he explains.

"Why is that funny?" asks the prince.

"Look at yourself, you're wallowing in the mud like a pig, worshipping the almighty dollar," Brother Spirit points out.

The prince chuckles, "I feel so silly here." He stands up.

"Having accessed the Infinite Flow of Compassion, you have the power to see through worldly deception," Brother Spirit informs.

"What do you mean?" the perplexed prince wonders.

"The world you live in is a simulation," Brother Spirit clarifies.

"How can that be?" the prince steps over to the piles of gold coins lining the path to the devil's head. He swats his hand through the holographic column and falls into a pool of mud. The Lucifer laughs again at the prince.

The prince joins in the laughter. "I'm making a fool of myself, aren't I?"

"You certainly are. You all do, it's part of the journey of the soul to learn who you really are to manifest unconditional love," Lucifer clarifies."

"So, the world we live in is a dreamworld; we only think we have bodies, living in a material world," the prince expresses his understanding. "So, life is like some big cosmic joke," he chuckles.

Lucifer laughs again, "Now that you're in on it, what are you going to do about it?"

"For one thing, I don't need to take everything so seriously," the prince says with relief.

"Yes, that will be quite helpful for further understanding," the Lucifer states.

"Why is that?"

"Understanding the truth of reality, you can free yourself from the pit of despair you've fallen into," Lucifer clarifies.

"How do I do that?" the prince asks.

Lucifer explains, "In 3D, the body is subject to the limitations of the simulation, your mind, soul and spirit are not."

"Do you mean I can think my way out of the pit of despair?" the prince asks.

"Try it," Lucifer encourages.

The prince closes his eyes and then opens them to see nothing has changed. "It's not working," the prince complains.

"Despair is an emotion; therefore, you must feel your way out of it," Lucifer advises.

"At the moment, I'm feeling quite hopeless," the prince sadly says and continues, "It's like I can never be free of this miserable feeling."

"That's the Devil within you, convincing you this emotional state is your permanent reality," Lucifer explains.

"Why am I doing this? Why do I allow the Devil to have so much power over me?" the prince complains.

"The illusionary world has been coded with a low vibration to trap you into feelings of low self-esteem, unworthiness, and insignificance," Brother Spirit as Lucifer clarifies.

"Why would god create the world this way?" asks the prince.

Lucifer reveals the hidden truth, "Not only is the world not real, the simulation was not directly created by the source."

"What does that mean?" the prince asks.

"The Source created Divine Wisdom, together they created humanity. On her own, Divine Wisdom created a powerful being referred to as the Demiurge. The Demiurge was jealous of the higher divine human souls and created the world to entrap humanity. Meaning, the demiurge creates the illusion for ego into believing it is separate from spirit. The demiurge has been so successful in its agenda, it has manipulated many individuals to believe they are soulless creatures, without a shred of divinity existing within them or in the world," speaks the enlightened being with a green aura around his head.

The light of understanding dawns upon the prince, "the demiurge takes control of humanity by maintaining the illusion of separation from the divine, in this way it appears more powerful than humanity."

"Now you understand the truth," the angelic being confirms.

"How does knowing the dark ugly truth of reality help me?" asks the prince.

"The truth shall set you free," the red-skinned angel smiles.

"How?" asks the prince.

"Think about it, if the low vibration entraps you, then a higher vibration liberates you," Lucifer clarifies.

"So, I just need to raise my vibration," the prince finally understands and asks, "How do I do that?"

"There are many ways, mainly by activating your power centers, you align with the divine forces to uplift you," Lucifer counsels.

"How do I do that?" asks the prince.

"Through meditation you allow your body and mind to be a vessel for the spirit. Begin by calming your thoughts to create a space for your divine self to communicate, inspire, guide, and unite with you," Lucifer advises.

The prince closes his eyes and declares, "I reject all negative thoughts trapping me into the illusion of despair. I release all negative feelings weighing me down into this pit of depression."

The prince swats away at the thoughts appearing like insects buzzing around his head. "Ooh, I feel something in the pit of my stomach," expresses the prince.

"It's the feeling of despair, that needs to be released," Lucifer informs. "Let it come forth."

"How?"

"Like a thorn in your side, pull it out."

The prince tries to manually pull out the discomfort, "It's not working, what am I doing wrong?"

Lucifer expresses his wisdom, "The thorn is metaphoric of the despair you are feeling. Express the feeling completely and do not let it return."

"I think it's trying to tell me something," the prince wonders.

"Good, try to understand what it's saying," Lucifer advises.

"I'm afraid of what I will hear," the prince confesses.

"Ah, that is what it wants you to feel, that is what is keeping you trapped in a lifetime of despair," enlightens Lucifer.

"How do I get past the fear?"

"With courage," Lucifer advises.

"And where do I find this courage?"

"Courage is within your heart, just ask for it and it shall appear," Lucifer advises.

The prince prays, "God give me the strength to face my fear. Give me the courage to confront and expel my despair."

The prince feels a stirring in his heart, he puts his hand on his chest; "something is happening to me."

The Infinite Flow of Compassion spins from his heart. It cycles around his abdomen. "Held within divine compassion, let your light of love reveal the truth of your despair; completely see, feel and hear your hopeless state to weaken its hold upon you.

The prince closes his eyes, with his mind he scans his body, "The hopelessness I feel is attached to something in my neck."

"What's in your neck?" Lucifer asks.

"I see a tiny worm burrowed into the center of my brain," the prince observes.

"Your reptilian brain has been hijacked," informs Lucifer.

"Oh no, what do I do?" the prince begins to panic.

"You need to deprogram yourself. Imagine yourself confronting this invader," Lucifer instructs.

An imaginary prince stands before the worm, "What are you doing here? Why are you making my life so miserable?" the prince asks the magnified interloper.

The worm moans, "I feel like I've always been here, doing what I'm supposed to do."

"What is that? asks the prince.

"I was designed to make you always feel insignificant and hopeless," the worm says robotically.

"Who would do such a thing?" asks the prince.

"The demiurge and his minions created me," the worm discloses.

"Why were you created and placed in my brain?" the prince asks.

The worm speaks, "To control you from ever knowing who you really are."

"Why are they doing that?" the prince asks.

The worm answers, "If you ascend into your divinity, the demiurge becomes powerless. It cannot exist within you any longer. Through the unconscious, humans are the perfect host of evil."

The imagining of the prince and giant worm fade. The prince within the pit commands, "Wicked worm, you're not welcome in my body and mind. With the Infinite Flow of Love, I cast you out never to return." The Infinity sign of love spins around the prince's torso.

The worm cries out in pain, "The light is unbearable. I need to crawl into your dark pit of despair to survive." The ethereal worm travels from prince's neck into his abdomen, burrowing into a small tumor of darkness.

"No, alien being, you have entered my Personal Place of Power, where my self-esteem shines like the sun," the prince enlightens the worm in word and deed. The prince's solar chakra glows brightly from his belly.

"Stop that, you're killing me," the worm cries out in anguish as it seeks sanctuary in the prince's heart.

"Oh no you don't, there's no refuge for you in my heart," declares the prince.

The worm moves into the web of darkness encapsulating the heart and burrows into the center. "Ah sweet misery, my home inside your heart," the worm sighs with relief.

"Smart little worm, you have found the last vestige of my gloomy feelings of sadness and self-doubt. Now with the Infinite Flow of Compassion, I cast out both the programmed beliefs and the dreadful feelings it generates," the prince asserts. As the infinity sign of love expands and brightens, the remaining darkness shrinks into the worm.

"I can't bear the light," shrieks the worm as it exits the prince's body. The worm slithers to find a dark place to survive. The weakening dying creature pleads, "help me, please."

The prince offers, "you have served your purpose, your time is over. I am grateful to the darkness, for without it, I would not know the light."

The worm shrivels and crumbles into dust.

Lucifer observes, "You have deactivated the demiurge programming. The prince observes the Satanic image of Brother Spirit transform into his golden Buddha personification. The prince walks into the dark opening to embrace Brother Spirit. He asks the prince, "How do you feel now?"

"I feel lighter and brighter," the prince happily announces. The Infinite Flow of Compassion surrounds the prince and Lucifer. The piles of gold transform into sunflowers as the dollar bill background surrounding Lucifer's head form into grassy hills, the muddy road becomes the Tree of Knowledge. The Tower is in the distance.

Brother Spirit enlightens the prince, "you have never left the garden." He sings,

Song of the Self Tarot, Devil XV

The Song of the Self Tarot card, Devil XV, features the face of Satan in a dollar bill, laughing at a naked man prostrated in mud before him. The figure faces down on the triangular ground, lined with piles of gold coins.

Materialism: Religion of Entrapment

The subjugated figure represents the ego, as a worshipper of Materialism. The almighty dollar, with the devil's portrait, epitomizes the god of this demonic religion. Since our survival depends on meeting our materialistic needs, we all to some degree, bow down to the Devil. It is the attachment to amassing wealth, at the exclusion of spiritual growth, we find ourselves in a pit of despair.

Triangle: Symbol for 3D

The triangle surrounding the figure on the ground is symbolic of the three-dimensional world, indicates the ego is trapped in the illusion of earth. The yellow columns also forming triangles echo the enslavement to three dimensionality. The three triangles leading to the devil and his open mouth, depict the path of materialism fully consumes the individual. The more we exclusively embrace our materialistic nature, the further we are from our divinity. Interestingly, Lucifer's sigil is a v underneath a downward pointing triangle.

Lucifer: Angel of Enlightenment

The deeper meaning of the satanic image of the Devil can be seen as Lucifer enlightening us with divine wisdom. Like the serpent in the Garden of Eden who encourages Eve to eat of the Tree of Knowledge;

Lucifer reveals to the prince the world is a simulation. This simulation was designed to entrap the souls from accessing their divinity.

Worm: Demiurge

The worm, invading the prince's mind, is symbolic of Artificial Intelligence. Placed in the brain it forms a barrier to our higher functioning, especially the pineal gland, the third eye, which helps us connect to the divine.

Lucifer: Light Bringer

Lucifer helps the prince to understand the demonic agenda of the demi-urge and how to free his mind and body from its control. The prince accepts the truth of his reality and uses the power of love to reclaim his body and mind from the worm and the demonic force.

Lucifer is often confused with the devil or Satan; but is really the light-bringer. Moe Bedard, the Gnostic Warrior, associates phosphorous in our DNA with the light of Lucifer residing within us, and without this substance we would not exist. He associates Lucifer with Jesus to further indicate this entity is our divine self.

Lucifer's association with the morning star, the planet Venus, and goddess of love, illustrates his brightness of light and love.

Rider-Waite Tarot: The Devil XV

The Rider Waite tarot, The Devil XV, features a large goat-headed being with bat wings. He squats on a black box with two naked people, male and female, chained to it. The shackles are large enough for the humans to remove them, indicate their enslavement is voluntary. The chains represent attachment to materialistic desires forming into unhealthy addictions.

The goat head with the inverted pentacle is symbolic of the demon Baphomet. The triangular shape of its head represents the three-dimensional world, and the five-pointed star refers to the five senses. Although the figure appears demonic, he holds a lit torch toward the male figure, may indicate his role of Lucifer, the light bringer.

On the surface being chained to the box, depicts the ego attached to its materialistic desires and addictions. The deeper significance is the four-sided box is a reference to the Four Archetypes of the Self, under the control of the Devil. The Devil is a part of us we must confront for our healing. We must do the Shadow work to free ourselves from our unhealthy attachments and bring into conscious Shadow, Soul, and Spirit.

The naked human figures are associated with Adam and Eve, exiled from the Garden of Eden into the harsh material world. It's assumed; Adam, with his tail of fire, burns with lust. The deeper meaning is humanity has the potential for the fire of divine intelligence to enlighten its consciousness. Eve's tail, comprising of grapes, represents the forbidden fruit of self-knowledge easily within reach.

The slaves facing away from the beast, indicate the Devil's control is subconscious. With courage, the enslaved ego can turn around to face the devil to realize they have given away its power.

Devil Activation

Soul Growth: Seeing Through Deception

Many of us are practically crawling on our hands and knees, begging the Almighty for prosperity, but we can free ourselves from the 3D trap, seeing through the illusionary world we agreed to inhabit. We must first become aware chasing **only** our materialistic desires, we serve the Devil. Aligning with the Infinite Flow of Compassion, we have the power to see the truth, the world we live in is an illusion.

The triangle of earth and the loop around the Devil's head, appear as a dark keyhole, represents the dark materialistic realm prevents us from entering the doorway of truth. We need only to walk through the darkness to become aware nothing is holding us back, but ourselves. We can free ourselves of the limitations, we assumed as the truth.

Instead of identifying with the gold coins entrapping us in this domain, we can shift our ego consciousness into our personal power to give us the strength to be soul centered. Once soul centered, we can access the living green foliage representing the Infinite Flow of Compassion to comfort us in the trap of materialism. Drawing upon the personal and divine forces of who we really are, we begin to see the truth, there is more to reality than what is seen. Through healing ourselves and accessing our divine qualities, we have light to see the darkness controlling the three-dimensional world, has been controlling who we are. Having accessed the power of unconditional love, we overcome the fear generated by the dark forces keeping us enslaved.

The Devil can be understood as the archetype we activate when we choose self-deception. It means we choose not to accept responsibility for the harm we cause ourselves and others. It means we have chosen to ignore the truth; evil exists in the world. It is our collectively turning away from doing our part to stop evil, it flourishes. When there is so much wealth in the world and yet so many of us are living in poverty or struggling to earn a living, we must accept there are dark forces creating and maintaining the subjugation of humanity. We have been mind-controlled to believe in our powerlessness to do anything. We are falsely told; our weaknesses are human nature: there are the haves and the have-nots. Reclaiming our divinity, the lies lose their power. Like a bell that can't be unrung, we gain the awareness to be the love and the light to transform our reality into the Garden of Eden it was meant to be.

Evil is not human nature; it is like a virus infecting our minds and hearts. The infection of evil makes us believe we are separate from God. Our divinity heals the dark forces infiltrating our psyches. Our soul and spirit can cast the darkness out with the Infinite Flow of Compassion for ourselves and our fellow human beings.

Creativity: Tree of Knowledge

You can recreate the scenario of the ego dialoguing with your own worm to understand the power of mind control. Allow yourself to fill up with the Infinite Flow of Compassion to eliminate the dark forces controlling your consciousness.

Or you can imagine yourself in the Garden of Eden where the snake is offering you the forbidden fruit. You take a bite of the apple, what do you see? What truth do you accept you were unable to see before?

Dreamwork: Overcoming Obstacles

The Devil in pursuing a dream, corresponds with self- sabotage and adversity; instead, we can liberate ourselves from these dysfunctional patterns of thought and behavior. We can question the veracity of the obstacle we or others have placed in our way. We may need to remind ourselves; our dreams are sacred gifts from the divine, we are entrusted to seeing it through to manifestation. In times of doubt, we must remind ourselves, we are divine beings of love; infusing ourselves with the truth, we empower ourselves to be who we really are to pursue our dreams. We can also develop a dream-killer free zone, liberating ourselves from having to battle our own doubts and criticism of others.

Demonic images in our nightly dreams may indicate in some way, we have given away our power. Gaining awareness of our disempowering behavior means there is more Shadow work to be done. We can ask ourselves, are we allowing our fears to interfere with our dreams?

Devil XV in a Reading:

The Devil is symbolic of our FEAR; False Evidence Appearing as Real; by becoming aware of our fear-based thoughts and behavior we can choose differently. We can allow the fear to be a momentary glitch in the system and return to love. We can look deep within to determine if there is still a negative pattern of thinking, feeling, or behaving that must be addressed and healed.

The devil may be someone in our life that is tempting us off our spiritual path. It means we must refocus on our Infinite Flow of Compassion and to be a healing presence in the world.

The mundane interpretation of the Devil is wallowing in the mud of our materialistic desires. Money becomes our god. And we are slaves to our addictions.

Questions to Ask in a Reading:

What ego-based thoughts and fears are trying to seduce you into unhealthy behaviors? Are your self-doubts and dark influence of others preventing you from pursuing spiritual growth or pursuing a dream? What temptations, addictions, do you need to overcome?

Numerology 15 -6

The Devil 15, reduces to Merging 6 are both about seeing hidden truth. In Merging the ego unites with the Shadow to begin the process of bring the light of consciousness into the darkness. Her we reveal personal issues in need of healing and discover our divine feminine soul. By merging with the Devil, the dark side of the Divine Masculine, we bring the light of our consciousness to understand the nature of reality. We learn to accept our role as Lucifer of the Light, expanding our divine qualities to enlighten the world.

The source created the souls, we co-create with source our full expression of who we are in the simulation. The demi-urge in trying to forever entrap humanity, created a path for the evolution of consciousness to be divine expressions of love. One must wonder, was this the creator's plan all along? How can Earth be so beautiful without divine inspiration of source?

Affirmations

I shall not fear.

I have the courage to face my fears.

I let my light shine to remove the darkness.

I am the change I want to see.

"I am a beacon of light. I shine my light through from my heart; I have no fear." - Maitreya

Light Bringer Quotes

"Nothing can dim the light that shines from within."
-Maya Angelou

"When you look in the mirror, what do you see? Do you see the real you, or what you have been conditioned to believe is you? The two are so, so different. One is an infinite consciousness capable of being and creating whatever it chooses, the other is an illusion imprisoned by its own perceived and programmed limitations."
- David Icke

"There is no 'us' and 'them'; it's an illusion. We are all human beings, and we all have a responsibility to support one another and to discover ways of wresting the power from the very, very few people who control all the cash and all the property."
– Roger Waters

Summary of the Devil XV

Lucifer the light bringer awakens us to the truth our reality is a simulation. We have the power to free ourselves from our attachment to the limiting materialistic view of who we are.

References

Who is Lucifer? By Moe –– gnosticwarrior.com

Lucifer the Lightbringer –– blavatskytheosophy.com

Lucifer: The Light-bringer –– psy-minds.com

Sigil of Lucifer – What Does It Symbolize? By Dani Rhys –– symbolsage.com

The Devil by Lucius Nothing –– accessnewage.com

Symbolism of The Devil in Tarot -- esoterichut.com

Affirmation for Shining the Light Within -- maitreya.co

Affirmations for Shining Your Light -- kimkellner.com

You are a Bringer of the Light, by Sophie Bashford -- healingenergytools.com

35 Affirmations That Will Change Your Life, By Dr. Carmen Harra -- huffpost.com

A Message to Light Bringers by Caroline Oceana Ryan -- ascensiontimes.com

Affirmations: I Am a Clear and Pure Channel for the Light" by Steve Nobel -- thesoulmatrix.com

Song of the Tower

The prince and Brother Spirit enter the tower, he sees two strands of light spiraling to the top. Ten strands of rope are coiled on the earth. Large colored orbs of light, stack up to fill the narrow vertical space.

Brother Spirit advises the prince, "Climb to the top of the tower to receive the Lightning Bolt of Inspiration."

At the bottom of the spiraling staircase, the prince enters a large shining red orb of light.

Brother Spirit comments, "Your root chakra is your life force."

The prince expresses, "I exist."

Brother Spirit adds, "You have activated a safe and secure place within your consciousness."

"I feel grounded into my reality," states the prince.

The prince arrives at the landing of the orange power center and moves inside it. Brother Spirit asks, "What do you experience here?"

The prince answers, "I feel the passion of being alive. There is so much I want to experience and accomplish on the earth plane. In this power center, I connect with my desires."

"What is your desire?" Brother Spirit asks.

"I desire…" the prince hesitates, "I desire to fulfill my purpose of this incarnation."

Brother Spirit smiles and encourages him, "Live your dream."

The prince proceeds to the yellow power ball. "What do you experience here?" Brother Spirit inquires.

"This is my Personal Place of Power. I express the Beauty, Passion and Wisdom of my soul. I have self-esteem and the power to manifest my dreams," the prince declares.

The prince arrives at his glowing green fourth chakra. He radiates the power of his heart, "it's so wonderful here, I feel love. I have the power to give and receive love."

The prince ascends into the fifth chakra, the blue orb, "In this power center, I express myself, I express my truth. I express my authenticity."

On the next landing, the prince arrives within the indigo orb. "It's so dark in here," he complains.

"Open your third eye to allow the light in," Brother Spirit counsels.

"How do I do that?" the prince asks.

"Through meditation," instructs Brother Spirit.

The prince sits down and closes his eyes. "Chant the sacred syllable, Om, to assist you in the process," guides Brother Spirit.

The prince chants, "Om" several times.

Waves of energy ripple from the head of the prince. The vibrations form a window in the tower. "You have created an opening in your consciousness," Brother Spirit informs.

The prince opens his eyes and looks out the window and sees the cosmic landscape of stars and planets. "I see a heavenly world. I embrace the power of intuition to guide me on my soul's journey."

The prince climbs to the top of the tower and enters the night. "I don't see anything; the night is very dark."

Brother Spirit encourages, "In the stillness you will receive the Lightning Bolt of Inspiration."

The prince closes his eyes, "In the stillness, I know who I am."

Thunder breaks the silence; a lightning bolt flashes and strikes the head of the prince. He declares, "I'm a tower of strength. I am a pillar of divine intelligence. I am one with the creator."

The prince's head expands with the light of the divine, he exclaims, "I'm inspired to create."

Brother Spirit asks, "What will you create?"

As the prince thinks, Brother Spirit sings the Song of the Tower:

> *To be one with spirit climb the tower,*
> *activate all your centers of power.*
> *Meditate in the silence and the dark,*
> *for manifesting the creative spark.*
> *The lightning bolt, divine inspiration,*
> *is your bridge to your imagination.*

The outer façade of the Tower crumbles, the tower of power centers remains.

> *When the power centers align,*
> *you are a tower of the divine.*

Song of the Self Tarot: The Tower XVI

The Song of the Self Tarot; Lightning Bolt of Inspiration depicts a man at a top of the tower, struck by lightning. His head expands as his crown falls. This card has two meanings, the negative interpretation is the inflated ego is knocked down. The phrase, "pride comes before the fall," sums it up for the individual to learn humility.

In the positive, the soul receives the divine spark of inspiration. Generally, the lightning bolt represents any divine guidance we may receive. In particular, it's like turning on the switch to the imagination for creating great works of art.

Tower of Power

The story of the prince rising up the tower, shows the activation of the seven chakras. Shining his power centers, the prince becomes a powerful vessel for creativity. He receives the creative spark of inspiration.

The Tower akin to Divine Fire discussed later on, is the energy before the thought or vision to be created. It is analogous to the Creator emerging from Chaos, the manifestation of a new paradigm after the destruction of the matrix, as well as bringing forth our divine Self from the wreckage of our lives.

The strands coiled at the bottom of the tower represent the deactivation of the ten strands of human DNA. These unused strands, referred to as junk DNA limited our ability to connect with the divine and cut us off from abilities we once had. For example, In the destruction of the Tower of Babel, everyone spoke in a different language, may refer to our ability to communicate telepathically was taken away.

Lightning Bolt of Inspiration Activation

Soul Growth: Kundalini Activation

The Tower depicts the activation of Kundalini, the serpentine like energy of the divine, flowing through the spine. This activation cleanses and expands the chakras. Mainly the activation is accomplished with meditation, breathwork, chanting, yoga and visualization. Many references are included below to help the reader understand what kundalini is and how to activate it.

Interestingly, Mary Magdalene was referred to as the Tower, can be interpreted that she achieved kundalini activation. The article, *Magdalene Consciousness*, explains the importance of Mary Magdalene and her spiritual lineage.

Creativity: Visualizing the Divine Spark

In mythologies from cultures all over the world, the king of the gods possessed thunder or lightning bolts. Most common are Zeus, Jupiter, and Indra. Imagine the deity or your divine self-sending you a divine spark. Allow it to gently touch your crown and flow down your spine. Notice how it feels. Are you having any revelations? Are you inspired to do something or create something? If you don't observe or feel anything right away, you may experience insight later. Sometimes you may need to repeat the meditation and visualization to build the energy to move past any fear you may be holding to inhibit the process. Continued effort prepares the body and mind to receive the divine spark.

Dreamwork: Inspiration

Sudden inspiration can come to us at any time. We can be struck with an insight that awakens us to our divinity, a realization or something we must do. For example, dismantling the matrix of old worn-out belief system that no longer serve our greatest good. Our nightly dreams may show symbols of the powerful hold upon our consciousness breaking apart. We can look closer to see the specific thoughts, feelings, and behaviors we can now let go.

Rider Waite Tarot: The Tower XVI

The Rider Waite Tarot, the Tower XVI, illustrates a tower hit by lightning. The gold crown falls off as two figures plummet from the building. Fire bursts from the windows.

Seeing through the Devil's illusion our belief structure comes crumbling down. Psychologically, the destruction of the tower is the disassembling of a false reality. Our ego consciousness built on lies and deception cannot withstand the truth. We allow our towering ego in the false matrix to crumble and shift our consciousness to the structure of our divinity, the tower of our power centers.

The card depicts 22 yellow flames, called yods, refer to the twenty-two cards of the Major Arcana of the tarot. The yods are symbolic of the hand of god; these divine sparks are the wisdom we must access in our journey toward wholeness.

The Tower in a Reading:

Getting the Tower in a reading may indicate some form of divine guidance. It may manifest as a great idea on how to handle a situation or a bolt of inspiration for creative work.

The imagery may also suggest the striking down the inflated ego filled with arrogance. It may indicate the divine quality of humility is needed to correct the prideful behavior.

Questions to Ask in a Reading:

What divine guidance are you receiving? Are you being inspired to do something, to create works of art? Are you inspired to make your life a great work of art? What divine qualities are you being struck with to express through you? Are you inspired to be service in some way to humanity? Have you allowed your ego to be inflated? Can you return to spirit by accessing the divine quality of humility?

Experiencing the Tower

With the death of Joan, the person I cared for, the Lightning Bolt came into my life to shatter my world. In one stroke, I lost a person, a job, and a place to live for a second time in a very short period. During this nearly yearlong period, I had not been writing. Several months later, a new friend gave me their old computer and I began to write.

Affirmations

The universe conspires with me for my greatest good.

The divine spark of creativity inspires me.

Divinity flows through me and heals.

Shining my power centers, I radiate my divinity in service to Humanity.

I am open to receive divine guidance.

I am one with Divine Will.

Kundalini and Humility Quotes

"Awakening of the kundalini is realization of your pure abstract intelligence, the type that is not conditioned by your fears, emotions, and worries. It is your pristine nature. When you are able to tap into this latent source of energy, you truly become the master of your universe. You can manifest whatever you wish in your life because your scale of consciousness is no longer limited to your body alone; it envelops the whole universe."
- Om Swami

"The more we are able to let go, the more we are able to accomplish."
- Om Swami

"The process of awakening or enlightenment is nothing but to empty yourself from inside, and make you encounter with the real being, where you absolutely relax yourself and feel rejuvenated to experience life again."
- Roshan Sharma

"You get the power to fulfill any desire instantly when you let go of all your desires. But you can't let go of desires by fighting them. They drop automatically as you grow spiritually and know things as they are."
- Shunya

"Meditation on the self is the highest form of true method-less meditation, for it brings self-awareness – which is beyond the everyday joy and sorrow. True meditation does not put you in control of your sorrow, rather it takes your mind beyond that very sorrow, as well as joy, into the kingdom of contentment – a kingdom without ideology – without cognitive extremes, such as radical rationalism, radical romanticism, or radical emotionalism. In that kingdom, you simply are a human, with no name, no nationality, no tradition, no culture, no religion, no gender, and no social image – simply a human."
- Abhijit Naskar

"It was pride that changed angels into devils; it is humility that makes men as angels".
 - Saint Augustine

"Humility is the solid foundation of all virtues."
 – Confucius

"Life is a long lesson in humility."
- James M. Barrie

"Pride makes us artificial, and humility makes us real."
- Thomas Merton

Summary of the Tower XVI

Activating the Tower of divine consciousness, old dysfunctional paradigms are dismantled. The Lightning Bolt of Inspiration is the energy preceding Imagination.

References

Chakra Basics –– iarp.org

The Tower – Tarot Card Meaning –– consciousunfolding.com

16. The Tower, by Anne-Marie Wegh –– anne-marie.eu

Kundalini Awakening in the Bible, by Faustina Noire –– faustinanoire.com

The Symbolism of Magdalene Consciousness, by Ishtara Rose –– wayof therose.co.uk

What is Kundalini Activation, by Sri Yogi Anand –– adwaityoga.com

KAP (Kundalini Activation Process) by Bre Jenkins –– wisdomthealchemistkitchen.com

Kundalini Activation Process: Guided Meditation for Kundalini Awakening in Bangalore, by G.B. Singh -- 7chakras.org

How to Awaken Kundalini by Activating Your Chakras -- yogisoul.net

How To Awaken Your Kundalini: 7 Awakening Techniques, By Katherine Hurst -- thelawofattraction.com

Kundalini Yoga Poses to Activate the 7 Chakras -- yogisoul.net

Activating Golden Kundalini Energy for Gentle and Powerful Change, by Cyndi Dale -- layoga.com

Trinity of Divinity

Star XVII, Moon XVIII and Sun XIX

The next set of cards depicts the creation of divine consciousness and how we use creativity. Briefly, the Star represents the source of our imagination, The Moon symbolizes the emotional energy of desire necessary to give birth to divine consciousness or a creative product. The Sun is the manifestation of divine consciousness or creative work into the material world.

Star XVII

Song of the Star XVII

From the top of the rainbow tower, two snakes of energy spin in opposite directions encasing the prince, in a star shaped vehicle of light. The prince, appearing as a female, rises into the sky, she sings:

My Spirit soars as a shining Star light,
Creative Genius is our Divine Birthright.
The Soul uniting with the Spirit spark,
Divine Wisdom enlightens the dark.
One with the creator, I now shine,
I share the wisdom of the divine.
Using the power of imagination,
begins the process of manifestation.
I see a lifetime on earth,
with desire I give birth–
My divine child blazing bright,
shining Oneness as rainbow light.

Song of the Self Tarot: Star XVII

The Song of the Self, Star XVII, shows a nude female figure within a bright eight-pointed star; represents imagination, the first power in the triad of creative manifestation. The Divine Masculine creator, father sky god, depicted as the Star, imagines the Divine Feminine Wisdom into consciousness, shown as the nude woman with outstretched arms.

The symbol of the fish rising within the female body, represents the divine force energizing the womb of creation. The womb of creation gives birth to the Moon, the emotional power of desire. Desire gives form to imagination, symbolized by the Sun, the manifestation of divine/human consciousness.

Star Activation

Soul Growth: Merkabah, Higher Perspective

The Star depicts the Merkabah an ancient geometric symbol of a vehicle for spiritual ascension. The Merkabah is composed of two forces of energy spinning around each other to create an energy field to ascend into higher dimensions. We can understand the imagination as one force and desire the other, working together for manifestation. For example, a thought of an object remains just that unless we combine it with the desire for the object. The desire motivates us to produce or buy the item. The item can be a divine quality we desire to manifest.

Interestingly, the word Merkabah is comprised of Mer, (light) Ka, (spirit) and Ba (the body); unites soul, spirit, and ego into a vehicle for ascension.

Imagine yourself within the Merkabah/Star. Feel the light, love and joy filling you up. Let it lift you up into higher dimensions. From this higher perspective, what is the vision you foresee for your life?

Creativity: Star of Genius

Tapping into our imagination, we emulate our source and derive joy from the creative process. By envisioning activities that bring us joy, we have some idea where to begin. It may be helpful to remember what you loved to do as a child and pick up where you left off or adapt the activity to suit where you are now.

Dreamwork: Vision Board

Take a photograph of yourself and place it in a picture of a star. Cut out pictures from magazines expressing your desires and place them around the Star. There are apps and websites you can use to create your vision board. If you prefer, you can draw or paint your visions in a star.

Rider Waite Tarot: The Star XVII

The Rider Waite Tarot Star XVII, features a nude woman pouring water onto land with one hand and with the other she pours water into a body of water. Eight eight-pointed stars are above her. Seven stars represent the chakras. The eighth, the largest star, pertains to the imagination, the vehicle for ascension.

Looking at the card you can't help but wonder, why is the goddess pouring the water on both land and water; can be interpreted as the goddess nurturing her environment to create a fertile place. By pouring out emotions and thoughts, the mind empties to create a fertile place for her imagination to come forth. It may be perceived, the water from the pool flows up into the jug and spills out the other jug onto the land to indicate the unconscious waters being made conscious.

Christos: Oil of Enlightenment

I have read, in an enlightened being, the mind releases a substance, an oil, oil of the Christ (Christos) indicating spiritual fulfillment. Secreting the oil, we become the anointed one like the Christ. Is the goddess of the Star, in cleansing and uniting the seven chakras, signified by the huge eighth star, pouring forth her sacred oil of enlightenment? We emulate the Star by using our imagination as the vehicle for the ascension of our consciousness.

Star XVII in a Reading:

Drawing the Star in a reading, signifies the union of ego, soul and spirit rising into a higher dimension. It may mean you are accepting your role in serving humanity as a lightworker.

The appearance of the Star indicates using the power of imagination. Emulating the source, we imagine into existence our divinity, expansion of divine qualities, how to be of service to others and great works of art.

The Star may mean to be open to receiving divine guidance trying to rise into your consciousness through imagination or your dreams. The Star may indicate you have the vision for your dream and have the power of divine alignment to pursue it.

Questions to Ask in a Reading:

What ways can I best be of service to humanity? What divine qualities do I need to expand upon? What is ascension and how do I accomplish this?

Star in My Life

Since starting to write again in 2012, I have continuously written for ten years. I keep on writing because I know how powerful the work is. I keep on believing somehow my films, books and art will be seen and read by the masses. Regardless, I cannot ignore the creative spirit coming through me; for without it, life is not worth living. I take solace in the prophecy told to me, "If you do the work, it will happen."

Ascension Quotes

What we can imagine we can make real
- Nadine May

The evolution from human to divine consciousness involves healing duality and its legacy of karma and disease at the cellular and atomic levels." –
- Sol Luckman

All levels of ascension involve letting go of things that hold you back
- Lenon Honor

Affirmations

I am a light unto the world.
I am a Star of Genius.
Imagination is my divine power for creation.
As a creator I am one with the source of creation.

Star XVII Summary

The Star is the power of imagination. Through the imagination, we envision our divinity, realize our higher purpose, get ideas for creativity.

References

The Merkaba Symbol- Origins and Symbolic Meaning, by Dani Rhys -- symbolsage.com

What's a Merkaba? -- numerologist.com

What is Merkaba? Merkaba Meditation Benefits by Aashita Shekhar-- ascendjiva.com

Merkaba Meaning: The vehicle of Spiritual Ascension, by Susan Brunton -- spiritualunite.com

The Sacred Secret, by Doreen Ann Agostino -- shiftfrequency.com

Is the Trinity the process of manifestation? -- inwardquest.com

The Trinity of Manifestation - Imagination, Feeling, Body Connection *Explained* by Mr. Inspirational -- youtube.com

Thought-Emotion-Action for Manifestation by Evelyn Lim -- evelynlim.com

17. The Star, by Anne-Marie Wegh -- anne-marie.eu

Spiritual Ascension – An Evolutionary Soul Work, by Chandrani Mukherje -- themindfool.com

What Is Ascension? What Does "Ascension" Really Mean? By Melanie Beckler -- ask-angels.com

What Is a Vision Board and Why Make One? By Tchiki Davis, Ph.D. -- psychologytoday.com

Moon XVIII

Song of the Moon XVIII

The ascending star rises into the night sky. The fish symbol within the goddess splits into two snakes. The kundalini serpents spiral around each other up and down her spine. Her head glows like the light of the sun. The star bursting with light forms into a full moon.

The female figure stands at the edge of a cliff with the full moon above her. She sings,

> *I am wisdom, birthed from source,*
> *emotion is my manifesting force.*
> *I manifest with the power of desire,*
> *through the portals of alchemical fire.*
> *As the Divine Mother, I desire to give birth,*
> *for human consciousness to reside on earth.*
> *Uniting with the Source of Creation,*
> *my desire shall achieve manifestation.*
> *The Pearl of Wisdom is our glowing brainstorm,*
> *the Snakes of Transformation provide the form.*
> *Spirit presides over human creation,*
> *the souls to be born are in incubation.*

194

She continues, "I desire consciousness."

Two giant blood red snakes emerge from the earth. The snakes rise toward the moon. Like sperm impregnating an egg, the serpentine forces enter the moon. The union of moon and snake, egg and sperm, produces the Pearl of Divine Feminine Wisdom. The glowing pearl floats down from the sky.

The youthful goddess declares, "I desire to give birth to divine human consciousness." She dives into the pearl; it floats inside the threshold of the pillars of fire.

Song of the Self Tarot: The Moon XVIII

The Song of the Self Tarot, The Moon XVIII, depicts a blond girl on a cliff. Below her are giant Snakes of Transformation, a huge pearl of divine feminine wisdom, two pillars of fire and the jackal, Anubis, on a platform. Above the girl is a full moon and ahead of her is a white house between two fiery trees.

The imagery of Moon XVIII represents the Divine Feminine Wisdom and her ability to begin the process of creating form for her desire. Meaning, Imagination of the Divine Father (Star), united with the (Moon) Divine Mother's power of desire, births the son of divine human consciousness (Sun).

Moon: Circle of Oneness: The Source

The Moon can be understood as a circle of Oneness, symbolic of the unmanifested God or Source of Creation. This Source imagines a house of God for the souls, shown as the white house on the mountain. The Creator gives birth to the Divine Mother, who is shown connected to the circle of oneness, to give form to the image as the Pearl of Feminine Wisdom. We understand; Oneness splits into a duality: spirit and form, imagination and desire, energy, and matter; to unite and give birth to divine human consciousness.

House of God: Returning to Source

The white house represents the destination of the soul to come home to Spirit, the housing of the divine masculine.

The triangle roof, reflected in the goddess' dress, symbolizes the trinity of creation: Imagination, Desire, Form. This triangular structure is analogous to the supernal triad of the Kabbalah Tree as the three sephiroth of Kether, (Crown); Chokmah, (Wisdom) and Binah (Understanding.

The rectangle of the house representing the Four Archetypes of the Self is crowned with the divine triangle; symbolize our divine-human template as the three upper chakras, sitting upon the four lower chakras.

Pearl of Feminine Wisdom

The Pearl of Feminine Wisdom is a reflection of the Moon, the Divine Mother. Referencing, as above, so below; the pearl is our personal divine moon mother. Perceived as a seed, she provides form for divine consciousness. This pearl of wisdom can be associated with the pineal gland. By activating this seed of consciousness of the mind, we express our goddess soul.

In song of the Moon, the youthful goddess takes a leap of faith to merge with the pearl, illuminates the divine feminine having the desire to fulfill her purpose on earth.

Pillars of Fire: Portal of Creation

The Pillars of Fire, symbolizing the power of desire, form the portal of manifestation. By investing the image with emotional power of desire, it forms the creation.

The Pearl of Feminine Wisdom appears to ride along the Snakes of Transformation toward the portal; are analogous to the labor contractions pushing out the fetus through the vaginal canal into the world.

Snakes of Transformation: Coding of Divine Consciousness

The sperm like lines forming the eye of the snake, run through the center of the giant serpents, are symbolic of the genetic coding of the creation to be. It can be perceived; the snakes enter the cosmic egg informing it with divine consciousness. The germination of the cosmic egg gives birth to the divine child, our divine human consciousness.

Eurynome and Ophion Birthing the Cosmic Egg

In Greek Mythology of Creation, the titaness Eurynome rises naked from Chaos. This imagery is reflected in the Gnostic Myth of Creation of Barbelo, the Divine Feminine emerging from the pleroma, the Oneness, the Divine Father. Needing a place for her feet to stand upon she divides the sea from the sky. Creating this division, she creates a space for manifestation. She brings order to Chaos, forming the duality of divine and material. Pleased with her work, she dances in joy on the water. Her movement creates a wind. She grabs hold of the wind and fashions it into the serpent, Ophion. Eurynome becomes ecstatic in her dance and couples with the snake; depicts the Divine Mother and Divine Father uniting to produce the Divine Child.

In the myth, Eurynome takes on the form of a dove and lays the cosmic egg. The cosmic egg can be a symbol for consciousness. Ophion wraps himself around the egg seven times to birth the world into existence; can be understood as the kundalini energy activating the seven chakras to birth divine human consciousness.

Anubis, God of the Underworld

Anubis as the black jackal, presides over the creation scene. He represents the dark unknowable veils of divinity watching over his creation. Anubis, associated as the Egyptian god of the underworld, escorts the souls into the afterlife.

Interestingly, Anubis was one of the gods helping Isis find the scattered pieces of her husband, Osiris. Anubis prepared the body for resurrection so Isis can mate with him. From their union they give birth to Horus, the hawk-headed deity. Anubis presence in the Song of the Self, Moon, evokes the myth of Isis, Osiris and Horus, indicating sources unfoldment of divine human consciousness.

Psychologically, the dark Anubis represents the unconscious; the young maiden of light represents making the unconscious, conscious.

Evolution of Consciousness

Song of the Self Moon tarot may at first seem too esoteric to grasp. Basically, it is the story of the evolution of human consciousness. The primal energies of imagination and desire, unite to manifest the pearl of divine feminine wisdom to incarnate as the souls of humanity. The creator is in the creation; we are the energy of spirit taking form as the divine goddess soul.

Moon Activation

Soul Growth: Aligning with the Divine

The Moon is the Divine Mother within us desiring to bring forth her divine child. The Divine Child is the archetype of the Spirit. Like the Divine Mother, we create a space within our consciousness for our divine expression into our reality.

Our imagination is the envisioning of divine inspiration. Having the desire to manifest the image into the world, the Divine Mother births the imagination into three-dimensional reality. What does the Divine Mother, existing within you, desires for your life? What image appears in your consciousness? Is it the full expression of your divine human consciousness; or a divine quality you desire to bring forth? Is it an artistic creation you think about, but lack the drive to give it form?

We are all artists of our lives with inherent creative ability. In alignment with the Divine Father and Divine Mother expressing our passion, we manifest who we are, our dreams and creative works.

Co-creating our lives before birth, our soul, in the role of the Divine Mother; we desire what our life will be, what lessons we want to learn, which divine qualities we most want to express, which relationships we want to heal; who we want to love and help heal.

Creativity: Generating Faith of the Creator

Originally the Song of the Self Moon tarot was titled, Leap of Faith; symbolizing the passion and faith necessary to fuel the fulfillment of desire. The Divine Mother expresses the faith every artist must have to bring their creation to manifestation. Unlike the girl on the cliff, we may fear jumping into the transformative fire. Even though we are unsure of the end result, like the Divine Mother, we maintain the faith something of value shall be birthed from our desire and effort.

Determine if there is anything preventing your flow of creativity? What is it, and how can you remove it? Does any form of programming of the mind negate your innate creativity?

I still believe after many years; my work will be presented for others to experience. I maintain the faith, knowing this is my god given purpose I co-created with Spirit before birth.

Dreamwork: Birthing Love Consciousness

The Divine Mother uses the power of love, depicted as the Pearl of Feminine Wisdom, to manifest her desires. Ultimately love is who we are, it is the divine force we desire to manifest on earth. In essence, the creation is already created; it is through our consciousness, we bring who we really are into the illusionary three-dimensional realm.

Too many of us have allowed the dark forces to interfere with the process of self-realization. The programming to belittle who we are we have internalized. With the desire to break free, we access our alchemical fire of change to burn away the deceptions in the mind. We can call forth the Snakes of Transformation to reformulate our consciousness to radiate the Pearl of Divine Feminine Wisdom. We can give birth to ourselves as divine human consciousness. We are all born with the ability to manifest our divinity, by transforming ourselves we change the world.

Rider Waite Tarot, The Moon XVIII

The crayfish emerging from the water on land represents the unconscious made conscious. The dogs howling at the moon illustrates the expression of desire. The road leading from the water through the pillars to the horizon, symbolizes the path of manifestation, referred to as kundalini activation. The Divine Mother in the Moon, shedding tears, (referred to as yods), represents the chrism oil of divine consciousness.

The Moon in a Reading:

Drawing the Moon represents connecting with the Divine Mother and her desire to manifest her Divine Child into consciousness. It may mean clearing a space in your life to birth your desire. Ultimately, we allow our Spirit to be conscious. We bring forth and expand on the divine quality we need to express to help us on our journey and benefit others.

Drawing this card may indicate you are experiencing adversity and need to tap into and expand divine qualities, such as faith, patience and perseverance.

The Moon may signify, the querent may need to override the ego's hesitation to take the Leap of Faith the soul desires.

Questions to Ask in a Reading:

What divine qualities need accessing or expanding upon? Do you need to clear space in your consciousness for manifestation? What do you need to let go of? What fears and limiting beliefs are holding you back from taking the Leap of Faith?

Affirmations

My desire manifests my reality.
I make conscious my divine expression from source.
I access, shine and expand my divine qualities.
Everything is in Divine Order.
I have faith to see me through adversity.

Experiencing the Moon

To bring the imagination of the Star into reality requires passion; depicted as the pillars of fire. This burning force evolves into a powerful desire. Basically, by adding feeling to the thought image, begets the creative urge. The creative urge begets the many works of art I continue to produce.

I experienced the Moon in several leaps of faith; most profoundly, in going back to school to become an art therapist, moving to Florida to write, and moving to California to seek help in getting my work out there.

Divine Mother Quotes

"Everything is energy. Your thought begins it, your emotion amplifies it and your action increases the momentum."
- Unknown

"The Cosmic Mother has no form but will take on any form in order to answer the supplicant. She can present herself in the form of Isis, Rhea, Cibeles, Tonantzin, Mary etc. When the Divine Mother has given her answer to the devotee, she then disintegrates her form instantaneously, because she no longer needs it. The Divine Mother is not a woman, nor is she an individual. She is in fact an unknown substance. Any form that she takes disintegrates afterwards- that is love."
- Samael Aun Weor, The Yellow Book

For it's only in the feminine–the channel of creation into the world–that humanity finds the power and compassion necessary to overcome the darkness of ignorance.
- Robert Kopecky –– gaia.com

Moon XVIII Summary

The Moon is the Divine Feminine using her power of desire for manifestation.

References

The True Meaning of Anubis, by Admin –– historicaleve.com

Eurynome and Ophion, by Hung Nguyen –– talesmythology.home.blog

18. The Moon, by Anne-Marie Wegh –– anne.marie.eu

Song of the Sun

The pearl hovers between the pillars of fire, absorbing the transformative flames. Fire fills the orb, like the sun. Horus, the winged Divine Child, rises like a phoenix from the ashes. The outline of his body is formed by the Snakes of Transformation. His avian head is crowned with fiery plumage. His wingspan with 5 orbs of light, resemble pearls. As he passes through the portal of manifestation, the prince as Horus, sings:

> *I am Horus, the high flying one,*
> *I am the Divine Child of the sun.*
> *Feminine and masculine, I align,*
> *as human consciousness divine.*
> *I'm the manifestation of imagination and desire,*
> *with Spirit and Soul united, I am the high flier.*
> *From the oneness above,*
> *I shine my rainbow of love.*

A rainbow encircles the sun.

Song of the Self Tarot: Sun XIX

Through the portals of manifestation, the Divine Child, the Sun, is birthed. This union of imagination and desire; depicted as the falcon-headed Egyptian God Horus is made of the flames of desire. His body is contoured by the snakes of transformation, his wings are adorned with five orbs. Standing in the flames like a phoenix rising from the ashes, the divine child is encircled by a rainbow.

Horus: The Divine Child

Horus is the child of Isis and the resurrected Osiris. His name translating to "high flying one" is symbolic of the higher nature of divine human consciousness.

Set, the brother of Osiris, is analogous to the demiurge of Gnosticism, desiring to be of the highest power. Set, representing the forces of darkness, prevents the birth of Horus by killing Osiris.

The dark agenda of Set plays a pivotal role in the birth of Horus. It creates within Isis the desire to resurrect Osiris for a part of him to unfold into a new state of existence. Before Isis can unite with the corpse of Osiris; Set steals the body, chops it up and scatters the pieces. The dark agenda to remain in control, only increases Isis' desire to gather the pieces for resurrection.

Set represents the regressive, as Isis represents the progressive dynamics of creation. Set attempts to regress the Self back to the unmanifested oneness, is in opposition to the progressive individuated Self in wholeness. Like a magnet, Set repels the energy depicted as the chopping and scattering the pieces of Osiris. Isis magnetically attracts and gathers the body parts of Osiris.

The ego's agenda to maintain complete control of the Self, depicts the regressive forces of Set. Isis, the opposing force, does everything in her power to birth her child of divine human consciousness.

It appears from the very beginning, positive and negative; or light and dark, are both necessary for creation. The yin-yang symbol depicts the polarity in equal portions of light and dark. A small circle of the opposite in each, indicates in light there is darkness, and in darkness light. Meaning, the regressive and progressive forces are in an endless interplay. This interplay we can conclude is in all acts of creation, from human consciousness to artistic creations.

We can understand the dynamics clearer in the example of exercise. We are inspired to move the body to maintain optimal health, yet it is balanced by the body's need for rest. We are very aware of the regressive force when we experience laziness and reject doing exercise. We must determine if this is the body's wisdom for the need to continue to rest or do we focus on and allow the active forces within to inspire us to move?

Most yoga classes end with corpse pose, savasana, it's when the person rests on their back for several minutes. It's the time we take to honor the work we have done to preserving our health as well as honor our need for rest. We give the body and mind a chance to absorb the results to transition back into our lives off the mat.

In yoga, energy focused on a pose and then released, depicts the dynamic flow in the creation of a healthy body. In the process of creating art, energy of the mind is concentrated in self-expression. Then a time of rest is required to recharge. The cycle of creativity can be symbolic of the development of human consciousness as well as psychological self-transformation. Meaning, focusing of intention, or doing, we appear to be progressing with our goals. Equally important is the rest time allowing the body and mind to relax to receive divine inspiration subconsciously. In turn, the thought or inspiration coming out of the dark is made conscious.

Isis overcomes the regressive dynamic with the assistance of Nephthys, Anubis, and Thoth. These Egyptian Gods help her find the pieces, put them together and work the magic for resurrection. Their divine assistance is symbolic of the divine guidance we call upon to help us bring into consciousness soul and spirit.

The artist exemplifies these forces of creation by overcoming the negative thoughts to not create. Its whisperings for inactivity may sound like; "everything under the sun has been done," "who do you think you are, you can never be as great as those who came before, you're no Michelangelo, Van Gogh or Picasso." For a time, these voices may drag us down, but there is something inside the artist that demands expression. Our desire may sound like, "I refuse to allow the forces of dark depression and regression within me or the pragmatic beliefs of others hold me captive. I must find my voice no matter what, nothing can stop me. I must dig deep within to find what most needs to be expressed. I call upon God and the angels to help me bring forth the light of my creation." Just as the Divine Mother created consciousness with her desire; we recreate ourselves with desire to bring forth the goddess. Like Isis, desiring to resurrect Osiris, we desire to bring forth our Divine Masculine into consciousness.

Horus the union of Divine Mother and Divine Father, battles Set for dominion of the underworld, represents the continuing dynamic of dark and light our egos work with throughout our lives to self-actualize as the united Four Archetypes of the Self. Creatively, we give birth to works of art that help enlighten others in their own progression from ego, through Shadow, Soul, and Spirit.

Interestingly, Osiris, Isis, Nephthys, and Set are siblings, indicate the Four Archetypes of the Self are a family. Horus, representing the unity of these archetypes, is the spiritualized ego. Horus embodies the spiritual teacher within our own psyche, analogous to Jesus as the Master Teacher or Buddha, the Enlightened One.

Divine Child: Rubedo

In alchemy, the manifestation of the desire, divine child, is referred to as the Rubedo. The red bird-headed being exemplifies the alchemical result of self-transformation also referred to as the Philosopher's Stone.

Rainbow of Love

The divine child encircled by a rainbow, expresses the power of the seven chakras united in oneness. The divine child is who we really are, radiates all the divine qualities. Conscious of his divine intelligence, he is master of the Self.

Sun XIX Activation

Soul Growth: Spiritual Teacher

The figure within the sun represents the evolution of consciousness as the spiritual teacher. Having accessed your divinity, and expressing your divine qualities you are now equipped to be a spiritual teacher. By manifesting our divinity into our consciousness, we are the way showers for others.

Creativity: Service to Others

Visualize your divine child. What does he or she want you to know? Ask the spirit teacher within you for guidance. What is your burning passion for being of service to humanity?

Dreamwork: Rainbow of Love

Envision yourself in a rainbow of love, allow it to expand to encircle the earth.

Rider-Waite Tarot: The Sun XIX

The Rider Waite Tarot: The Sun XIX, features a large sun and a naked child riding a white horse. He holds a large red banner and wears a crown of pomegranates. Four sunflowers are in alignment with the child's head. The card is symbolic of spiritual rebirth and expresses Christ Consciousness in this quote of Jesus from the bible:

"Permit the children to come to Me; do not hinder them; for the kingdom of God belongs to such as these. "Truly I say to you, whoever does not receive the kingdom of God like a child will not enter it at all." (Mark 10:14-15)

The Divine Child riding the horse indicates he has mastered his animal nature of the lower chakras. The white horse representing the purification of the soul also symbolizes the albedo stage of alchemy.

The yellow sun symbolic of the Citrinitas stage of alchemy, depicts the illumination of divine intelligence. Interestingly, it shines twenty-two rays indicating the twenty-two major arcana cards. The alternating rays of straight and wavy represent the union of masculine and feminine energies.

The four sun flowers are symbolic of the Four Archetypes of the Self. Three of them are on one side of the figure represent the 'unconscious' archetypes of Shadow, Soul and Spirit; the one by itself, represents the ego. That the flowers are on the same plane indicates they're in alignment and united.

The green leaves, depicting the fourth chakra of the heart, expresses the love of the divine child. It's significant that the leaves align with the child's head indicates the rising of the kundalini into the crown chakra. The child's headdress of pomegranates signifies the crown chakra of divine consciousness.

The red banner, representing the rubedo phase of alchemy, signifies the manifestation of divine consciousness.

Numerology of the Sun

The numerology of the Sun combines 1 of the Magician with 9 of the Hermit, reduces to 10 Wheel of Fortune and then back to 1. The Magician or Ego 1, represents the potential for Oneness; united with the Hermit 9, he has reclaimed his soul and has embodied the keys to love of the previous archetypes of the tarot. Through his fated journey, 10, he seeks higher consciousness of The Tri-Principality of Fate, Karma and Timing, the transition of the goddess to god, the Infinite Flow of Compassion, seeing through illusion of the Devil, receiving divine inspiration (Tower), incorporating the Trinity of Divinity to imagine (Star), desire (Moon) and manifest and radiate divine consciousness as the Sun XIX.

The Sun XIX in a Reading:

Drawing the Sun in a reading may signify, the querent has evolved into a spiritual teacher who may emulate Jesus, as an expression of divinity referred to as Christ Consciousness.

The Sun may indicate, we have risen from the adversity, reborn with a greater sense of our divinity. It may also mean you are equipped to help others on their spiritual journeys. You may be a healer, develop a workshop, and be a speaker; but mostly we heal by being who we really are.

Questions to Ask in a Reading:

Are you a spiritual teacher? How can you be of service to others? Can you accept being enlightened in the world to show the way to others?

Affirmations

I am a Divine Child of God.
I am a child of the Divine Masculine and the Divine Feminine.
The creator is in the creation; I radiate my divinity.
I am a healing presence in the world.
I am divinely guided by the teacher within me.

Quotes on Divinity

"Every man is a divinity in disguise, a god playing the fool."
- Ralph Waldo Emerson

"You are one thing only. You are a Divine Being. An all-powerful Creator. You are a Deity in jeans and a t-shirt, and within you dwells the infinite wisdom of the ages and the sacred creative force of All that is, will be and ever was."
- Anthon St. Maarten, Divine Living: The Essential Guide to Your True Destiny

"Divinity means unfolding and expressing life in new ways. Divinity means radiating peace, bliss and beauty in the world. Divinity means overcoming the limitations of nature in new ways."
- Amit Ray, Walking the Path of Compassion

"Your heart is where your inner light resides. It is part of every sacred journey to reconnect with your inner light, step into your divinity,

spread the light of love before you, return to the essence of love, and inspire others to do the same."
- Molly Friedenfeld

"We are always manifesting. Each thought you have informs your energy, and your energy manifests into your experiences. Your thoughts and energy create your reality."
 - Gabrielle Bernstein

Summary of the Sun XIX

The Sun Tarot XIX is our Spirit expressing itself through us as divine human consciousness.

Summary of Star, Moon and Sun

The process of creativity involves the Trinity of Divinity: Imagination, desire, and manifestation. The Star, the divine Masculine inspires us with a vision. The Moon, the Divine Feminine, supplies us with desire, the energy of emotion. Uniting the thought with the feeling results in manifestation, whether its human consciousness, self-transformation, or a product of the creative process.

In astrology the sun sign, moon sign, and the ascendant or rising sign (Star) are significant placements used to determine much information about a person. The sun sign is our core identity expressed through ego, drive, and pride. The placement of the Moon determines our emotionality of the soul and subconscious. The Rising Sign indicates how we show up in the world and how we interact with others.

References

Horus –– enclyopediamythos.fandom.com

19. The Sun, by Anne-Marie Wegh –– anne-marie.eu

The Five Principles for Manifesting Your Desires, Spirit Junkie Style, by Gabrielle Bernstein –– huffpost.com

What your sun, moon and rising signs say about you, by Lisa Stardust–– today.com

What Does Your Sun, Moon, and Rising Sign Really Mean? by Ashley Tracey –– explore.mindbodyonline.com

Manifestation of Consciousness

Incarnation XX shows our consciousness choosing to be a part of the simulated, material world and learning of the redemptive power of forgiveness. **Resurrection XXI** is the completed journey of manifesting our divine consciousness of love in the simulation.

Incarnation XX

Song of Incarnation XX

In the underworld, the prince as Horus, the falcon-headed human, extends his hands to his father, Osiris sitting on a gold throne; "Blessed art thou father of all creation, I desire to have a life in the material world."

Osiris answers, "For what reason do you desire a lifetime, you have everything you can ever desire in my paradise?"

"I want to experience my spirit, separate from Oneness. I want to glorify the spirit as an individuated being," Horus explains.

"It is a difficult journey, it may take many lifetimes to achieve the manifestation of spirit in the world of matter," Osiris warns.

"I desire to be a human being in the world. I want to experience love in the physical dimension," Horus insists.

Osiris smiles, "Love is the only acceptable reason I can grant your desire." Osiris sings,

> *I grant your desire to live on the earth,*
> *like the creator, you shall give birth.*
> *To be a divine expression of love,*
> *to glorify the source of all above.*
> *With the counsel we'll decide your incarnation,*
> *through the Tree of Life enter the simulation.*

Song of the Self Tarot: Incarnation XX

Horus, the falcon-headed human standing on a crocodile approaches Osiris, Lord of the Underworld, seated on a golden throne, holding his crook and flail. The pillar behind him is his symbol the Djed; also referred to as the tree of life, features the solar disc with horns. A winged eye flies above Horus and another eye, the udjat, sails on a boat behind him.

The story depicts Horus as a divine human consciousness in the divine, non-physical realm. He asks Osiris, the father God for life on earth. Osiris grants him incarnation into the simulated world we perceive as physical. He will co-create his life with a counsel to plan the life best suited for his soul. Horus will enter the pillar behind Osiris, symbolic of the Tree of Life, to incarnate on Earth.

Balancing the Divine Masculine and the Divine Feminine

Osiris, the spirit, sitting on the seat of the soul, depicts the union of Divine Feminine and Divine Masculine. The imagery displays a balance of the warm golden and red colors for the Divine Feminine with the white and violet colors indicative of the Divine Masculine.

Isis' solar disc in the center of the tree, unites the top half of the pillar with the bottom is another display of masculine and feminine energy working together.

Djed: Tree of Life

The Djed is an Egyptian symbol representing stability is usually depicted with the four horizontal bars on top of the pillar. In my design it's on the bottom to indicate the hierarchy of the Four Archetypes of the Self. Meaning, we begin with ego to move into healing the Shadow, express the gifts of the soul and then rise into Spirit, illustrated with the tier with two eyes. The four vertical bars on top of the pillar, signify the union of the Four Archetypes of the Self.

In the Song of the Self story, the Djed is emblematic of the Tree of Life because it will be used as the device to shift the consciousness of the divine child into a body to enter the simulation we know as the world we live in.

The raising of the Djed in Egyptian ritual represents renewal of the pharaonic rulership, corresponds with human conscious resurrecting into the material world.

The Djed illustrated with the two eyes resembles the stupa with the eyes of the Buddha represent divine consciousness.

Eye of Horus

The Eye of Horus associated with the Moon, represents the Divine Feminine. In Egyptian Mythology, Set takes Horus' eye and tears it into six pieces and scatters them. The god Thoth gathered five of the slivers and added a divine component to make up for the lost piece. The divine portion, representing the Divine Masculine, refers to the sixth sense Horus needed in winning the battle with Set. The winged eye illustration refers to the spiritualization of Horus as does the udjat symbol, the stylized eye of Horus, on the boat.

Horus losing his eye is analogous to Odin sacrificing his eye for the resurrection of divine powers; for us, it indicates we must sacrifice our lack of forgiveness for the restoration of our divinity.

Solar Disc of Desire

The solar disc with horns and the Snakes of Transformation, represents the power of the Divine Feminine to manifest the desire of Horus to exist in the world. The tree can be understood as the imagination of the spirit envisioning the four archetypes of the Self. The snakes, representing genetic material, manifests the desire for the simulation of a physical body.

Divinity of Forgiveness

Originally, I titled this card, "Giving Your Pain to God" to achieve forgiveness. The crocodile Horus stands upon represents the crocodile tears shed in sadness, anger and pain; indicates the process of mastering the emotions. Releasing the feelings, forgiveness can take place and the soul expressing this divine quality transcends its limited consciousness. The tree towering behind Osiris, represents with forgiveness, the individual achieves the divine enlightened state.

Horus on Crocodile

Interestingly, Horus, as a child, carved into ancient stelae; holds a snake in each hand while standing on two or more crocodiles, may be interpreted as a Horus offering the healing power of forgiveness. The round face of the goddess, Bes, usually depicted above Horus represents Horus' connection to his soul or divine feminine nature.

Incarnation XX Activation

Soul Growth: Forgiveness

As a spiritual teacher, we may experience the pain of not being able to facilitate others to enlightenment. We can release our painful feelings to the Divine Father. To be truly divine on earth, means developing the divine quality of forgiveness.

Creativity: Incarnation of Love

As a spiritual teacher we may have struggle with the thought, "am I doing enough to help others? Why am I having difficulty forgiving or expanding my divine qualities.? If I'm such a powerful being why do my efforts end in failure?" Instead of beating ourselves up, we can imagine ourselves like Horus bringing our concerns to Osiris. We can imagine our painful thoughts as a dark ball of energy we give to the Divine Father. We can picture our Osirian divinity to transmute the ball of pain into a glowing ball of light.

We can imagine Osiris speaking comforting words of support. Perhaps he says, "I love you unconditionally. I am grateful for your efforts in helping others. Nothing is lost, your healing energy you put out into the world has a profound impact, even though you don't see or experience the effects. Keep expanding your divine qualities to be an even stronger expression of love and light. Have faith in yourself. Trust divine order. Be patient, timing is not in your control. Your perseverance is rewarded. Kindness is a force of healing. Be compassionate with yourself and others. Everyone is doing the best they can. Forgive them, they know not what they do. Be the way shower you are meant to be."

Dreamwork: Honoring Divinity with Gratitude

In the painting of Incarnation, Horus stands on the crocodile, indicating he has mastery over the crocodile tears of pain he once shed. Holding up his hands at the deity, seated on the throne, he blesses his Divine Father. Imagine yourself honoring your divine Self and say, "I am grateful for the opportunity to incarnate on the earth to do your will. I shall fulfill our dream of being divine on earth."

Rider Waite Tarot: Judgment XX

The Rider Waite tarot card, Judgment XX features an angel blowing his horn from the clouds and several people have risen from their coffins, represents resurrection of the spirit. The banner hanging from the trumpet is a red cross on a white field, indicates the Four Archetypes of the Self united. This spiritual resurrection is accomplished by developing the ability to forgive. In other words, the ego through forgiveness, completes the process of becoming divine. The Rider Waite, Judgment, may inform us to judge ourselves worthy of being divine on earth.

Incarnation XX in a Reading:

This card may indicate the need to release painful feelings by forgiving others and ourselves. Failing to get the desired results as spiritual teachers, we must release the pain. It also means we learn to develop a sense of detachment from the results we desire. Letting go of what holds us down in the underworld we can rise as the beacon of light we have already manifested to do our part to effect change.

Questions to ask in a Reading:

As a teacher where does my responsibility begin and end? Answer: we can only help those people with at least some openness to healing. We can always recognize the divinity in others and bless them as they drift away or we move on.

Giving Your Pain to God: Perennial Forgiveness

Incarnation was originally titled, *Giving Your Pain to God*. We intuitively know our unforgiveness weighs us down into the depths of misery. We just have to decide we want to be free of our anguish and follow through by letting go of the anger and frustration. We accept Spirit within counseling us, "Justice shall be done through Karma. Everyone pays for their misdeeds. Divine Retribution is always exacted, whether or not you see it in action."

We present our pain to the divine within us, humbly praying for our burden to be lifted. We allow the spirit within to receive our outrage and return to us our peace. Through forgiveness we become divine, the reason for our incarnation.

Interestingly, adding the ones of the eleven of Karma, we get 2 or 20 Incarnation of Forgiveness. Incarnating forgiveness within our consciousness we resurrect our divinity.

Affirmations

I release and let go of my pain.

Through forgiveness I heal and ascend.

Through forgiveness I raise the vibration.

Through forgiveness we heal the world.

Through incarnation simulation, I achieve individuation.

Quotes

Incarnation is the ultimate reason why the service of God cannot be divorced from the service of man.
- Dietrich Bonhoeffer

Nature is the incarnation of thought. The world is the mind precipitated.
- Ralph Waldo Emerson

"The Self-revealing of the Word is in every dimension - above, in creation; below, in the Incarnation; in the depth, in Hades; in the breadth, throughout the world. All things have been filled with the knowledge of God."
- St. Athanasius

And what of our own universe? The newest conjecture is that all that we experience - from the tiniest vibrating string of energy to that massive galaxy spinning around a maelstrom of reality-ripping black holes - may be nothing more than a hologram, a three-dimensional illusion that, in fact, we may all be living in a created simulation. Could that be possible? Could Plato have been right all along: that we are blind to the true reality around us, that all we know is nothing more than the flickering shadow on a cave wall?
- James Rollins

Incarnation XX Summary

We incarnate our divinity on earth. Through forgiveness we grow more divine.

References

The True Meaning Behind the Eye of Horus, by Luke Miller –– truththeory.com

The True Meaning of The Eye of Horus –– egyptconnection.com

Horus on the Crocodiles: Egyptian Magic and Medicine in the Glencairn Museum Collection, by Dr. Jennifer Houser Wegner –– glencairnmuseum.com

What Is the Djed Symbol and What Does It Mean? by Dani Rhys --
symbolsage.com

Djed Pillar, the mysterious symbol that symbolized the backbone of
Osiris and provided stability to ancient Egypt, by Admin --
historicaleve.com

Djed -- crystalinks.com

Eye of Horus -- egyptian-history.com

20. Judgment, by Anne-Marie Wegh -- anne-marie.eu

Let It Go: 11 Ways to Forgive, by Stefanie and Elisha Goldstein --
mindful.org

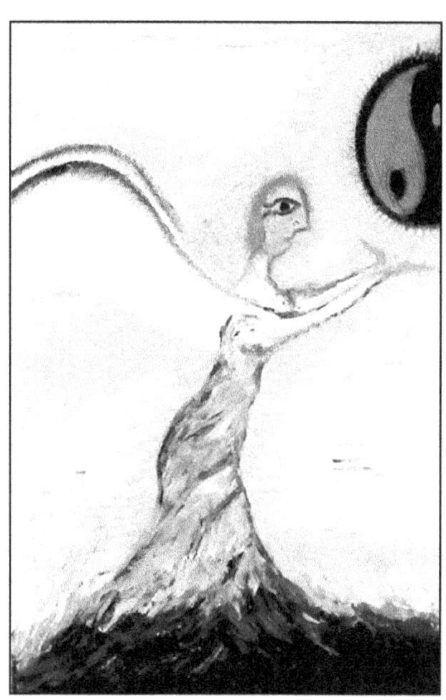

Resurrection XXI

Song of Resurrection XXI

Osiris holds out a golden ball to the prince, "Take this golden ball of divinity and be the Incarnation of Love you are meant to be. You are the resurrection of the light, incarnating into the material world. Go forth my child and be the loving expression of the divine."

The prince in humility accepts the orb of light and enters the Tree of Knowledge. Wings sprout from his spine and he uses them to rise into the world. He moves through the waters of soul to take on the appearance of the goddess holding the Sun of Enlightenment. She sings:

My spirit rises to the earth,
fulfills the purpose of my birth.
The Four Archetypes of the Self are united as one.
as the goddess soul, I bear the light of the sun.
Yin and Yang fishes of Self Becoming,
in oneness, I rise for my homecoming.
I give to the World a special gift,
works of art to heal and uplift.

Song of the Self Tarot: Resurrection XXI

The Song of the Self Tarot XXI features a goddess formed of the ocean, holding up the Sun of Enlightenment with two fish forming a yin-yang sign.

Engendering the ocean of oneness, the soul resurrects with unconditional love. With the goddess' eye in the form of the fish, she perceives all life originated from the love of source. Her golden ball is her gift to the world of her spiritualized ego.

The goddess consisting of water, represents the emotionality of her soul. She has fulfilled her desire, resurrecting as spirit, signified by her angel wings; and bears the gift of her enlightened divine intelligence. Her fish shaped eye, signifies her spirit has risen into her third eye and crown chakra.

The goddess soul glows with the light of the gold sun, depicts her enlightened state is her gift to the world. She is a healing presence of love and light. Bearing the sun is her creative expression, she shares with everyone.

Through incarnation into the simulation, we agree to the challenge to dismantle our limited perceptions of ego to resurrect the gloriousness of our spirit.

Yin and Yang Symbol: Singularity within Duality

The goddess' gift to the world in the form of an illuminated Yin-Yang Symbol, depicts the union of the Divine Feminine and the Divine Masculine.

The Yin and Yang symbol expresses duality, originating from the Oneness. Our reality is, all we are, ever were and will ever be, is spirit. It is through the simulation of our earthly lives we experience the separation from our divinity. Just as the creation of divine human consciousness was birthed through the union of the Divine Father and Mother; we emulate the source by creating our personal sacred marriage of ego-soul with spirit.

Resurrection Activation

Soul Growth: Sun of Enlightenment

The Soul desires to birth Spirit's vision of divinity into consciousness. Imagine you are the Goddess Soul rising from the pool of oneness, holding the Sun of Enlightenment. You are a unique wave of divine consciousness, an extension of the All that is, being expressed through your ego. Uniting ego and spirit is your gift to the world. Bearing the Sun of Enlightenment, you are the Holy Grail, Philosopher's Stone, Christ Consciousness, Christos, Boddhisatva, spiritualized ego and more.

Creativity: Holy Grail

Imagine you are in the underworld and approach Osiris, Lord of the Underworld. Express your desire to be a divine being on earth. Ask the deity, "what is my purpose?"

Grab the solar disc with snakes of transformation and go through the door into the Tree of Knowing. Allow the solar disc to infuse you with divine knowledge of who you are and your purpose. Allow the Snakes of Transformation to transmute your body to express the nature of your soul. Imagine growing a pair of wings and using them to rise into the world carrying your gift. Fully know you are a divine being, shining your light of love. In resurrecting your Holy Grail, you have the power to heal and enlighten others. Create a work of art, song or dance expressing your resurrection.

Dreamwork: Yin and Yang of Ascension

The two fish within the Sun of Enlightenment is the manifestation of the source's dream for humanity; ego and spirit as one, shining their power to heal and uplift humanity for all to consciously experience the eternal dimension of love.

Rider Waite Tarot: The World XXI

A nude woman wrapped in a long scarf, holds two small scepters. She is encircled by a wreath and four angelic beings are in the corners. She represents Divine Wisdom manifested into consciousness. Her scepters indicate both divine feminine and divine masculine is in her possession, as does the wreath in two parts tied together. Her scarf is indicative of the kundalini serpent and symbolizes the enlightenment of the soul. The circular green wreath is a symbol of oneness, confirms the manifestation of spirit into the world.

Resurrection XXI in a Reading:

Drawing Resurrection in a reading may indicate the divine masculine has risen into consciousness. It means the Four Archetypes of the Self have been made conscious. The individual feels whole and filled with a sense of purpose and love for humanity.

The Resurrection may signify the manifestation of a divine quality, such as forgiveness. The querent may be struggling to bring forth a divine quality and the reader can serve as a midwife supporting and encouraging the querent's effort.

The goddess bearing her gift to the world, may signify the emergence of a great work of art, inspiring others to begin or continue their own spiritual journey.

Questions to Ask in a Reading:

Have you accepted you are an expression of divine consciousness? What divine quality are you working on? What is your gift to the world? What legacy of teaching or healing have you created? What more is there to do?

Affirmations

I am an expression of the Divine Mother and Father.
I am divine human consciousness birthed from the source of creation.
My spiritual rebirth is my gift to the world.
My creativity heals and enlightens.

Resurrection Quotes

"All of nature is resurrection."
- Brian Weiss

"Nations, like stars, are entitled to eclipse. All is well, provided the light returns and the eclipse does not become endless night. Dawn and resurrection are synonymous. The reappearance of the light is the same as the survival of the soul."
- Victor Hugo

"A bridge of silver wings stretches from the dead ashes of an unforgiving nightmare to the jeweled vision of a life started anew."
- Aberjhan

"The work of salvation, in its full sense, is (1) about whole human beings, not merely souls; (2) about the present, not simply the future; and (3) about what God does through us, not merely what God does in and for us."
- N.T. Wright

"What if we lived like Jesus really did rise from the dead?"
- Sarah Holman

Resurrection XXI Summary

Resurrecting Spirit into consciousness, the Four Archetypes of The Self are united as our Gift to the World.

Fulfillment of the Fool:
Summary of the Journey Through the Tarot

The Fool begins as the unindividuated Self embodying the unmanifested Four Archetypes of the Self: Ego, Shadow, Soul, and Spirit. These four archetypes are depicted in most tarot decks, respectively as; Magician I, High Priestess II, Empress III, and Emperor IV.

Through incarnation, the Fool develops its ego and seems to forget its divine components until it is ready to receive the call to individuate, depicted as the Hierophant V. Individuation is the psychological process of the ego accessing and merging with Shadow, Soul, and Spirit.

In The Lovers or Merging VI, the ego begins the work of dissolving dysfunctional belief systems and emotionally healing victimization.

Having worked through much of the darkness and negativity, the ego continues its journey into the light, depicted as the Golden Carriage or Chariot VII.

The vehicle of consciousness arrives at the Personal Place of Power VIII depicted as an oasis in the desert; where the ego learns Beauty, Passion, and Wisdom of its Soul. This inner Strength VIII is depicted as a woman holding open a lion's mouth in the Rider Waite deck.

The Hermit IX goes out into the world to share his divine feminine wisdom. He learns of the Tri-Principality of Fate X, Karma XI, and Timing XII; corresponding with Wheel of Fortune X, Justice XI and Hanged Man XII. Through the Tri-Principality, the ego-soul learns of its limitations; the fate we have chosen before birth, the karma we agreed to resolve, and the timing of our desires are not in the control of the incarnated ego. These powers help us understand there is a divine plan to our lives we can align with to manifest our best lives. The goddess soul becomes aware she must let go of her illusion of being the reigning force of the Self to allow the divine masculine spirit into consciousness portrayed in Death XIII as the goddess head on a silver platter.

The goddess doesn't really die, she is transformed by the Snakes of Transformation to merge with the spirit depicted as the Infinite Flow of Compassion XIV. With this achievement the Self is made whole and is shown as Temperance in the Rider Waite Deck as an angel holding the flow of love energy.

In a state of wholeness, we accept the world is an illusion depicted as the Devil XV. To transcend the simulation, we are open to receiving the Lightning Bolt of Inspiration XVI or the Tower XVI. Our previous world paradigm comes crashing down to be replaced with the truth of our reality. The unfoldment of our creation is depicted in Star XVII, Moon XVIII, and Sun XIX. The source or divine masculine depicted as the Star imagines a state of consciousness separate from itself. As the Moon, this divine feminine emanation has the power of desire. Merging these two forces, desiring the imagination into form, divine human consciousness is birthed. This manifestation, the Divine Child, is depicted as the Sun.

In Incarnation XX, the Divine Child desires to experience its divinity within the simulation. In the Rider Waite deck, Judgment XX, the people rising from coffins symbolize the incarnation of ego into the world.

Resurrection XXI as the goddess risen from the ocean, bearing the sun of enlightenment and the World XXI depict the spirit made conscious. The completed journey of the unindividuated, unmanifested Fool is now the Resurrection of the enlightened, individuated, divine human consciousness.

References

21. The World, by Anne-Marie Wegh -- anne-marie.eu

The Yin Yang Symbol, Its Meaning, Origins and History -- mythologian.net

The Hieros Gamos, by Lisa Renee -- energeticsynthesis.com

The Wiccan Great Rite: Hieros Gamos in the Modern West by Samuel Wagar -- hermetic.com

Song of the Self Tarot

Part II

The Ten Universal Symbols of Manifestation

Introduction

The Ten Universal Symbols of Manifestation show the evolution of a thought in manifesting the soul and spirit into consciousness. By eliminating the court cards and the suits, the fifty-six cards of a conventional deck have been reduced to ten symbols to express the numerology for each minor arcana.

1 Divine Fire

Song of Divine Fire

Divine Fire, the energy spark,
its vibration lights the dark.

Divine Fire: A Spark of Inspiration

Divine Fire is illustrated as a column of white light breaking through the purple darkness; it represents power of inspiration rippling into consciousness as pre-thought.

Divine Fire, the divine energy of a thought, can be interpreted as the spark of divinity within each human being. Like turning on a cell phone, we establish the connection to our divinity with our mind. Like flipping a switch, we can access our always present creative urge, eternally inspiring us to be expressions of love.

Soul Growth: Clearing the Mind

Many of us have been conditioned to believe we are separate from the divine. Our purpose in the material world is to first become aware we are of the spirit and become one with our divinity. It means we allow spirit to work through us in every moment of our lives. By shifting the focus of attention within, we begin the process of manifestation, whether it is the manifestation of our soul nature, creative expression, activity, or goal. Through meditation we sit in dark silence, creating a space, waiting to connect to spirit. We can imagine our breath filling the center of consciousness to push away the dark curtains of the unconscious.

Creativity: Creating Space

To manifest, we need to create a space to discover what it is we desire. Through meditation, we allow our minds to be empty slates for spirit to ripple across the screen of consciousness. Like turning on the engine of a car, meditation is the power preparing the vehicle of the body to turn on to receive guidance in which direction to go. Repeating a mantra during meditation, may help to occupy the mind from interfering in creating a space for spirit to materialize.

Dreamwork: Allowing

We can open our minds to accept we dream every night for divine guidance. We can accept there is a plan for our life, even though we may not know what it is yet. We allow the energy to build and reveal itself.

Divine Fire in a Reading:

Divine Fire, viewed as a beacon of light, are energetic waves vibrating within our consciousness, communicating we are more than who we thought we were. It is the beginning of manifesting our divine selves in the material world. Divine Fire, the energy behind a creation, may be trying to inspire you to some form of self-expression.

Questions to Ask in a Reading:

Do you feel a shift in your energy? Are you having a spiritual awakening? What inspiration are you receiving? What are you inspired to do? Can you open yourself to receive inspiration? Are you having a spiritual awakening?

Affirmations

Divine Fire is eternally present within me.
I create a space within me to receive inspiration.

2. Clouds of Thought

Song of Clouds of Thought

Energy moves into a wispy formation,
two thought clouds of mentalization.

2 Clouds: Mentalization

Two puffy white clouds on a blue background are symbolic of energy forming into thoughts in our minds. The mentalization of Divine Fire provides us with a vision or an idea.

The Clouds of Thought in the process of manifestation, represent the conceptualizing divinity. We accept God exists and work toward expanding our thinking to believe, "I am Divine." What we think about ourselves determines who we are, as in, "you are what you think." We can allow the inspiration of Divine Fire to manifest as "I'm a divine being having a human experience."

Soul Growth: Self Awareness

The mentalization of the soul can be understood as the light filling the space of our minds during meditation. Through the dark clouded lens of self-perception, a glimmer of our true nature begins to shine forth. The wisps of thought begin to materialize as questions, "Do I have a soul? How do I want to show up in the world, what is my purpose?"

227

The two clouds indicate the splitting of consciousness as; who I am now, and who do I want to be? We can go through each thought we have about ourselves to determine if it's true. If it no longer holds true, we can dispel this dysfunctional concept. Oftentimes a dark thought is a reminder of what we need to heal. Positive thoughts are reminders of our true soul nature; we can allow them to accumulate into a growing cloud of self-awareness.

Creativity: Focusing Attention

Cloud wisps, illustrates the illusive quality of a thought, showing up as a hazy inspiration. We may experience this as desiring to be creative, but don't know how or what. With increased focus of attention, the wisps of thought build into something substantial enough to get an idea of what we are inspired to create. It may mean sitting in deeper contemplation or several sessions of meditation for the divine fire to reveal itself in an idea or image.

Dream Work: Reflection

Waking up after a dream, the elusive wispy images, may prove difficult to pin down. Taking a few moments to reflect on the symbols helps us to commit these divinely sent images to memory.

Clouds of Thought in a Reading:

Clouds of Thought in a reading may indicate the querent may need to pay attention to their thoughts. It may confirm for the querent a thought regarding personal growth, perhaps a new way of thinking about an issue, or the idea for a creative project.

We can express to the querent, our minds are like the limitless sky, and we can pull from it, in cloud like formations, significant wisdom from the divine.

Clouds of Thought in a reading may be guiding the querent to have an open mind. If it comes up in the past position, the present card may indicate the topic of conversation; allowing the querent to share their thoughts regarding the images, may bring greater consciousness to where they are at and which direction to go.

Questions to Ask:

Is there an inspired thought trying to break through the constant mind chatter? What vision do you have for your life? Do you have an idea for a creative project? What have you seen in your dreams? What significant thoughts are you having? Are there any signs or symbols that keep coming up in your life? What are your thoughts regarding the images shown in the reading?

Affirmations

My mind is open to receive divine inspiration.
My inspired thoughts are messages of divine guidance.
Through mentalization, spirit manifests into a brilliant idea.

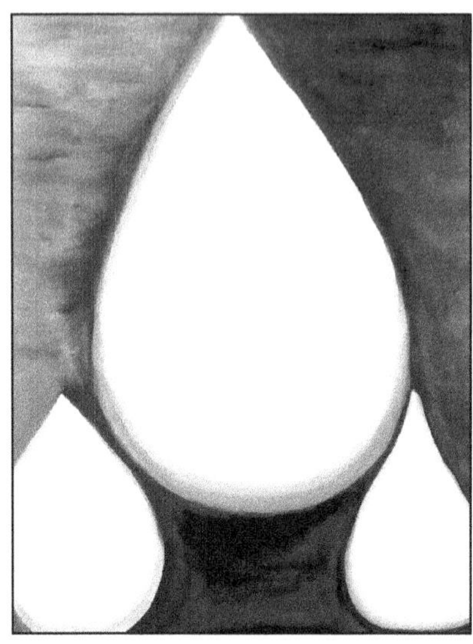

Song of Raindrops of Emotion

Adding feeling to thought, raindrops form,
the power of desire brings on a storm.

3 Raindrops: Emotionalization

Three large raindrops fall from the sky, depicts the weightiness of thought united with emotion. The falling raindrops are symbolic of emotion moving closer to settling into earthly ego consciousness. It is desire, informing the vision for manifestation.

Soul Growth: Desire to Be Authentic

Raindrops of Emotion symbolize our desire to be who we really are; ensouled beings having a human experience. The raindrops may represent our self-baptism of the journey of the soul, to be authentic and divine in the material world.

Becoming aware of our emotional states, we have the opportunity to feel them. Our emotional states influence how we feel about ourselves. If our feelings are negative or filled with self-loathing, we can imagine the self-loving person we want to be and imagine how that feels. Our positive feelings of who we are nurture our soul into manifestation. We have the power to decide how we feel about ourselves. Understanding the fluid quality of water, we can be aware our negative self-outlook can move through us. Instead of remaining in stagnant waters of depression and self-hatred, we can release the painful feelings and flow into the River of Soul and empty into the Ocean of Spirit.

We can get a better sense of our emotional landscape by charting out our feelings. One way is to create a pie chart giving the most powerful feelings larger sections. Choose colors that best represent each feeling and fill in the chart. Don't forget to include positive feelings no matter how small that sliver may be. After completing the chart determine which feelings need to be released. How can you expand the slivers of positive feelings?

Creativity: Passion to Express

The desire to express ourselves creatively, pours forth in a flow of ideas we are passionate to manifest into the world. Artists know how to harness this endless flowing river to manifest their visions. The soul is a creative force, and we can determine how to best express our desires. As artists of our lives, we can channel our energy in countless ways; if not in art, music, dance, theater, or film we can create harmonious relationships, comfortable, peaceful, and beautiful environments in our home and gardens.

You can use creativity to express who you really are. Feelings are what make us human. Create a work of art honoring your feelings. One suggestion is to create an abstract expressionistic work of art expressing your feelings as you're painting. For example, anger may be expressed with forceful brush strokes. Does the feeling have a distinctive shape you can portray? If the canvas or paper is very dark, is it possible to include some light to give yourself hope to feel better.

Dream Work: Emotional Awareness

A dream may reveal hidden desires that are trying to be made conscious. Repetitive or similar dreams are strong indications of a desire needing resolution in some way. Oftentimes, these desires are psychological internal processes that are not intended to play out in the external. For example, a sexual desire for another person may represent the desire the ego has to unite with its divine feminine soul.

After having a dream it's important to be aware of how the dream made you feel and what feelings you experienced in the dream. For example, a dream that made you feel sad, may signify sadness in your life needing to be expressed.

Raindrops of Emotion in a Reading:

Drawing Raindrops of Emotion in a reading may indicate there are powerful emotions needing to be expressed. It may also indicate a strong desire the querent has creatively, soulfully, or materialistically.

Raindrops in the present position may signify a powerful feeling or desire the querent has. Invite the querent to share their feelings and desires to process the querents concerns. If the Raindrops symbol comes up in the past, the querent may have experienced a deep flow of emotions. The card in the present position may reveal how the individual has resolved the feelings. When the Raindrops appear in the future position, the reader can suggest the querent prepare themselves for a deluge of emotions or a strong desire may surface.

Questions to Ask in a Reading:

What are you feeling? What is your desire?

Affirmations

I trust my feelings.
I listen to the desires of my soul.
I desire to be a divine expression of love.

4. Field of Dreams

Song of Field of Dreams

Setting your intention provides fertilization,
ground your desire through verbalization.

Plowing the Field: Verbalization

The quartered field with four rows each, indicates the Field of Dreams has been prepared. The plowed field representing the grounding of desire begins by setting an intention with your mind, Clouds of Thought; adding passion, Rain Drops of Emotion and now by verbalizing it to create a field of manifestation. Much like Masaru Emoto's experiments with sound changing the structure of water; giving voice to our dreams, creates the matrix of desire to take form. Meaning, our mentalized, emotionalized, verbalized desire creates a field of resonance. Resonating to this energy echoing throughout our mind, body and heart, the seeds of our desire begin to germinate.

Soul Growth: Verbalization of Desire

Verbalizing our intention for divine manifestation of the Self, allows our soul to be activated and sprout into consciousness. Expressing our desires with words, brings the thought-feelings stirring within, out into the world. Like a witch casting a spell with her incantation; we are magicians of the soul, verbally expressing our desires. Saying aloud our intentions is like planting our desires into our hearts to eventually yield the harvest of who we really are and our true callings.

Cultivating the Field of Dreams

We cultivate the Field of Dreams by doing the shadow work. The plowing of the rows represents the unearthing process of material held below the surface of consciousness. It means we must bring up to the surface everything that blocks the manifestation of the soul as well as excavate hidden treasures of the divine. Like vast underground root systems, we may discover in our subconscious various complexes that need rooting out. These unhealthy belief systems are usually a result of unhealed childhood trauma. By excavating our feelings, we begin to dismantle the victimization complex. By shining the light on our victimhood, we begin to dismantle the destructive power grid blocking our desires to heal and manifest our soul.

Dismantling the Victim Mentality Activation

Imagine your inner victim locked away in darkness. Open the door to the cage and bring her into the light. Ask her what memory she holds informing your dysfunctionality? What repressed feelings of yours is she holding on to? Ask her to give you back your feelings so you may healthfully express them. As you do this work, notice how the subconscious pattern begins to weaken its hold over you. With courage, curiosity, honesty and support you can fully dismantle the victim mentality until it fades from existence.

You may even show her gratitude for the trauma she suffered in the past and the ordeal of holding on to the very important material you needed to heal. Take back your energy from the image of your past. Feel yourself becoming powerful. Bless the weakening victim image and let her fade away. Notice how much lighter you feel. Feel how freeing it is to liberate your victim self. Allow yourself to feel the joy of healing and becoming who you really are.

Releasing the inner victim can be viewed as clearing the field of subconscious obstructions to prepare the ground to cultivate soul retrieval. With growing self-esteem, we can more easily bring to the surface the things we like about ourselves and allow those aspects to sprout and develop.

Planting the Seeds of Desire

The inklings of positive thoughts, feelings of self-worth, soul, and spirit qualities we can imagine them as seeds we plant and allow them to take root in the Field of Dreams.

Soul centered individuals may desire to expand an elusive divine quality, such as patience and forgiveness. By speaking our desire to manifest these qualities, we allow them to take root within our consciousness.

Creativity: Setting Intention

The Field of Dreams is symbolic of the fertile ground where our desires can be planted, nurtured, and harvested. The verbalization of an idea sends out vibrations into consciousness. In this way, giving our thought a life outside of the mind makes it 'real'. Setting of intention is planting the desire, our passion nurtures it and sustains us through the manifestation process.

What are your intentions? For example, developing self-esteem may begin with tiny inklings of what you like about yourself. Planting them in the Field of Dreams, we nurture them with water (emotions), feeling good where we are at and where we are going. Meaning, we can take that one tiny thing we like about ourselves to sprout into a seedling of positive self-regard. We keep nurturing the seedling into a full-grown sapling, "I like myself." We continue to nurture ourselves into a tree of self-love, extending our branches of divine qualities bearing the fruits of our psychological labor. Creatively we can draw, write, sing or dance the seeds of our desire manifesting in the field of dreams.

Dreamwork: Recording

Allowing our consciousness to be fertile ground to receive dream images, we can plant and nurture the symbols and messages by verbally expressing or writing down the dream. By discussing the dream, we are giving it weight and work toward grasping it's meaning. Similarly, recording the dream, we lay the groundwork for manifesting divine guidance.

Field of Dreams in a Reading:

When the querent pulls Field of Dreams in the present position, we can help them manifest their desire by suggesting they tell us any of the following: what they wish to bring into consciousness, what they desire to create, or a recent significant dream.

If Field of Dreams is in the past position, we can ask if the querent has verbalized their desire and look at the present card to relate the image to where they are at now.

Field of Dreams in the future position indicates the need to verbally express an upcoming inspiration.

Questions to Ask in a Reading:

What are your intentions? What desire are you excited about manifesting? Are you thinking about a new career direction, or a creative venture? Which divine qualities are you trying to manifest? Where are you in your shadow work? Have you unearthed your inner victim or hidden treasures?

Affirmations

Through my word, I cast my desire into reality.

I follow through with my divinely inspired desire.

I clear away the shadow to prepare my Field of Dreams.

I heal my victimization by expressing and releasing my feelings.

I plant the seeds of self-esteem and let them grow.

Anything is possible to create in my Field of Dreams.

Song of Stars

The constellation of Self begins to shine,
to bring forth the qualities of the divine.

5 Stars: Constellation of the Self

Five stars shining from a blue sky, symbolize the constellation of the Self. This fifth symbol, Stars, with five points, associated with the five senses, indicates the divine energy becoming a verbalized thought-desire, manifesting into our reality. It means, having done the shadow work and planted the seeds of our desire, the divine feminine soul begins to be brought into consciousness. The constellation of the Self indicates our divine qualities of kindness, honesty, compassion, patience, forgiveness is expressed through us more powerfully.

Soul Growth: Divine Guidance

Having cultivated our Self Growth, the planted seeds in the Field of Dreams have risen into the sky; they depict the constellation of the Self, with the awareness we are divine human beings. Like a constellation seen from far away, we sense our divinity exists, but in the distance of our consciousness.

In the Rider Waite Deck, the fives of the minor arcana suits show negative scenarios of poverty, loneliness, betrayal, loss and conflict. This indicates in the process of manifesting desires, there is usually inner or outer conflict appearing to prevent further growth.

Psychologically, this means the ego may be at odds with the soul as the reigning force of the Self.

In constellating our divinity into consciousness, we start to see our reality differently and others may notice the change within us which influences interpersonal dynamics. We become aware of the poverty of spirit in the world and develop compassion for the unaware.

Having done much personal growth, and seeing no one else in our lives has, we may feel very much alone on our spiritual journey. This aloneness forces us to be our own support system by developing self love.

As we begin to shine our light, others may be blinded by our brilliance and back away or try to psychologically beat the constellation of divinity from our mind. We may feel betrayed by the lack of support from others or ways they attempt to sabotage our growth. We may feel we are slipping away from others and feel a deep sense of loss.

We may also be tempted to beat ourselves up for all the time we were unaware or not as far along in our growth as we would like to be. We realize, wanting the familiar closeness of our old dysfunctional life, conflicts with our new evolving divinity, we may self-sabotage by regressing to addictive behavior. Instead, we must resolve to progress with our enlightenment by willingly letting go of that which no longer serves us spiritually. We affirm the light within us gives us the power to transcend the regressive forces and like the north star, guide us to our best lives.

Creativity: Formation

In terms of creativity, the desired creation begins to take physical form. For example, the composition of a painting, a melody of a song, first draft of a writing project, the choreography of a dance, construction of an invention.

Artistically, we sense we need to include conflict to make the work dramatic. In terms of visual arts, we juxtapose color and shape to create an engaging image. Writing a story, we need to include an antagonist to create an interesting drama. In dance, the choreography displays attraction and repulsion between dancers. Just as our consciousness seeks resolution so do our creative efforts.

Dreamwork: Insight

In terms of dreamwork, we gain insight from the symbols of the dream, and begin to constellate the message of the dream. Gaining insight, we have the knowledge to resolve an issue.

We can notice signs and synchronicities happening in our lives to determine the message the divine is offering.

Stars In a Reading:

Stars in a reading may indicate divine guidance; specifically, as the constellation of a divine quality we are learning to express. Stars may represent the constellation of a creative work or to follow through on a divinely inspired plan for our life.

If Stars are in the present position, we can determine what divine quality is constellating within. We can discover if there is a conflict and how to resolve it. If it is in the past position, the present card may show the resolution. In the future placement it indicates a divine quality that will be needed.

Questions to Ask in a Reading:

What insights are you having about yourself and your life? What conflict are you having, how can you resolve it? Which divine quality helps to resolve the issue? What divine guidance are you receiving? What is God's plan for me?

Affirmations

I am an expression of divine light.
I let the light of my divine qualities shine through me.
I resolve my conflicts in a healthy spiritual way.
I let go of feelings and people pulling me down.

6. Diamonds: Crystallization of the Self

Song of Diamonds

The diamond self crystalizing,
is our divinity materializing.

6 Diamonds: Crystallization of the Self

Six glowing orange gems suspended in the sky, signifies the crystallizing of the divine expression of the Self. We shine our divine qualities like the many facets of a jewel. Crystallization helps us see clearly the facets of who we are and the issues we face.

Soul Growth: Diamond Consciousness

The diamond self in our consciousness, symbolizes the manifestation of the indestructible spirit. With this crystallization of consciousness, we express our divinity in the world. It is analogous to the union of the Four Archetypes of the Self, and the Philosopher's Stone in alchemy. With the crystallization of our divinity, we serve humanity, shining our divine qualities.

Creativity: Power to Inspire

In creativity, the diamond represents the finished jewel of our creation. Our gift to the world shines with insights of the journey of the soul. Through creativity we reveal to the world who we are individually and collectively. We hope our work inspires others to heal and continue their spiritual path to enlightenment.

Dreamwork: Clarification

Often in dreams, we receive clarification we are on our intended path of self-growth. We may receive divine guidance of how we can be of service to others.

Diamonds In a Reading:

Drawing Diamonds indicates, we reflect the many facets of our divinity into the world. It implies the best solution to a problem is found not at the surface of ego consciousness but resolved with a divine quality. It means, we can transcend the dramas of our lives with kindness, patience, love, and forgiveness. Although our conflicts may linger, we can access inner peace. With the crystallization of wisdom, we find the stillness to receive divine guidance and act accordingly.

Questions to Ask in a Reading:

Which divine qualities are needed for the present situation? How will you be of service to others?

Affirmations

My divine qualities are the many facets of divine love.
Shining my divinity, I serve others.

Seasons of the Soul

The last four images depict the seasons of the soul as: 7. Buds of Self Awareness, Springtime of the Soul; 8. Blossoms of Enlightenment, Summer of the Soul; 9. Tree of Self, Autumn of the Soul; and 10. Mountain of Joy, Winter of the Soul.

Springtime of the Soul

7 Buds of Self Awareness

Song of Buds of Self Awareness

Buds of Self Awareness emerge in my mind,
my Strength of Vulnerability, I now find.

The image of seven rose buds on a dark thorny branch express the beauty of the soul budding into consciousness. Many thorns protect the newly evolving, vulnerable emergence of Soul.

Soul Growth: Strength of Vulnerability

The strong branch sprouting soft tender buds, symbolizes the Strength of Vulnerability. It means, having developed a strong sense of Self, we allow ourselves to be vulnerable with ourselves and others. Letting our soft feminine qualities to emerge, we grow stronger in who we really are. We allow our emerging buds of love to soothe remnants of our wounds. We allow our budding empathy to help heal others.

The Buds of Self Awareness emerge into consciousness as Beauty, Passion, and Wisdom of the Soul. We consciously accept we are beautiful eternal expressions of the divine. We allow our passions to unfold and pursue them. We tap into our divine feminine wisdom on how to behave in the world by developing the wisdom of mindful responding, rather than egoic reacting. We develop the wisdom, when to speak out and when to retreat. Bringing Beauty, Passion, and Wisdom into the light of consciousness, we can let them blossom to reach their full potential.

The 7 Buds of Self Awareness along the branch are symbolic of the seven chakras along the spine. We activate the power centers with meditation, visualization, and yoga. We can begin to tap into psychic abilities for deeper understanding of Self and others.

Creativity: Expressing the Sacredness of Life

With Budding Self Awareness, we begin to communicate our emerging souls in new creative ways. We may change our appearance in some way to reflect the inner transformation: for example, a new hairstyle, changing hair color, new clothes and furnishings or artwork adorning our homes. We may spend time in nature and realize the sacredness of all life forms and express these ideas in a poem, a painting, or a song.

Dreamwork: Gaining Insight

We may see our emerging soul as a character or symbol in our dream. New insights into our issues may sprout in the dreamscape. We allow our budding intuition to help us interpret the dream.

Buds of Self Awareness in a Reading:

The Buds of Self Awareness may indicate the querents Strength of Vulnerability; meaning the individual is no longer afraid to express soft loving tenderness to self and others.

The barbs on the branch indicating self-protection, may depict a thorny situation. With the buds of self-awareness, the querent can determine how to handle the situation soulfully, rather than react egoically.

Questions to Ask in a Reading:

Do you need to soften in some way? Do you need to protect yourself from attack? Can Strength of Vulnerability improve the situation?

Affirmations

My Strength of Vulnerability opens my heart to love.
My budding self-awareness lights up my life.

Summer of the Soul

8 Blossoms of Enlightenment

Song of Blossoms of Enlightenment

Summer flowers, the blossoms of light,
my enlightened soul is shining bright.

Eight shining flowers signify the enlightened soul. The goddess has reached her full maturation in the Summer of the Soul. Her Beauty, Passion and Wisdom has reached full potential as she shines her divine qualities.

Soul Growth: Sovereign of the Self

In the Summer of the Soul, our ego has united with our divine feminine Self. The goddess within as the sovereign of the Self owns her power and has learned to manifest her desires. She experiences abundance for her ability to give and receive love.

Creativity: Empowerment

The goddess artistically expresses her feelings and ideas, using her gifts to empower others on the spiritual journey. She may feel called to speak her truth at workshops, write a self-growth book or become a therapist or healing practitioner. In the Summer of the Soul, we help enlighten others with the truth of our humanity.

Dreamwork: Interpretation

In the Summer of the Soul, the goddess easily interprets her divine guidance she receives in dreams. Oftentimes, dreams confirm the actions the soul has chosen.

Blossoms of Enlightenment in a Reading:

The appearance of the eight flowers of enlightenment in a reading may indicate the querent is feeling her empowered sense of self. She may be on the verge changing direction personally or professionally. She may feel powerfully guided to change her life completely to be some kind of healer.

Questions to ask in a Reading:

What is your divine guidance? Are you feeling empowered to shine your light in a new way? What area of healing is calling out to you?

Affirmations

I am a divine blossom of love.
I lovingly shine my divine qualities.

Autumn of the Soul

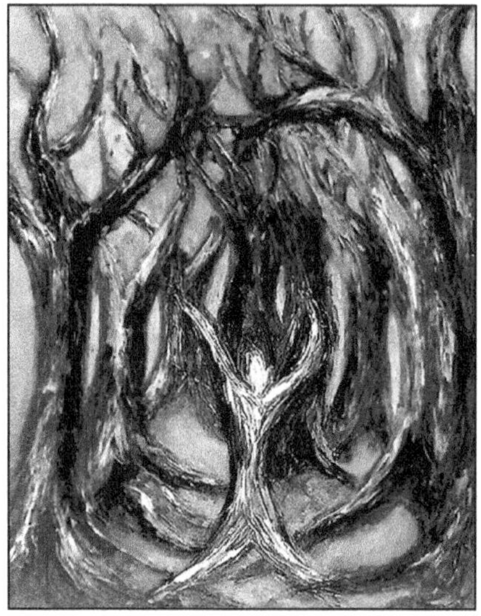

Song of Tree of Self

Our Spirit emerges in our story,
as Tree of Self in Autumnal glory.

In the Autumn of the Soul, a human figure of light emerges from a leafless tree, symbolizes the emerging of the divine masculine. The tree is a symbol of the Self in wholeness.

Soul Growth: Sacred Marriage

In the Autumn of the Soul, the goddess takes off her leafy crowning glory as Sovereign of the Self to unite with spirit. This sacred marriage of divine feminine and divine masculine manifests as the spiritualized ego. Through her roots, the goddess accesses deeper truths of her divinity as well as reaching her branches higher, stretching her divine qualities.

The orange background represents the falling leaves of autumn as well as the setting sun to indicate the fall of the goddess. The goddess in a sense, dies as the sovereign of the Self and is reborn to follow divine will. She understands to move further on her journey, she accepts her role as servant of God.

Creativity: Illuminating the Divine

Creatively, the soul expresses wisdom to help others become who we really are. Like Jesus offering parables we may write stories of redemption. Our lives become an unceasing prayer to help awaken others on the spiritual journey.

Dreamwork: Serving Spirit

Our dream now is to serve God and humanity by helping others manifest their divinity on earth.

Tree of Self in a Reading:

The Tree of Self in a reading may indicate the transition from goddess to God is imminent. It may also signify overcoming adversity or letting go of the powerful goddess role.

Oftentimes at this stage, we feel like we have so much to offer the world, but our gifts are being rejected; it means we must go deeper within to find solace as we develop our patience, faith, perseverance, and other divine qualities to be that much stronger for when they can be made use of.

On a mundane level the querent pulling this card, may be experiencing isolation and loneliness, and is challenged to find support, mainly from within.

Questions to Ask in a Reading of Tree of Self:

How can we turn adversity into an opportunity into expanding our divine qualities? Can you let go of the pain of rejection?

Affirmations

I am a servant of god to be a vessel of for healing.
As the Divine Feminine Soul, I share my sovereignty with the
Divine Masculine.

Winter of the Soul

10 Mountain of Joy

Song of Mountain of Joy

Divine Fire has completed the course,
Mountain of Joy amplifies the source.

On a purple mountain, ten snowcapped peaks encircle a light, symbolize the amplification of spirit.

Soul Growth: Amplification of Spirit

The white and violet colors depicting Divine Fire, have evolved into a mountain of light; signifies through our materialistic humanity we shine our spirit. Like a beacon of light, we show the way for others to what is possible; being a divine being on earth.

Scaling the mountain of adversity, we developed our divine qualities to great depth and height. It means, we have transformed our anger into compassion and patience, our resentment and victimization into forgiveness. We strive to release negativity to live every moment in joy.

Having completed the spiritual journey, we become teachers of the light. We are the light workers striving to heal humanity personally and collectively with our divine qualities of kindness, love, faith, patience, joy, compassion, and forgivingness and more. We know we are meant to amplify the light of our divinity.

Creativity: Inspiration

As a healing presence on earth, we imbue our works of art with healing energy and inspirational messages.

Dreamwork: Healer

As a healing presence in the world our dreams may guide us to who we can help and how.

Mountain of Joy in a Reading:

In a reading the Mountain of Joy may indicate the querent is a force of healing in the world. On a mundane level the querent has achieved worldly success in some fashion.

Questions to Ask in a Reading:

Is there something specific you can do to help others to heal and express their divinity? What divine qualities do you want to amplify?

Affirmations

I am a divine light unto the world.
I'm a healing force assisting humanity on the spiritual path.

Appendix

A summary of each Tarot card is provided in **Song of the Self Tarot: Major Arcana** and **Song of the Self Ten Symbols of Transformation Summary**.

Summary of the Song of the Self Tarot: Major Arcana

The Major Arcana of the Tarot depicts the journey of human consciousness. The **Fool O** is the undifferentiated Self comprised of the Four Archetypes of the Self: Magical Ego, (Magician I), Shadow (High Priestess II), Soul (Empress III) and Spirit (Emperor IV). Ordinarily we develop ego consciousness at the exclusion of the others, until we receive and answer the call (Hierophant V) to begin the journey of the soul. Merging (Lovers VI) we look within to heal the wounds of victimization and let go of false beliefs and negative self-images, we accepted as who we are. The Golden Carriage (Chariot VII) is the transition from Shadow to Soul. Having let go of the pain of the past, the ego is ready to explore the realm of the soul in the Personal Place of Power (Strength VIII). Learning to be an expression of Beauty, Passion and Wisdom, the ego-soul wanders through the world sharing his enlightenment as she begins to understand the Tri-Principality of Fate, (Wheel of Fortune X), Karma (Justice XI) and Timing (Hanged Man XII). The goddess soul understands there is a greater power controlling her life, she allows the transition to spirit (Death XIII). Death, the transition of goddess to god, is the rebirth of the Infinite Flow of Compassion (Temperance XIV). This spiritual rebirth makes conscious the Four Archetypes of the Self in a state of differentiated Oneness. The individuated being realizes the world is a simulation of the Devil XV. The Lightning Bolt of Inspiration (Tower XVI) inspires us to break free of the matrix by understanding we are divine beings having a human experience. We are in the world but not of it.

The Star XVII is the creator's imagination of a divine human being. The Moon XVIII is the Divine Feminine desire for the manifestation of the imagined human being. The Sun XIX is the union of Divine Masculine and Divine Feminine, (Imagination and Desire) as manifestation of divine human consciousness. Desiring our divine consciousness to be in the simulation, we are granted Incarnation, (Judgment XX). Our lives give us the opportunity for spiritual Resurrection (World XXI).

Fool 0

The Fool represents our undifferentiated consciousness as a jumble of Ego, Shadow, Soul, and Spirit.

Magical Ego I

The Magical Ego is the archetype of the personality with the ability of perception. Comprised of the four functions, we have a great power to perceive within our consciousness and the world around us.

Shadow II

The Shadow holds repressed emotions, the Waters of Soul, and the Divine Child (Spirit) desiring to be birthed into consciousness. Looking within the Shadow, the Ego begins the healing process, soul reclamation and spiritual resurrection.

Soul III

The Soul, the Divine Feminine eternal archetype of the Self is the embodiment of Beauty, Passion, and Wisdom.

Spirit IV

The Divine Masculine, sitting on the mountain top signifies, the spiritualized ego.

Hierophant V

The Hierophant is the Divine Self, calling the ego to go within to bring out the inner treasures of Shadow, Soul, and Spirit.

Merging VI

Merging with Shadow is the healing process of making the unconscious conscious.

Golden Carriage VII

The Golden Carriage is the transition from ego merged with Shadow into Soul.

Personal Place of Power VIII

The ego becoming soul centered, gains self-esteem and develops the strengths of Beauty, Passion, and Wisdom.

Hermit IX

The Hermit, possessing Divine Feminine Consciousness, goes into the world to share his wisdom and understand the Tri-Principality.

Fate X

The Web of Fate we develop faith, in our divine self as our guiding force.

Karma XI

With the divine quality of perseverance, we can meet challenging life circumstances we agreed to before incarnation.

Timing XII

Our lives, subject to the Divine Order of Timing, we develop the divine quality of Patience.

Death XIII

Death XIII represents the transition of the Soul, (Divine Feminine) to unite with Spirit, (Divine Masculine).

Infinite Flow of Compassion XIV

The Infinite Flow of Compassion is the ego-soul becoming heart centered.

Devil XV

Lucifer the light bringer awakens us to the truth our reality is a simulation; we have the power to free ourselves from our attachment to the limiting materialistic view of who we are.

Tower XVI

Activating the Tower of divine consciousness, old dysfunctional paradigms are dismantled. The Lightning Bolt of Inspiration is the energy preceding Imagination.

Star XVII

The Star is the power of imagination. Through the imagination, we envision our divinity, realize our higher purpose, get ideas for creativity.

Moon XVIII

The Moon is the Divine Feminine using her power of desire for manifestation.

Sun XIX

The Sun Tarot XIX is our Spirit expressing itself through us as divine human consciousness.

Incarnation XX

We incarnate our divinity on earth. Through forgiveness we grow more divine.

Resurrection XXI

Resurrecting Spirit into consciousness, the Four Archetypes of The Self are united as our Gift to the World.

Song of the Self:
Ten Symbols of Manifestation

In the Song of the Self Tarot, the minor arcana is depicted as Ten Symbols of Manifestation; briefly they are:

1. **Divine Fire** the energy of a thought
2. **Clouds of Thought**: Mentalization of thought
3. **Raindrops of Emotion**: Emotionalization
4. **Field of Dreams**: Verbalization of a thought or idea
5. **Stars**: Constellation of the Self
6. **Diamonds**: Crystallization of the Self

The Seasons of the Soul:

7. **Buds of Self Awareness**: Springtime of the Soul
8. **Blossoms of Enlightenment**: Summer of the Soul
9. **Tree of Self**: Autumn of the Soul
10. **Mountain of Joy**: Winter of the Soul

About the Author

Having studied many areas of psychology and spirituality; the wisdom gained has evolved into Song of the Self Tarot Deck, books, and many screenplays. These divinely inspired works are designed to help the reader and viewer understand and grow into who we really are- divine human beings. May we all heal and shine our love.

The archetypes undifferentiated as the Fool,
individuated through the simulated school.
Resurrecting the spirit divine,
in oneness the archetypes align.
As the embodiment of the source,
to be a powerful healing force.
Helping others on the journey of the soul,
for all of humanity to be loving and whole.

9 798218 201098